How Very Effective Primary Schools Work

British Educational Leadership, Management & Administration Society

Published in Association with the British Educational Leadership, Management and Administration Society

This series of books published for BELMAS aims to be directly relevant to the concerns and professional development needs of emergent leaders and experienced leaders in schools. The series editor is Dr Hugh Busher, School of Education, University of Leicester.

Titles include:

Educational Leadership: Personal Growth for Professional Development (2004)
By Harry Tomlinson

Developing Educational Leadership: Using Evidence for Policy and Practice (2003)
By Lesley Anderson and Nigel Bennett

Performance Management in Education: Improving Practice (2002)
By Jenny Reeves, Pauline Smith, Harry Tomlinson and Christine Ford

Strategic Management for School Development: Leading Your School's Improvement Strategy (2002)
By Brian Fidler

Subject Leadership and School Improvement (2000)
By Hugh Busher and Alma Harris with Christine Wise

How Very Effective Primary Schools Work

Chris James, Michael Connolly,
Gerald Dunning and Tony Elliott

Paul Chapman
Publishing

Paul Chapman Publishing
A SAGE Publications Company
1 Oliver's Yard
55 City Road
London EC1Y 1SP

SAGE Publications Inc
2455 Teller Road
Thousand Oaks, California 91320

SAGE Publications India Pvt Ltd
B-42 Panchsheel Enclave
New Delhi 110 017

Library of Congress Control Number: 2005931205

A catalogue record for this book is available from the British Library

ISBN-10 1-4129-2007-8   ISBN-13 978-1-4129-2007-0
ISBN-10 1-4129-2008-6   ISBN-13 978-1-4129-2008-7 (pbk)

Typeset by GCS, Leighton Buzzard, Bedfordshire
Printed in Great Britain by Athenaeum Press Ltd, Gateshead, Tyne & Wear
Printed on paper from sustainable resources

Contents

Series editor's preface

I am delighted to welcome this book by Chris James and his collaborators to this series as it offers a landmark in several ways. Unlike many books on school improvement/school effectiveness it is focused on primary schools, and in this case on primary schools in Wales, a country that has not received sufficient attention for its innovatory work in education, although the concern of its peoples for education has been legendary. One consequence of this location that emerges in the stories of the success of these schools is the creative and positive relationships they had with their local authorities in sustaining their development of inclusive schooling.

For those readers who want it, James and his colleagues adumbrate an overview of the concepts and literature on school effectiveness, focusing on its systems perspectives and noting its inability to explain the interactions of individual people with organisations except in a crude and simplistic way. To address this important gap in knowledge about why people behave in the way they actually do in organisations, the authors develop a discussion of systems psychodynamic theory. This allows them to conceptualise and explain the complexities of the relationships between people and organisational systems (or powerful groups of people) in such ways that the contradictions and discontinuities that emerge in these are seen as legitimate and understandable from the perspective of the individual, and not merely evidence of obtuse obstructionism or of ineffective leadership. As Ball (1987) in an earlier work suggested, conflict in organisations is normal, not pathological. It is how that conflict is used that is important, whether for constructive development through creative dialogue or for confrontation and retrenchment. Later in the book James and his co-authors argue that focusing on the former is one of the key elements to understanding why some schools may be very effective. From their conceptual framework they draw out the main parameters through which they intend to explore the schools in their study – all of them chosen because there was strong circumstantial evidence that they were successful schools that served areas and communities that were disadvantaged socially and economically.

Unlike many studies on school improvement this work focuses on schools serving socially challenged and economically disadvantaged communities that appear to have made a difference to the quality of learning of the students that attend them. The nature of these communities is clearly described in one of the early chapters of this book so that readers understand the contexts in which the research was carried out. Yet the people from those communities are closely drawn in to supporting the work of the schools in helping children develop their learning, contradicting the usual view that people from disadvantaged communities tend to be distant from the schools their children attend. The explanation offered by the authors of this book for this is the effort put in by headteachers and other staff to encouraging and helping parents to become part of the school communities. Such success fits with work by other authors such as Vincent (2000) on the importance and means of involving people from the communities in which schools are nested to support the development of students' learning.

At the core of these successful schools, James and his colleagues argue, is effective leadership. This type of leadership focuses on particular values of inclusion and high expectations of achievement, that helps to construct a creative and inclusive culture supporting, passionately, norms and beliefs of success and achievement in learning of as good a quality as possible by everybody. In these learning communities staff encouraged students to be active co-constructors of the schools by using a variety of formal and informal channels to make their voices heard constructively. The mindsets of the people in these schools were said to be empowered, pro-active and optimistic in tackling the problems they faced to improve teaching and learning. This culture is described as the central characteristic of these schools and explicitly encompasses the importance of continuing professional development by all staff. Supporting this leadership and sharing in it, the authors found committed teachers and other staff with high expectations of themselves and strong positive interpersonal relationships who had often been carefully selected on appointment. They worked in an information-rich environment that allowed them to monitor their and their students' progress and offer formative feedback on it.

If you are a reader busy in the everyday press of education, with little time to enjoy the full detail of the book, then at least read Chapter 12 which provides a very useful summary of this important and illuminating piece of research. But it is a book that repays closer reading when you have the time, not least because the way in which the authors have conducted their research offers a blueprint for ways in which a school could evaluate its own practice and consider why it might not yet be very effective but might achieve that state in due course.

Hugh Busher
School of Education
University of Leicester

Acknowledgements

This book is dedicated to all those who work in and work for the schools we studied. Thank you for your Good Work.

1

Introduction

INTRODUCTION

It was not until the late 1970s that the idea that some schools may be more effective than others in achieving a higher level of educational outcomes began to be accepted. Since that time, the characterisation of effective schools has been the focus of much research endeavour. In fact, there has been so much research into effective schools that it could be argued that that we know all we need to know about them and that what we should do now is focus on how we improve those that are ineffective. There is, however, an equally strong, if not stronger, case for a different view.

Firstly, we may in fact not know all there is to know about what makes schools effective and we may not have a way of describing successful practice and explaining why it works. There may still be something missing that remains to be captured in the ways we look at effective schools and attempt to understand what they do. Our knowledge of them is thus incomplete. We may not have a way of describing what those schools do – a form of knowledge – that encapsulates their practice. So, although we think our descriptions are accurate, they do not actually capture the essence of successful practice. Finally, we may not have a fully developed way of explaining, understanding and theorising the good practice we observe. As a result, although we can describe 'good practice', we may not be making the correct interpretation of it and explaining why it works.

Secondly, as society continually changes, so do schools and so do society's requirements of schools. As a consequence, a set of 'effective school characteristics' that might have been adequate in the past may not be so now and may not be so in the future. Such a view argues for a constant exploration of what *currently* works and why. As schools reform and reconfigure, we need to try to continually understand what is going on in them. We also need to attempt to explain why current successful practice works and, equally, why current unsuccessful practice does not.

1

Thirdly, there is a growing recognition that context is a very significant but very varied influence on the effectiveness of schools. It is becoming increasingly apparent that schools need to work in particular ways according to the complex and varied nature of their local and national settings. What is needed therefore is more study of the ways in which schools work well in particular settings to find out the reasons for their particular success.

There are thus three reasons why we undertook the research we report in this book. Firstly, we wanted to discover more about schools where pupil attainment is high. In particular, we wanted to find out about schools where levels of attainment and disadvantage are both high, which is a relatively unusual occurrence given the effect that disadvantage can have on pupil attainment. Secondly, we wanted to understand why some schools are currently successful. Understandings of schools generally, the ways they are viewed and the potential to explain their workings are all developing and changing which gives a new opportunity to look afresh at why some schools are effective. Thirdly, we wanted to begin to clarify why some schools work well in specific settings. Since schools work in very different contexts, the more we can understand about how schools respond to their contexts the better, especially if the response is successful.

THE ISSUE WE ADDRESSED

The research we report here addresses an important issue which we outline fully in Chapter 4. In essence, it is as follows.

In Wales, as in many countries, the educational attainment of primary school pupils (aged 3–11) has improved over the last ten years or so. The problem is that the gap between the attainments of pupils in schools where pupil attainment overall is high and those in schools where overall it is low has not narrowed significantly. In effect, educational attainment in all schools has improved but the attainments of pupils in 'low attainment schools' have not substantially caught up with those in 'high attainment schools'.

In Wales, again, as elsewhere, socio-economic disadvantage can have a significant influence on pupil attainment. Generally, high levels of disadvantage correlate with low levels of attainment; the higher the level of disadvantage, the lower the level of attainment.

Despite the overall correlation between pupil attainment and socio-economic disadvantage, there are primary schools in Wales where the level of pupil attainment is high even though the pupils experience high levels of disadvantage. These schools appear to have overcome a negative influence on attainment – socio-economic disadvantage. They must be very effective in the way they work. We studied some of these very effective schools to find out what they do, how they do it and why it works.

OUR INTENTION IN WRITING THIS BOOK

Our intention in writing this book is to report the outcomes of our research to as wide an audience as possible. We envisage the readers of the book will be those who are interested in finding out what works in the schools we studied and why it works. We hope that reporting our findings in this way will help those who work in and with primary schools in all settings, including disadvantaged settings, to improve their schools. We also want to interpret the findings of the research in relation to various theoretical frameworks in order to make sense of what works and to understand why 'what works' works. This kind of sense-making and interpretation will inform theoretical understandings of why some schools in disadvantaged settings are successful.

THE STRUCTURE OF THE BOOK

The book has a 'theory–research–interpretation' structure. The early chapters of the book describe some of what is already known about effective schools. They also outline a theoretical perspective known as 'system psychodynamics' or 'institutional transformation' as we also call it, which gives a way of interpreting and theorising the main findings. The middle section of the book explains how we went about the research and describes the outcomes. From our analysis of the data, we identified seven important characteristics. We call the main one of these *the central characteristic* and the others *key characteristics*. All the key characteristics contributed to and sustained the central characteristic. There are seven chapters in the middle part of the book, each of which describes a characteristic. The later chapters examine the findings in relation to what is known about effective schools and interpret the findings in relation to the system psychodynamic concepts and ideas. The book ends with some reflective thoughts and comments. Thus the content of the various chapters following this introduction is as follows.

Chapter 2 summarises key aspects of the literature on the characteristics of effective schools. Our intention in this chapter is to provide a way of comparing practice in the schools we studied with what is already known about effective and successful schools. In Chapter 3, we describe the important underpinnings of system psychodynamics, which is the theoretical framework which we use to interpret the findings and to explain why the schools were successful.

In Chapter 4, we describe the context of the research, explore the key issue we addressed and explain how we undertook the research so that readers can fully understand the research process and the setting. Chapter 5 describes the central characteristic and the way it is represented in the schools. This central characteristic is a productive, strong and highly inclusive culture that is focused on ensuring effective and enriched teaching for learning for all pupils and improving and enriching further teaching for learning for all pupils. Chapter 6 discusses leadership in the schools. In particular, we focus on the two key dimensions of the work of the headteacher. The first is the headteacher's role in setting, driving and reinforcing the school culture. The second dimension is developing leadership capability in others in order to create leadership density and depth in the school. This chapter also looks at the contribution of the governing body to the work of the schools.

In all the schools, there was a clearly discernable way of thinking, an attitude of mind and an overall approach which we have termed 'the mindset'. We describe the various components of this mindset in Chapter 7. In Chapter 8, which is entitled 'The teaching team', we describe the way in which the teachers and all those who had a teaching role in the classroom – teaching assistants and nursery nurses, for example – *all* worked together to fully utilise and to improve their expertise. Chapter 9 describes the way the schools sought to fully engage the commitment of all the pupils and all the parents in their work. An important characteristic, which we describe in Chapter 10, was the way all the schools were very efficiently and effectively organised and managed. The final characteristic was the very real sense of support the schools received for their work and the validation and valuing of it from all those connected with them. We outline this contribution of the wider system in Chapter 11.

In Chapter 12, we examine the findings in relation to what is known about effective schools. We outline some of the key issues to emerge and explore how the various characteristics might work together to make these schools successful. Chapter 13 theorises some of the main findings and focuses in particular on issues such as the significance of the core work of the school, which we term the primary task, leadership, boundary management, why inclusivity is important, the containment of emotion and passion for 'Good Work', and systemic leadership for schools. We also offer a perspective on organising in the schools, which we have termed 'collaborative practice'. It was widespread in these schools and was a significant feature. The main dimensions of collaborative practice are collaboration, reflective practice and a focus on the primary task. In Chapter 14, we offer some final thoughts, reflections and concluding comments.

HOW TO USE THE BOOK

We have deliberately structured the book so that it can be used in a variety of ways. Here are some suggestions for how you might use the book.

If you want to get a very quick sense of what these schools did and how they did it then read Chapter 11. You will get an idea of the main outcomes of the research and a sense of how the characteristics of these schools compare with the widely accepted characteristics of 'effective schools'. You will also get a feel for how the ways the schools worked contributed to their success.

If you are interested in finding out in detail what the schools were like – their features and characteristics – then we suggest you read Chapters 5 to 11. These chapters describe *what* the schools do.

Reading Chapter 2 and Chapters 4 to 12 will give you a sense of the issue we addressed, the research we undertook, the characteristics of the schools, how the features of the schools compared to those of 'effective schools' and *how* the characteristics contributed to the schools' success.

To find out why we think the schools were successful from a theoretical standpoint, we suggest you read Chapters 3 and 13. These two chapters together explain *why* the schools were successful.

If you want to know about very effective primary schools, what they do, how they do it and why it works, we suggest you read the whole book!

ACKNOWLEDGEMENTS

The research reported here was undertaken by the Educational Leadership and Management Research Unit at the University of Glamorgan, Wales, UK and by the School of Education at the University of Wales, Bangor, Wales, UK. It was supported by the Narrowing the Gap Initiative, which is sponsored by the Welsh Assembly Government and the Welsh Local Government Association. David Hopkins of Caerphilly Local Education Authority, Chris Llewellyn of the Welsh Local Government Association, Elizabeth Taylor of the Welsh Assembly Government and Maggie Turford of Estyn have been particularly supportive. Some of the data collection was undertaken by Ian Lewis and Jean Williams both of whom are independent educational research and development consultants. We are very grateful indeed for their expert assistance.

We are also very grateful to the schools we worked with on this project. We thank them for their time, their openness and for the clarity of their views. We are especially appreciative of their Good Work. These are Good Schools. They are doing excellent work and giving their pupils the best possible educational start in life.

2

A review of the literature

INTRODUCTION

Such is the breadth of scope of the issue we address in this book, it is difficult to imagine an aspect of the published literature on schools that would not be relevant in a literature review. We have thus decided to focus on a smaller number of particularly significant themes. In doing so, we acknowledge that we are being very selective and that we are clearly anticipating some of the key outcomes and setting a framework within which those outcomes can be considered. The way we have undertaken the review is to explore the literature that we thought would be relevant before we began collecting the data. This literature largely relates to the characteristics of effective schools. When the data collection was complete and we had categorised it into various themes, we then looked at the literature again to see what was relevant to what we had found that would enable us to understand the findings better.

Our intention in this chapter is to review the most important and relevant themes in the literature. The themes are as follows.

- key issues in school effectiveness;
- the characteristics of effective schools;
- organisational culture;
- contextual influences on effectiveness.

KEY ISSUES IN SCHOOL EFFECTIVENESS

History and background

Over the last thirty years or so, there has been extensive research into school effectiveness and the factors that impact on effectiveness. During that time, school effectiveness has grown into a substantial field in educational research and its development continues. A key text in the field edited by Charles Teddlie and David Reynolds (Teddlie and Reynolds 2000) cites over 1,100 references on various aspects of school effectiveness which is a testament to the substantial amount of work that has been amassed.

The major impetus for the initial development of school effectiveness research is generally acknowledged to have been the reaction to the view, prevalent in the 1960s, that the results pupils achieve at the end of their schooling are largely determined by their abilities when they start. This somewhat pessimistic, deterministic and, on reflection, counter-intuitive judgement that 'schools make no difference' was advanced by researchers such as Coleman et al. (1966) and Jencks et al. (1972). It was a widespread point of view in both in the UK and the US at that time. Those who held this view argued that the 'outcome' of schooling (pupil attainment) is determined by the input (pupil ability) and that the work of schools (the processes) has very little, if any, impact on pupil achievement (the outcomes).

Two important studies, one in the US and one in the UK, and the resultant publications were central in countering the 'schools make no difference' argument. In 1979 in the US, *School Social Systems and Student Achievements: Schools Can Make A Difference* was published by Wilbur B. Brookover and his co-workers (Brookover et al. 1979). In the same year in the UK, *Fifteen Thousand Hours* by Michael Rutter and his colleagues (Rutter et al. 1979) was published. Both studies indicated that schools in broadly similar settings and with similar intakes can exert very different effects on pupil outcomes, thus countering the deterministic and somewhat depressing orthodoxy. Other research undertaken during the 1980s supported these two studies and in 1990, Reynolds and Creemers were able to assert in the first edition of the journal *School Effectiveness and School Improvement* that:

schools matter, that schools do have major effects on children's development and that, to put it simply, schools do make a difference.

(Reynolds and Creemers 1990: 1)

This notion that 'schools do make a difference' has remained the central tenet of school effectiveness research and a considerable body of evidence now exists to support that view. Sammons (1999) cites 23 studies conducted in a variety of contexts on different age groups and in different countries that confirm the 'schools do make a difference' standpoint. She concludes that, although ability and family backgrounds exert a major influence on pupil attainment, "*schools in similar social circumstances can achieve very different levels of educational progress*" (Sammons, 1999: 191). Thus some schools are more effective than others, a conclusion which gives rise to a number of important questions, for example: 'How do we know some schools are more effective than others?' 'What is the nature of the effects that different schools have?' and 'What are effective schools like?' A question that was important in the research we report here is 'Are there aspects of educational practice, which are not yet fully understood, that impact on educational effectiveness?'

Deciding which schools are effective

Mortimore (1991) defined an effective school as one in which students progress further than might be expected from a consideration of its intake. This simple and straightforward definition is helpful. It takes into account the starting capabilities and characteristics of the pupils at the beginning of their experience in a school and then seeks to define effectiveness by the amount of 'value added'. However, developing that definition and working with the notion that effectiveness is inherently comparative in nature is somewhat problematic.

Deciding on which schools are effective is not straightforward. The criteria for effectiveness are difficult to derive in both a non-normative and a normative way. Thus deriving a comprehensive and widely accepted definition of effectiveness is very complicated. Deciding on the criteria will always be affected by our value-laden expectations of schools that are derived from our experience and will thus be normative. So, for example, the government and the population at large may conclude that the aim of schools is to ensure that young people pass examinations. Regardless of the prevalence and the authority of such a view, it remains a value judgement, a normative statement. Hence the problem is complicated because there is no agreement on the aims for schools on which criteria and then judgements of effectiveness will be based. So a normative basis for effectiveness is difficult to derive. What is the aim of schooling? To prepare children to participate in a democracy? To enable young people to become independent thinkers? To prepare the young to become compliant workers in the capitalist economy? To fit children for their predetermined place in society? To make sure they gain essential skills? Probably most of these are valid aims and because of the diverse aims for schools, making judgements about school effectiveness even in a normative way is difficult. Furthermore, once the aims have been decided, determining the specific criteria by which these can be assessed is also complex and difficult. For example, if it is agreed that the aim of schools is to ensure that young people pass examinations, we could use examination results as a readily accessible measure and the criterion would be a certain percentage passing. We may use this measure and criterion even though we may not be sure exactly what they are measuring (the results may reflect for example the amount of privately funded support parents can afford to provide their children). But because the results are available we may use these despite any misgivings we have. In other words, the measure ends up determining the criteria and not the other way around.

Sammons (1994) argues that decisions about effectiveness are dependent upon a range of factors including the following.

- *The sample of schools studied.* Effectiveness is situated; it relates to a particular context. Thus, as Mortimore's definition (Mortimore 1991) implies, effectiveness in one setting may not be appropriate in another. For example, effectiveness in a school in an area where there was a high level of pupil disaffection may be judged on attendance rates and attitudinal measures to show how the school had impacted positively upon the ways the students viewed their school. Such a definition may not be appropriate in other settings with low levels of pupil disaffection.

- *The choice of effectiveness measures.* A narrow focus on examination results may give an incomplete picture of the entirety of particular school's work with its pupils. Schools may impact on a whole range of pupil capabilities, not simply those tested in examinations. Arguably, it is important to focus on a range of cognitive measures and affective/social outcomes in the way that Mortimore et al. (1988) did in an early large-scale study of effective schools.

- *Control for pupil intake.* It is important to control for differences in intakes between schools to ensure that similar schools are compared when deciding which are effective and which are not. A school may not be effective for all pupils and, if not, it is important to understand the kind of pupil for which it is effective. A school may be very effective with pupils with a high starting ability but not so effective with pupils with a low starting ability. The composition of the student population of a school can have a significant impact on its overall effectiveness and importantly on the difficulty of the task of improving effectiveness (Thrupp 1999; Lauder, Robinson and Thrupp 2002). So, understanding the overall balance of the pupil intake is important. The differences in pupil intake include: prior attainment and personal, socio-economic and family characteristics. Ideally, this information should be at the individual pupil level, not at the group or cohort level.

- *Methodology.* Value added approaches that focus on students' progress over time can give a better picture of effectiveness than 'snapshots' of the progress of a particular cohort. Statistical techniques such as multilevel modelling can give more accurate estimates of effectiveness because they take into account pupils' background and prior attainment and thus give a better estimate of a school's effect on pupil achievement.

- *Timescale.* 'One-off' changes in effectiveness may be the result of unusual events, unrepeatable episodes or spurious reasons, which, while interesting, do not provide the basis for searching for ways of securing effectiveness in the long term. Furthermore, such changes do not provide a realistic benchmark for effectiveness. Longitudinal approaches, which study effectiveness over a long period, are preferable. Following one or more cohorts over a period of time allows the stability and consistency of a school's effectiveness from year to year to be analysed.

Making clear, unambiguous and indisputable comparisons of the effectiveness of different schools is thus highly problematic.

The nature of the effects

This section briefly explores some of characteristics of the effects that schools can have on pupil progress.

The impact of different degrees of effectiveness

Once the background of the students such as prior attainment and socio-economic status is taken into account, the influence of the classroom and school on educational outcomes is generally small. Estimates of the variation in pupil outcomes that can be attributed to the school vary between 8 and 10 per cent (Daly 1991) and 12 and 18 per cent (Creemers 1994). Thus the bulk of the variation in student outcomes arises from the pupils' background and prior attainment. These differences in school effects may appear to be small but they can have significant educational consequences. For example, at secondary level, the effect on a school's value added score can be between seven Grade E results and seven Grade C results at GCSE or 14 points (Thomas and Mortimore 1996). Differences of this size can have major implications for students' subsequent educational and employment prospects (Sammons 1999). The extent of a school's impact on pupil achievement varies in different subjects (Thomas, Sammons and Mortimore 1995). Perhaps somewhat predictably, it is higher for those subjects taught primarily in school such as history (20 per cent), English literature (12 per cent) and mathematics (9 per cent), and lower for those that are not – around 6 per cent.

Primary school effects may be larger than those identified in the secondary phase and can have a significant long-term impact on subsequent attainment at GCSE (Sammons et al. 1994; Goldstein and Sammons 1997). At both primary and secondary levels, there is a high correlation between different kinds of academic outcomes. At the primary school level, academic and social/affective outcomes are positively related but only weakly so and may be independent. At the secondary level, the link may be closer, in particular between attendance and examination results and between behaviour and examination results.

Consistency of school effects

School effects on overall measures of academic achievement in secondary schools are fairly stable over time. The same is true in the primary sector for basic skills such as numeracy and literacy, though correlations are lower. There is less evidence to indicate stability for specific subjects in secondary schools or for social/affective (non-cognitive) outcomes for any age groups (Sammons 1999).

Differential effectiveness for different groups

There is mixed evidence as to whether schools differ in their effectiveness with different pupil groups, such as those groups with different prior attainment and socio-economic background. Thomas et al. (1995, cited in Sammons 1999) did not find any evidence that more effective schools closed the gap in achievement between different student groups. Pupils with disadvantaged backgrounds did better in schools that were generally more effective than they did in schools that were less effective overall, but then so did pupils from advantaged backgrounds. Sammons (1999) concludes that in general:

> Effective schools tend to be more effective for all pupil groups and, conversely, ineffective schools tend to be ineffective for all groups. (p. 125)

The effects of primary school attended

Sammons (1999) argues that the importance of primary schools in determining students' later school performance may have been underrated. This 'primary effect' may be twofold. Firstly, it may affect the rate of progress made during primary school in basic skills such as reading and mathematics and raising or lowering the level of attainment reached at the point of transfer to secondary school. Secondly, it also affects attainment at age 16 in some way.

THE CHARACTERISTICS OF EFFECTIVE SCHOOLS

There have been a number of seminal studies that have examined the characteristics of schools that are deemed to be effective. These studies are very helpful to practitioners and a number have significantly impacted on educational practice and policy in the UK. However, the outcomes of such studies need to be interpreted and used with a degree of caution (Gray 1990). For example, studies of effective schools need to be reflected upon by those in schools and applied appropriately according to the context. Studies of effective schools identify characteristics that tend to get results; they do not provide certain answers. Moreover, Willms (1992) and Reynolds and Cuttance (1992) suggest that there is no simple combination of factors that can produce an effective school.

Choosing which effective schools to characterise is problematic for a variety of reasons (Sammons 1994). These reasons include the following.

- *Ensuring that contextual variations in the sample of effective schools chosen to study are taken into account.* Schools may be similarly effective but may be so in very different settings. They may thus achieve their effectiveness in very different ways.

- *Deciding on the measures by which schools are deemed to be effective.* Narrowing the sample down to focus on a particular set of measures will inevitably exclude schools that could be deemed to be effective on the basis of another set of measures.

- *Identifying 'control schools' against which the effective schools are to be compared.* It is important to compare 'like with like'. Given the complex nature of schools such comparisons are very difficult.

- *Ensuring that the schools studied are consistently effective and that the characteristics identified are directly relevant to sustaining continual effectiveness.* Although it might be interesting to find out why a school has suddenly but perhaps temporarily become more effective, arguably it is more interesting to study those schools that can sustain a high level of pupil progress.

Key studies

Early studies by Reynolds and co-workers (Reynolds 1976; Reynolds and Murgatroyd 1977; Reynolds and Sullivan 1979) studied schools with differing levels of effectiveness based upon an analysis of a range of pupil intake data. This data related to prior achievement, family background and outcome measures of achievement, attendance and delinquency. Reynolds and his colleagues identified a number of factors including:

- extensive involvement of pupils in positions of authority;
- low levels of involvement of the senior staff of the school in managing pupil behaviour;
- positive expectations of pupil achievement;
- extensive involvement of teachers in the organisation of the school;
- flexibility on the pupils' compliance to rules on uniform and manners;
- considerable involvement of the pupils in extra-curricular activities such as after-school clubs and societies.

Rutter et al. (1979) studied 12 inner London secondary schools and found significant differences between them on four measures:

- behaviour in school;
- attendance;
- examination success;
- delinquency.

They found substantial disparities even when the variation in pupil intake was taken into account. Several aspects of the school process were found to be important in achieving these outcomes, including the following.

- *Academic emphasis.* A number of 'academic' processes contributed to achieving the positive student outcomes which included: the setting of homework and the checking by teachers that it had been completed; teachers having high expectations; the display of students' work around the school; a high proportion of teacher time devoted to teaching; teachers collaborating to plan courses; and students regularly using the school library.

- *The leadership of the headteacher.* Key features were the combination of firm leadership from the headteacher and the headteacher involving the staff in decision-making.

- *Teacher actions in lessons.* These actions included: the amount of time spent communicating about work rather than routine organisational matters; good time-keeping; effective planning and organisation; and teachers addressing the whole class during lessons. They all contributed to positive pupil outcomes.

- *The use of rewards and punishments.* These included: the ample use of rewards; praise and appreciation; unobtrusive discipline management; the rewarding of good behaviour; and minimising the disruption of lessons.

- *The school environment.* Good working conditions for the students and a high standard of care and decoration had a positive effect on pupil outcomes.

- *Student responsibility and participation.* In schools which had a significant positive effect on pupil outcomes, there were large numbers of pupils in positions of responsibility.

- *Staff organisation and the skills of the teachers.* The way the staff were organised and the capabilities of the staff had a significant effect on positive pupil outcomes.

The Mortimore et al. (1988) study tracked the educational progress of 2,000 pupils in 50 randomly selected London primary schools. Mortimore and his colleagues identified a number of characteristics as follows.

- *Purposeful leadership by the headteacher*. The headteacher understood the needs of the school and was actively involved. He or she did not exert total control over the rest of the staff but had an inclusive approach. The headteacher shaped curriculum practices, influenced in-service training and was involved in maintaining records of pupil progress.

- *The involvement of the deputy headteacher*. The deputy headteacher clearly had a significant role. Mortimore and his colleagues found that where the deputy headteacher was involved in policy decisions, there was a positive impact on pupil progress. Conversely, when the deputy headteacher was absent or there was a change of deputy headteacher, there was a negative impact on effectiveness.

- *The involvement of teachers*. In effective schools, teachers were involved in making decisions about curriculum matters and had a significant role in developing both schemes of work and guidelines on teaching and learning. They were also consulted about finance and policy decisions.

- *Consistency among teachers*. Continuity of staffing was important as were stability and consistency in teacher approach. Teachers following agreed guidelines had a positive impact on pupil progress – and vice versa.

- *Structured sessions*. Pupil progress was greater when the school day was more structured. Ensuring there were sufficient learning activities for the pupils enhanced progress. Pupils being given appropriate responsibility for their own work also had a positive impact. There was a negative impact when they were given unlimited responsibility and little supervision for a long list of tasks.

- *Intellectually challenging teaching*. It was important that teaching was stimulating and challenging. Teaching of this kind was characterised by:
  - the use of higher order questions and statements;
  - communicating interest and enthusiasm;
  - explaining the purpose of tasks to students.

The level of communication was more important than the frequency of communication. High expectations and a well-established positive classroom culture enhanced pupil progress.

- *Work-centred environment.* In effective schools, there were high levels of student activity and endeavour. The pupils enjoyed their work and were keen to undertake new tasks. In classes, noise levels were low and movement around the class was work-related and not excessive. There were positive effects from teachers discussing the content of the work rather than spending time discussing routine organisational matters. Giving feedback to pupils benefited their progress.

- *Limited focus within sessions.* Learning was enhanced when teachers devoted their energies to one or perhaps two particular topics within one session. 'Mixed' activities reduced pupil progress perhaps because the pupils worked less hard, noise and pupil movements were greater, teachers spent less time on content and more on routine organisational matters, and perhaps because there were fewer opportunities for communication between pupils and teachers. Matching the level of work to the pupils' needs was important.

- *Maximum communication between teachers and students.* More communication enhanced pupil progress. Teachers addressing the whole class was important. It raised the intellectual level of teacher–pupil communication and the extent to which all pupils were exposed to 'higher order' communications.

- *Record-keeping.* Keeping records of pupil progress was beneficial. It was an important aspect of the teachers' planning and assessment.

- *Parental involvement.* The involvement of parents in a variety of ways exerted a positive impact. For example, parents helping in the classroom, attending meetings to discuss pupil progress, reading to their children at home, all had a beneficial effect on effectiveness. The headteachers' accessibility to parents was important. The Mortimore et al. study concluded that parent–teacher associations were not universally beneficial because some parents found the formality of them somewhat intimidating.

- *Positive climate.* Effective schools had a positive ethos and pleasant atmosphere. In such schools, there was an emphasis on praise rather than punishment and teachers encouraged self-control by the pupils.

Sammons, Hillman and Mortimore (1995), following a review of the literature on the nature of effective schools, identified 11 key features of effective schools as follows.

1. Professional leadership

The leadership of the headteacher consistently featured in the literature describing the features of effective schools. The impact of the headteacher on pupil attainment is likely to be indirect, a view that has been subsequently confirmed by others, for example Hallinger and Heck (1998, 1999).

Firm and purposeful leadership.   The headteacher:

- was proactive especially in the recruitment and selection of staff;
- had the ability to mediate or buffer the school from unhelpful change agents and initiatives;
- had the capacity to challenge and even violate externally set guidelines;
- played a key role in initiating and maintaining the school improvement processes.

A participative approach.   The headteacher involved others in decision-making in particular and showed a readiness to delegate – a characteristic especially prevalent in larger schools. Good 'middle management' was important.

The leading professional.   The headteacher:

- was involved in and knew what was going on in the classrooms;
- was ready to support teachers;
- had a high profile and visibility around the school.

2. Shared vision and goals

Effective schools build consensus on the aims and values of the school. They put this shared view into practice consistently, in particular by working and making decisions collaboratively. There are three themes in this characteristic.

Unity of purpose. Shared vision raises aspirations and encourages a collective sense of purpose, especially where schools are in demanding circumstances.

Consistency of practice.   In effective schools there is:

- consensus among the staff;

- a consistent approach among the staff to their work;
- adherence to common and agreed approaches to matters such as assessment, the enforcement of rules, and giving rewards and sanctions.

Collegiality and collaboration. Mortimore et al. (1988) in particular drew attention to the importance of teacher involvement in decision-making and in the development of school plans and procedures in order to create a sense of 'policy ownership'. They concluded that a climate of collegiality and collaboration:

- is fostered by mutually supportive and respectful relationships;
- comes through the sharing of ideas, observing each other and giving feedback and learning from each other;
- is enhanced by working together to improve the teaching programme.

3. A learning environment

The climate in which the pupils work – the learning environment – is important in determining the ethos of the school. Mortimore at al. (1988) concluded that two particular aspects are important.

An orderly atmosphere. Successful schools are more likely to be characterised by calmness rather than chaos. This finding confirms those of the earliest effectiveness studies in the late 1970s, which emphasised the importance of maintaining a task-oriented and orderly learning environment. Mortimore et al. (1988) pointed to the importance of encouraging self-control among pupils in creating a positive ethos in the classroom. They also drew attention to the negative impact of the disruption of pupil concentration by noise and pupil movement around the class that was not task-related. It is not that schools become more effective as they become more orderly but that order is an important prerequisite for effectiveness. As Creemers (1994) points out, an orderly atmosphere that has the purpose of stimulating learning has a positive impact on pupil achievement.

An attractive working environment. School effectiveness research suggests that a pleasant and attractive physical environment can have a beneficial effect on both pupil attitudes and achievements. Some of the earliest studies, for example Rutter et al. (1979), drew attention to the link between an attractive working environment and effectiveness. Mortimore et al. (1988) pointed out the importance of creating a pleasant physical environment which included the display of pupils' work.

4. Concentration on teaching and learning

Sammons, Hillman and Mortimore (1995) assert that the primary purposes of schools concern teaching and learning. Thus, while it would be expected that these would be activities upon which schools would focus, research indicates that schools differ in the extent to which they focus on their primary purpose. A number of authors, for example Cohen (1983), Scheerens (1992), Mortimore (1993) and Creemers (1994), have reported that school effectiveness is dependent upon effective classroom teaching. Many studies have focused on teacher time and related it to school effectiveness, but the issue is not simply the time spent on teaching. Schools and teachers need to focus on the quality of teaching as well.

Maximisation of learning time. A number of measures of 'learning time' have been shown to have a positive impact on effectiveness including:

- the proportion of the day devoted to academic subjects;
- the amount of time in lessons devoted to learning;
- the time teachers spent discussing content of work with pupils as opposed to talking about routine organisational matters;
- teachers' concerns with cognitive objectives rather than personal relationships and affective objectives;
- punctuality of lessons;
- a low level of disruption from outside the classroom.

Scheerens (1992) reported four time-related factors as follows.

1   The institutional time spent on learning such as the length of school day/week/year. These institutional constraints can affect the total learning time available which will in turn impact on effectiveness.
2   The quantity of homework set. Time spent learning outside the institution will also impact on effectiveness.
3   The total amount of effective learning time within institutional time constraints. The amount of learning time may vary between schools in which the pupils are present in the schools for the same time overall.
4   The amount of learning time for different subjects. The balance of time spent on the various subjects in the curriculum will impact on attainment in the different subjects.

Sammons, Hillman and Mortimore (1995) identified two important characteristics as follows.

An academic emphasis. Effective schools are characterised by:

- the sense that teachers and pupils have of the academic emphasis;

- high levels of pupil diligence in the classroom;
- regular setting and marking of homework with monitoring of homework setting and marking by senior staff;
- mastery of academic content by the pupils;
- teachers having an adequate level of subject knowledge;
- complete curriculum coverage.

A focus on achievement. Given that pupil achievement as measured by tests of various kinds is a measure of effectiveness, it is perhaps understandable that effective schools concentrate on the achievements of their pupils in these tests. Early studies especially in US primary schools, for example Brookover et al. (1979), showed that stressing the acquisition of basic skills or having an 'achievement orientation' have a positive influence on school effectiveness.

5. Purposeful teaching

Sammons, Hillman and Mortimore concluded that it is difficult to draw general conclusions on effective teaching practices because effective teaching is measured by pupil learning which can itself be difficult to measure. From their review of the literature, they concluded that the outstanding factor was 'purposeful teaching' which had three dimensions.

Efficient organisation. In effective settings:

- teachers were well organised;
- teaching was prepared in advance of rather than during lessons;
- there was appropriate pacing of lessons.

Clarity of purpose. It is important that pupils are always aware of the purpose of the content of lessons. Sammons, Hillman and Mortimore point out that one way of ensuring this awareness is to begin the lesson with an initial explanation of the purpose and intentions which is then followed by the substance of the lesson, and the lesson ends with a recap.

Structured lessons. From a review of the literature, Scheerens (1992) defines 'structured teaching' as:

- making clear what is to be learnt;
- splitting teaching material into manageable units for the pupils and offering these in a well-considered sequence;
- the extensive use of 'exercise material' in which pupils make use of their intuition and instincts with appropriate triggers and prompts;
- regular testing of progress with immediate feedback on results.

Scheerens admits this list is probably more valid for primary schools but argues that it can be adapted for other settings. Gray (1993) offers a note of caution on structure suggesting that it may not be necessary beyond the early years. Moreover, it has been given too much weight because early school effectiveness research focused on disadvantaged schools thus giving especial emphasis to the teaching of basic skills.

Adaptive practice.   Pupil progress is enhanced when teachers are sensitive to differences in the ways different pupils learn and, as appropriate and feasible, identify and deploy a range of teaching strategies. This way of working may require teachers to be flexible in their approach and to be capable of modifying their teaching methods and strategies.

6. High expectations

Sammons, Hillman and Mortimore concluded that positive expectations of pupil achievement by teachers, and also by the pupils themselves and their parents, is one of the most important characteristics of effective schools. A substantial body of evidence indicates that when teachers set high standards for their pupils, let the pupils know they are expected to meet those standards and provide intellectually challenging lessons that match those expectations, then the impact on achievement can be considerable. There are three particular themes in the literature related to high expectations.

High expectations all round.   Sammons, Hillman and Mortimore cited 15 studies in various countries that have all shown a strong relationship between high expectations and effective learning. High expectations are a part of proactive teaching, which is a way of describing a teacher's sense of being able to influence pupil learning, to overcome the pupils' learning difficulties, and a sense of a teacher's high level of agency and efficacy. High expectations have a greater impact when they are part of a general culture – hence the notion of high expectations *all round*. Levine and Lezotte (1990) consider that high expectations are a feature of virtually all unusually effective schools.

Communicating expectations.   When 'high expectations' are communicated to pupils, there is a consequent impact on pupil esteem which then leads through to an impact on pupil achievement. Further, teachers conveying the conviction that pupils have the capacity to 'do better' can have a powerful effect. Sammons, Hillman and Mortimore suggest that high expectations do not impact directly on pupil achievement but when those high expectations are *communicated* that they have an effect.

Providing intellectual challenge.   A common cause of under-achievement in pupils is the failure to challenge them (Mortimore et al. 1988). The use of higher order questions and statements and encouraging pupils to use their imagination and problem-solving capabilities can be particularly significant in giving pupils intellectual challenge.

7. Positive reinforcement

Reinforcement, whether in terms of routines for ensuring a high standard of pupil behaviour or through giving of feedback to pupils, emerged even in the earliest studies to be an important element of school effectiveness. Walberg's study of teaching methods (Walberg 1984) indicated that reinforcement was the most powerful factor of all in effective teaching. Rewards, other positive incentives and clear rules are more likely than punishment to be associated with better outcomes.

Clear and fair discipline. Effective discipline contributes to school effectiveness. It involves keeping good order, consistently enforcing fair, clear and well-understood rules and the infrequent use of punishment.

Feedback. Praise or reprimand as forms of feedback are best given to pupils immediately while feedback in the form of rewards, incentives and prizes may be delayed. Rutter et al. (1979) indicated that praise had a greater effect than rewards because:

- it affects a greater number of pupils;
- the lack of delay allows more definite links to the behaviours that are being encouraged;
- it is more likely to increase the intrinsic value of that which is being reinforced.

Praise should be directed in relation to correct answers or to achievement and should be used sparingly. Sammons, Hillman and Mortimore found that various studies report the need for praise to be specific, contingent, spontaneous and varied. It should use students' own prior accomplishments as a context for describing present achievements and to attribute success to effort and ability.

8. Monitoring progress

Effective schools typically have well-established mechanisms for monitoring the progress of pupils, classes, the whole school and improvement programmes. There appear to be particular benefits from headteacher involvement in monitoring pupil achievement and progress. Within this characteristic, Sammons, Hillman and Mortimore identified two strands in the literature as follows.

Monitoring pupil performance. Checking and keeping track of pupil progress is an important 'ingredient' of the work of an effective school even though it may have little direct impact on achievement. Monitoring pupil performance:

- provides a means of determining the extent to which the school's goals are being achieved;
- focuses the attention of staff, parents and pupils on these goals;
- informs planning, teaching methods and assessment;
- indicates clearly to pupils that teachers are interested in their progress.

Appropriate monitoring is the key. Levine and Lezotte (1990) argue that too much time and energy can be spent on monitoring or on monitoring inappropriately. Mortimore et al. (1988) reported that keeping records of pupils' academic progress – not just their personal and social development – was important.

Evaluating school performance. Scheerens (1992) argues that evaluation is an essential prerequisite to effectiveness. It enhances measures of effectiveness at all levels. The headteacher should be actively involved in whole-school evaluation.

9. Pupil rights and responsibilities

There can be quite substantial gains in effectiveness when:

- the self-esteem of pupils is raised;
- pupils are actively involved in the life of the school;
- pupils have some responsibility for their own learning.

Within this characteristic there are three themes.

Raising pupils' self-esteem. Sammons, Hillman and Mortimore report that early studies showed that a sound and positive student–teacher relationship was important in bringing about pupil achievement. There were beneficial effects from teachers communicating enthusiasm to pupils and where teachers show an individual interest in the pupils (Mortimore et al. 1988). Extra-curricular activities can be used to enhance pupil–teacher relationships. Positive outcomes resulted when pupils felt able to talk to teachers about their problems.

Positions of responsibility. Giving pupils positions of responsibility conveys trust, sets standards for mature behaviour and has positive effects overall.

Control of work.   When pupils have greater control over what happens to them at school there are beneficial effects on outcomes.

10. Home–school partnership

Research into effective schools generally shows the positive effects of supportive and cooperative relationships between home and school. A key dimension is parents being involved in their children's learning.

Parental involvement in their children's learning.   The literature indicates marked differences between the nature of parental involvement in primary and secondary schools. In primary schools, parents helping in the classroom and with school trips, regular pupil progress meetings, a designated parent's room in the school and an 'open-door' policy by the headteacher all had beneficial effects.

Hallinger and Murphy (1986) showed that parental involvement can be more influential in schools with more poor or working-class pupils. The combined support of parents and teachers for learning can be a powerful force. Macbeath (1994) asserts that successful schools support and make demands on parents and Coleman, Collinge and Tabin (1994) argue that the positive interrelationships between the teacher, parent and pupil are crucial in creating support from the pupil's home for their learning.

11. A learning organisation

In effective schools, teachers and senior managers keep up to date with their subjects and with advances in understanding about effective practice. This 'learning orientation' is school-wide and Sammons, Hillman and Mortimore use the term 'learning organisation' to capture the sense of it. The literature indicates that school-based staff development is a key feature of the school as a learning organisation.

School-based staff development.   Staff development in effective schools generally takes place at the school site and is focused on enhancing classroom teaching and improving teaching plans. It is continuous and incremental. Embedding staff development within collegial and collaborative planning is important as is ensuring that ideas from development activities are routinely shared.

Some thoughts on the characteristics of effective schools

The findings of Sammons, Hillman and Mortimore (1995) in particular provide a very helpful framework, which, although open to attack for being *"platitudinous or tautological ... are reasonably robust"* (Hargreaves 2001: 487). Other researchers have subsequently described similar groupings of characteristics, most notably Stoll and Fink (1996), MacGilchrist, Myers and Reed (1997) and Teddlie et al. (2002). The lists give rise to five points for consideration.

1   There is a remarkable consistency and unanimity to the lists. At their core they are very similar. They seem to build successively, each one adding more to the previous lists, embellishing, extending and clarifying them. In many ways, this accretion of understanding is reassuring in that it confirms their validity. But the changes do add weight to the argument that we may not know all there is to know about effective schools and that we should continue to look for new – perhaps significant – aspects. Also the newer lists may recognise and acknowledge the important changes as schools shift and adapt their ways of working.

2   These lists of characteristics are valuable and useful but we consider that they accord insufficient status to pupil learning. Although it could be argued that 'ensuring pupil learning' is threaded through the various characteristics, particularly those of Levine and Lezotte (1990), it appears to be but one of a range of characteristics. Sammons, Hillman and Mortimore report a number of studies that link effectiveness with the quality and quantity of classroom teaching. However, teaching, especially teaching that brings about pupil learning, is not accorded any particular status despite its obvious importance.

3   The lists pay insufficient attention to the influence that a school's wider community might have on the school beyond that which parents may bring to bear. Schools do not exist in isolation. In the UK, for example, schools have governing bodies, work in local authorities and are part of a wider educational community that includes other schools, professional associations, school inspection services, central government and various national agencies. Nowadays, those agencies would include organisations such as the Teacher Development Agency and the General Teaching Council, for example. Arguably, all the members of this wider community have a part to play in bringing about the effectiveness of a school.

4   The lists are essentially content lists. They have very little to say, for example, about the way teachers in effective schools go about their work, what the general attitude is and how the various characteristics are worked with. What is the overall approach? Is it enthusiastic, positive and optimistic? Or is it apathetic, negative and pessimistic? Is 'purposeful teaching' undertaken with energy, vitality and commitment? Or is teaching, despite its purposefulness, carried out in a slightly flat, somewhat lacklustre and perhaps unexceptional way?

5   Although adaptive practice is stressed, arguably this quality is not given sufficient status. The ability to adapt practice in the way that reflective practitioner (Schön 1983) models of teaching explain is fundamental to good teaching. Without the ability to modify teaching

in the moment of practice and to learn from that experience and subsequently improve, a teacher's work is likely to be inadequate and, moreover, its quality will almost certainly decline over time.

SCHOOLS IN CHALLENGING CIRCUMSTANCES

There has been a recent upsurge of interest in the characteristics of schools in 'challenging' or 'difficult' circumstances and identifying how schools respond positively to those circumstances. In this section, we look at the nature of challenging and difficult circumstances and how schools respond to them.

The nature of challenging circumstances

Schools in challenging circumstances have been defined by Keys et al. (2003) as those:

- where 25 per cent of the pupils or less achieve five or more A*–C grades at GCSE (or equivalent in other Key Stages);
- which serve communities with high levels of socio-economic disadvantage;
- that face one or more school-related issues such as:
  - poor management
  - a budget deficit
  - unsatisfactory buildings
  - staffing problems
  - low levels of pupil attainment on entry
  - behaviour management problems
  - high rates of unauthorised absence and pupil exclusion
  - low levels of parental involvement
  - falling rolls
  - high pupil turnover
  - a lack of public confidence in the school.

The notion of challenging circumstances is clearly complex and wide-ranging. This list identifies the whole range of challenges and difficulties that cover input characteristics such as falling rolls, process characteristics (for example behaviour management problems) and output characteristics (for example, a low percentage of pupils achieving higher grades in national tests). The sources of challenge are linked and intersect and because of their varied nature will require very different strategies to overcome them.

The characteristics of schools in challenging circumstances

An important study of schools in a particular kind of challenging circumstance – those working in disadvantaged areas – was that undertaken as part of the National Commission on Education in the UK in the mid-1990s (NCE 1995). *Success Against the Odds*, the publication that resulted from the study, describes the work of 11 schools in England and Wales that were successful in disadvantaged settings and identified a number of common themes as follows.

Visions of success. There was a pride in the schools' achievements and success, a collective sense of vision among all those who worked in the schools, unity of purpose and a 'can-do' philosophy.

Whole-school policies and practices. Within this theme, making the school an environment fit for learning, good pupil behaviour, high expectations that were communicated to pupils and the monitoring pupil progress were significant. Inclusion, *"where staff share ownership, involvement and responsibility with pupils, parents and the wider community"* (p. 327) also featured.

The leadership and management of the school. This theme included the judgement, the presence, visibility and style of the headteacher. It also included shared leadership and *"building and developing a team"* (p. 327).

The impact of educational reforms. Because of the timing of the study, the schools would have been working with the implications of the substantial reforms initiated by the 1988 Education Reform Act, which among other things gave the schools considerable managerial autonomy and required them to follow the National Curriculum. The response of the schools to these reforms was interesting. Firstly, the schools did not passively accept the requirements of the National Curriculum. They retained a considerable sense of control over curricular matters despite the obligations of the National Curriculum. Secondly, what emerged was a focus on 'the school', and most notably the headteacher and the staff as the driving force for improvement. Governors were not considered to be a particularly powerful driving force for change. The role of the local authority was unclear, although the definition of that role will have been sharpened as a result of subsequent legislation. OfSTED, despite its slogan of 'Improvement through Inspection', was not seen to be driving change. The 'cross-case analysis' concluded that:

> The important lesson to be learned is that the energy released in these schools is generated primarily by what that school believes it can and must do. (p. 354)

This finding is particularly important in the context of one of the outcomes of the study reported here. In Chapters 11 and 12 we explore the notion of systemic support for the schools in this study and explain its importance. Five years later, Maden repeated the original study (Maden 2001) and drew a number of conclusions, the most significant of which is the importance of the role of the headteacher in involving, energising and nurturing staff. Again, the drive to ensure effectiveness and to bring about improvement originates and resides within the school.

From a study of the literature, Keys and her co-workers (2003) found that schools that were effective in challenging contexts:

- had effective leadership;
- created a shared vision;
- involved staff in the leadership process;
- improved the curriculum and the quality of learning and teaching;
- raised achievement;
- improved attitudes and behaviour;
- involved others and engaged external support.

The leaders of schools in challenging settings are constantly managing tensions and problems, are people-centred and are able to combine a moral purpose with a willingness to be collaborative and to promote collaboration (Harris and Chapman 2002). The published literature on improving schools in disadvantaged settings, which is wide-ranging and comprises several different and overlapping sets (Muijs et al. 2004), covers:

- a focus on teaching and learning;
- leadership;
- creating an information-rich environment;
- creating a positive school culture;
- building a learning community;
- continuous professional development;
- involving parents;
- external support.

The problematic nature of challenging circumstances

For a variety of reasons, the notion of 'challenging circumstances' is problematic.

Firstly, many schools may respond to a 'challenge' and may overcome it and yet in a sense the challenging circumstance remains. The challenge may still be present even after the school has successfully responded to it. For example, the school may still serve a community with high levels of socio-economic disadvantage even though it works very successfully with the challenges that such a community can present.

Secondly, a school's performance in a particular aspect of its practice will regress unless efforts to respond to keep the challenge at bay are sustained. For example, behaviour management problems will recur unless successful behaviour management strategies remain in place.

Thirdly, there is a case for arguing that all schools and all those who work in them or who are connected with them should be continually experiencing a sense of challenge to improve regardless of their current effectiveness. This sense of challenge may come from sources outside the school such as the local authority, school inspection or changes in government policy. It may also come from the work of the teaching staff individually and collectively reflecting on their practice in order to improve it. The challenge to improve may come from formalised procedures such as performance management and self-evaluation. It may come from the enthusiasms, passions and desires to undertake 'Good Educational Work'. The motivation to respond to and overcome challenging circumstances may come from all of these sources.

ORGANISATIONAL CULTURE

Arguably, efforts to describe the characteristics of effective schools are attempts to capture their culture and make it explicit. In this section, we review the notion of culture in order to explore it as an organising framework for understanding how the schools we studied worked. We examine in particular the origins of the term, what it means and its recent history, the usefulness of the term, approaches to understanding culture and the origins of organisational culture.

Organisational culture – the origins, meaning and recent history of the term

The term 'culture' is borrowed from anthropology, where 'there is no agreement on its meaning' (Alvesson 2004: 3). Unsurprisingly, Smircich (1983) argues that *"organisational analysts hold varying conceptions of culture"* (p. 339). Allaire and Firsirotu (1984) reviewed the organisation/culture literature and identified 164 definitions of the term. In a general sense, however, culture refers to the meanings, values, beliefs, myths and stories, as well as the rites, rituals and ceremonies that abound in organisations. Frost et al. (1985) add that it also refers to the interpretation of events, ideas and experiences that are influenced and shaped by the groups within which people live. Alvesson (2002) goes even further and includes values and assumptions about social reality, though he considers that values are less central and useful than meanings and symbolism in cultural analysis. The functional importance of the concept lies in the fact that patterns of belief or shared meaning, fragmented or integrated and supported by various operating norms and rituals, can exert a decisive influence on the overall ability of the organisation to deal with the challenges it faces.

Peters and Waterman helped to bring about the popularity of 'culture' as a term with their hugely successful (if deeply flawed) book *In Search of Excellence* (Peters and Waterman 1982). Its rise to eminence coincided with the success of Japanese companies and the Japanese economy generally in which culture was thought to be a success factor. It was envisaged by many that the emulation of those much admired approaches would bring success in other settings. The term was employed before then, however, and its early use in organisation theory can be traced to at least 1951, when Elliot Jacques of the Tavistock Institute in London published his dissertation entitled *The Changing Culture of a Factory*. In recent years, the term has come under some attack, in part because some of the exemplar companies identified by Peters and Waterman ran into difficulties and many Japanese companies – and indeed the whole Japanese economy – have had problems. Further, the slipperiness of the concept has led academics to be wary of it and the evidence indicates that efforts to change cultures to a more desirable form are difficult and may not be successful (see, for example, Weeks 2004).

A number of commentators have applied the concept to public sector institutions, for example the civil service (Metcalfe and Richards 1984, 1990), local government (Newman 1996) and schools (Nias, Southworth and Yeomans 1989). The popularity of the term in the 1980s and 1990s owed much to the supposed linkage between (strong) cultures and organisational performance. That linkage is central to the Peters and Waterman arguments and to the apparent importance of the culture of Japanese companies in what was then a highly successful economy. As a result much effort went into seeking ways of developing – strengthening – organisational cultures which enhanced the performance of the organisation.

The concept remains of interest and Alvesson (2002) in a major review writes that culture is:

> Highly significant for how … organizations function: from strategic change, to everyday leadership and how managers and employees relate to and interact with customers as well as how knowledge is created, shared, maintained and utilized.

(Alvesson 2002: 2)

Culture – the usefulness of the term

Practitioners – including managers – use the term 'culture' when talking about the nature of organisations and institutions – including schools. The culture metaphor (arguably, that is what it is) enables many traditional management concepts to be interpreted in interesting ways. For example, it allows the roles played by managers/leaders in the social construction of reality to be recognised. Leadership in this sense is the management of meaning. In addition, organisation–environment links can be understood as a process of social enactment. Finally, managers themselves value the concept. The notion of culture may well have a particular resonance for 'professional organisations', partly because of government efforts to secure performance targets from public sector institutions, including schools.

Understanding culture

Commentators have sought to define ways of understanding culture (see, for example, Meyerson and Martin 1987; Bate 1994; Martin 2002; Alvesson 2002). One major fault line is Smircich's (1983) distinction between culture as a variable and as a root metaphor, or as Bate (1994) puts it, between culture as something an organisation has and something an organisation is. The former case is illustrated by the 'McKinsey 7S diagram' where it is described as shared values (see Peters and Waterman 1982). It is a function of an organisation, and is treated in a way that is similar to, say, an organisation's structure. This view of organisational culture is important, not least because managers are themselves interested in it. Culture is seen by some writers in this tradition as the:

> Social or normative glue that holds an organisation together ... It expresses the values or social ideals that organisation members come to share ... These values or patterns of belief are manifested by symbolic devices such as myths ..., stories ..., legends ..., and specialised language.

(Smircich 1983: 344)

Culture provides:

> The shared rules governing cognitive and affective aspects of membership in an organization and the means whereby they are shaped and expressed.

(Kunda 1992: 8, quoted by Alvesson 2002: 3)

Alvesson goes on to argue that culture in this view is not inside people's heads but somewhere 'between' the heads of a group of people where symbols and meanings are publicly expressed. Culture is seen as a key contingency, which organisations must get right if they are to succeed. Culture is functional to the organisation, ensuring that organisational members have a sense of loyalty to and identity with the organisation. From this notion comes the idea that organisational culture:

> May be another critical lever or key by which strategic managers can influence and direct the course of their organisations The belief is that firms that have internal cultures supportive of their strategies are more likely to be successful.

(Smircich 1983: 346)

An alternative view sees culture as a way of understanding organisations. Strategy therefore is seen through a cultural prism: it is culture. Bate

(1994), for example, quotes Weick (1979) who uses definitions of strategy and culture to demonstrate their identity. This relationship is referred to by writers who view organisations as paradigms, that is *"organised patterns of thought with accompanying understanding of what constitutes adequate knowledge and legitimate activity"* (Smircich 1983: 350). Authors in this tradition see organisations as 'cognitive enterprises' (Argyris and Schön 1978). Thus, in talking about culture, we are really talking about a process of organisational reality that allows people to see and understand particular events, actions, utterances or situations in distinctive ways. Karl Weick (1979) talks about a process of enactment, of people unconsciously creating their own world.

Alvesson (2002) argues that the base metaphor of 'culture' itself requires metaphors to understand it:

> When people talk about culture in organization studies, for example, what do they think of? What are their gestalts? Is culture seen as 'personality' writ large, 'an overall control mechanism', a 'community' or what?

> (Alvesson 2002: 29)

His point really is that the concept of culture is a heavily burdened one and we need to be careful about how we use it and what we want from it.

The origins of organisational culture

If we begin by asking about the origins of organisational culture, the first view (culture as a variable) tends to suggest that management creates the culture, a process sometimes referred to as cultural engineering. This perspective gives a prominent role to 'the leader', especially the organisational creator. In turn, that implies that there is a coherent, unifying culture. While leaders may well be a crucial element in determining cultures, especially where they are the creators of their organisations, there is more to organisational culture than leadership style. Williams, Dobson and Walters (1989) argue that:

> some consultancy-based authors have drawn conclusions far beyond the available evidence. It is really extraordinary that, for example, Deal and Kennedy and Peters and Waterman have made statements about the nature of organizational culture mainly based on the statements of CEOs and senior executives of multi-nationals; these interesting, but largely second-hand, executive stories are probably truly the myths of culture. (p. 10)

In organisations there are often many different and competing value systems that create a mosaic of organisational realities rather than a uniform corporate culture. As Riley (1983) puts it:

Increasingly people are warned that organisations are not the rational monoliths they appear, but complex mixtures of game-playing, rule-following, self-promotion, competition, and hidden agendas.

(Riley 1983)

So, for example, different professional groups may create their own culture and guide their activities with reference to a common and integrated set of norms and priorities. This in turn raises questions about the nature of the relationship between power and the creation of corporate culture.

In schools, professional values will be an important dimension in the creation of organisational culture. But this might imply that all schools are the same. Indeed, we have clearly established that that is not the case. So, from where might the differences arise? The role of heads and other leaders may well be important, especially in small schools, but at least two other factors are significant. The first is the history and traditions of the school. If culture is a socially constructed phenomenon, its development takes place within a social environment, which is interpreted, for example, by long-serving staff members. Secondly, the school is part of a broader community or set of communities and these communities and the pupils and their parents will interact with the school in various ways. They will have expectations and experiences which will inform the culture and the way 'the school' interacts with them will also influence and be influenced by the culture. There is a substantial managerialist literature which is devoted to changing the ways customers are viewed by organisational members, something which, despite the limitations of the marketing perspective on public sector organisations, occupies the time of many senior members in the public sector. The nature of these (two-way) interactions will inform the culture of the organisation.

In the analysis and interpretation of the data from this study, we draw heavily on the notion of culture: it is part of the central characteristic of these schools. At this juncture, it is worth making two points about culture. Firstly, and as our data bears out, culture has a purpose. To put it colloquially, 'We do things round here the way we do for a reason'. It may be the 'right' reason, it may not, but nonetheless culture represents purposeful activity of some kind. In our analysis, the culture and its various aspects and contributing characteristics address what we call the main task or the primary task. It was a very significant feature of the schools. Secondly, we draw attention to a number of aspects of practice in the schools that contribute to the culture. One interesting characteristic is what we call 'the mindset' (see Chapter 7). The term is intended to describe an overall approach, a predominant way of thinking, a prevailing attitude. The mindset affects actions, shapes agency and underpins practices, which if engaged in recursively affects 'the way we do things round here' – the culture.

The impact of culture on organisational performance

The impact of the culture of the organisation on performance is a significant issue. The managerialist literature tends to emphasise that strong cultures (that is, unitary and deeply held cultures) impact positively on performance and as we have already argued above was a factor in encouraging the growth of interest in culture. There are a number of points to be made. Firstly, if the shape of the organisational culture is not in the gift of senior managers, they may be wasting resources by attempting to engineer the culture. That assertion does not invalidate the argument that strong cultures may impact positively on performance. Secondly, it is possible that culture helps to influence performance evaluations. Whether a university judges research output of a particular sort as the core activity may well in part reflect its culture. Thus the core task may well be partially defined by the organisation's culture. Third, there is an argument within the literature that causation runs from performance to culture. Success is determined by factors other than culture, and that success then shapes the culture. Fourth, it is perfectly possible for strong cultures to inhibit success. New headteachers may find themselves faced by a culture that is complacent and hostile to their notions of success. Finally, this point in turn leads to the argument made by Alvesson that *"There are no recipes for success that just can be copied and applied without consideration of time and space"* (Alvesson 2002: 69), an assertion that resonates with Gray's note of caution (Gray 1990) about using the characteristics of effective schools as blueprints or magic formulas that will guarantee effectiveness.

CONTEXTUAL INFLUENCES ON EFFECTIVENESS

The context of a school, which can have a significant influence on its overall effectiveness (Teddlie, Stringfield and Reynolds 2000), covers a range of factors, including the following:

- the socio-economic status of the students attending the school, which is perhaps the most significant contextual feature;
- the community in which the school is set;
- the grade of school – for example whether the schools are elementary grade or high schools in the US, or primary or secondary in the UK;
- the governance structure of the school, for example whether the school is in the maintained sector and is funded by public means or is in the private sector and is funded by the fees paid by the pupils, or whether the school is supported by the church.

The first two of these contextual influences – the socio-economic status of the students attending the school and the communities in which the schools are located – are of most interest given our focus in this book.

The socio-economic status of the students attending the schools

Numerous studies, from the earliest by Brookover and Rutter and their co-workers in 1979, point to the influence that the socio-economic status of the students attending a school can have on its effectiveness. All the studies draw attention to the negative effect that the low overall socio-economic status of a school's pupil intake can have on student attainment. This effect goes beyond the effects associated with the students' individual social class and/or ability. In a study of schools in Scotland in 1986, Willms showed that contextual effects were more strongly related to the proportion of students of high socio-economic status than the proportion of students with low socio-economic status (Willms 1986). Further, students of all abilities benefited academically from attending high socio-economic status schools. This finding confirmed the outcome of a US-based study by Murnane (1981) which found that pupils with low initial levels of attainment or low socio-economic status benefited from attending schools where the pupils' initial levels of attainment or socio-economic status were high. However, the effect on the achievements of the more able and advantaged pupils in such schools was small. Later Willms (1992) reported that, in addition to peer group influences, schools with a greater proportion of students with high socio-economic status may gain additional benefit because they:

- receive greater support from parents;
- experience fewer discipline problems;
- have atmospheres that are conducive to learning;
- are more likely to attract and retain excellent teachers.

Teddlie and Reynolds (2000) in a comprehensive review of research into contextual influences on school effectiveness draw attention to two main studies, one by Teddlie and Stringfield (1985) carried out in Louisiana in the US and one by Hallinger and Murphy (1986) also undertaken in the US in California.

Teddlie and Stringfield (1985) looked at 76 schools which they categorised as 'more effective', 'typical' and 'less effective', and where the students overall were of middle and low socio-economic status. They found some similarities and some differences among the various types of school as follows.

- *Promotion of educational expectations*. Low socio-economic status schools stressed present expectations whereas middle socio-economic status schools promoted both high present expectations and high future expectations.

- *Principal leadership style*. The principals of effective low socio-economic status schools tended to be initiators who wanted to make changes in the schools, whereas the principals of effective middle socio-economic status schools tended to be good managers.

- *The use of external reward structures.* Visible external rewards for academic achievement were significant in low socio-economic status schools whereas they were not emphasised in middle socio-economic status schools.

- *Emphasis in the school curriculum.* Effective low socio-economic status schools emphasised basic skills whereas effective middle socio-economic status schools had an expanded curriculum.

- *Parental contact with school.* Parental involvement was encouraged in middle socio-economic status schools. However, many low socio-economic status schools did not encourage contact with the community in order to shield themselves from negative community influences.

- *The level of experience of the teachers.* Effective middle socio-economic status schools had more experienced teachers whereas effective low socio-economic status schools had less experienced teachers.

The Hallinger and Murphy study (1986) researched eight schools in four levels of socio-economic status. It confirmed the findings of Teddlie and Stringfield with the main outcomes as follows.

- *Differences in the curriculum.* In low socio-economic status schools, the curriculum was narrow and focused on basic skills, whereas in high socio-economic status schools it was broad and focused on a variety of academic skills.

- *Differential student expectations.* In those schools of low socio-economic status, expectations were low and the source of expectations tended to come from within the schools. In high socio-economic status schools, the sources tended to come from the home and tended to be high.

- *Differences in leadership style.* Principal leadership styles in effective low socio-economic status schools tended to focus upon the control of instruction and task orientation. In effective high socio-economic status schools, the leadership was low to moderate with regard to control of instruction and moderate with regard to task orientation.

- *Parental involvement.* Home linkages were weak in effective low socio-economic status schools and strong in effective high socio-economic status schools.

The community type of schools

The influence on school effectiveness of the type of community in which the school is located is complex. Although it has been the subject of less research than the effects of socio-economic status of the pupils, studies by Cuttance (1988) in Scotland and by Freeman and Teddlie (1997, cited in Teddlie and Reynolds 2000) in the US give some valuable insights.

Cuttance (1988) studied the differences in achievement associated with three typologies – type of school, type of community and local authority. Using multilevel modelling to take account of the socio-economic status of the pupils and other background factors, Cuttance concluded that the range of variation in effectiveness within community types decreases as they become less urban. That is, the more urban the community the greater the variation in effectiveness of schools within that community. Further, schools in city and urban sectors had lower median levels of adjusted attainment than those in borough and new town sectors. The findings are particularly interesting because there was a similarity in the socio-economic status of students attending the various types of schools. There must therefore be another explanation. Cuttance suggested that the reason for the difference in effectiveness might be other factors such as the denominational status of the school or the period when the school was established.

Freeman and Teddlie (1997), in a replication in the US of the Cuttance study, found a greater incidence of naturally occurring school improvement in elementary schools located in small city/suburban areas than was found in either urban areas or rural/town areas. They suggest that small city suburban areas have greater community resources, both human and fiscal, than are found in many urban and rural areas in the USA.

CONCLUDING COMMENTS

In this chapter, we have sought to summarise the key themes that have emerged in school effectiveness research over the last thirty years. Not unexpectedly, consistent themes emerge. There is, for example, broad unanimity about the characteristics of effective schools. We have drawn attention to a number of issues about those characteristics, which are in essence the lack of status given to ensuring pupil learning, the notion that the lists are essentially content lists which describe what schools do with little focus on how they do it, and there is insufficient value accorded to reflective teaching. We also ask the question 'Are the lists complete?'

The recent attention given to schools in challenging/difficult circumstances indicates that those circumstances, and indeed the circumstances of all schools, are diverse and different. Moreover, we argue that all schools should be experiencing a sense of challenge to improve on their previous best. What is needed therefore is individual support and assistance for schools regardless of whether their circumstances are 'challenging' or not.

It would be helpful if that support could be offered within a coherent framework within which the question 'Why do the various characteristics make effective schools effective?' is answered.

In this chapter, we have also looked at the notion of culture; it is a metaphor that we draw on to capture the practice of the schools we studied. An important consideration for us is the perplexing question of whether the culture brings about success ('We do things this way in order to be successful') or whether culture is the outcome of success ('We have found we were successful by doing things this way'). Regardless, culture for all its paradoxes remains an important way of portraying the nature of the organisations, including the schools we studied.

An emergent but underdeveloped theme in the research is the influence of a school's wider community on its effectiveness. The move to school autonomy and perhaps the competitive pressures of the education market have created the feeling and overall impression that schools are 'on their own' when it comes to finding the energy, drive and commitment to engage in meaningful change for improvement. But schools do not operate in isolation. They are part of a much wider system. In the UK, and in many other countries especially in the developed world, almost everyone is or has been connected to schools in some way and a large number of organisations, institutions and agencies have an interest in schools. An important question then becomes 'What influence does that systemic connection with the wider community currently have on schools and what positive effect could it have in the future?'

The context – broader characteristics, the setting and the history – of each school is unique. How each school works with its context is crucially important and indeed how that context works with the school is important too. Each school needs to find a way of working as appropriately as possible with its context. Thus research into schools in disadvantaged settings might give insights into how schools work with particular kinds of setting, which was one of the key rationales for the research we report in the coming chapters.

3

A way of understanding schools as institutions

INTRODUCTION

In this chapter, we develop a conceptual framework with which to begin understanding the work of schools in disadvantaged settings. The theoretical perspective is called 'system psychodynamics' because it combines social systems theory with psychodynamics. We also use the term 'institutional transformation' to describe it because the insight gained through the system psychodynamics perspective can change the conditions in which institutions as social systems work and thus has the potential to bring about radical change or transformation. System psychodynamics is a collection of concepts that interlink synergistically – the different concepts add value to each other.

Institutions, such as schools, hospitals, the legal profession, Parliament or the police, are established organisations which have an important social purpose and a special place in society. As such, they attract our conscious and unconscious psychological attention and they have a significant representation in our minds. This inner representation endows them with greater significance than we might expect. Thus we have stressed the notion of 'schools as institutions' in the chapter title.

The system psychodynamics perspective is especially relevant and particularly useful for considering the work of schools. For a variety of reasons, schools are places where there are particularly high levels of emotion (James 1999). Their main task, the nature of learning, the work of teaching, the quality of relationships in educational institutions, the characteristics of professional practice, policy changes that affect the curriculum and management of schools, technological changes and, importantly, the centrality of schools to people's lives all make schools particular locales for emotions, especially anxiety. Understanding the origins, movement and effects of these emotions can be very helpful both in understanding schools as institutions and in guiding leadership and management actions. System psychodynamics provides both a framework for analysing organisational actions and a basis for acting appropriately in organisations. It is thus both a theory *of* organising in schools and a theory *for* organising in schools. We develop this notion more fully in the following section.

Our intention in this chapter is to explain and develop some of the significant concepts in system psychodynamics and institutional transformation. We start with a straightforward discussion of the nature of theory in order to 'clear some ground'. We then introduce the two main conceptual themes, psychodynamics and social systems theory, develop those two themes further and explore some of the main components of the framework.

THEORIES – PURPOSES AND PROBLEMS

In this section, we consider some aspects of the nature of theory. In considering 'theory', we intend to concern ourselves with theories that relate to organising in a particular kind of institution, schools. We use the term 'organising' to encompass the whole range of actions that can take place in schools. In a sense, all actions are organising actions in that they create organisations. Our concern is with 'organising theories'.

Our central thesis is that there is a significant difference between theories *of* organising and theories *for* organising. From our standpoint, 'organising theories' have two main purposes. The first is to enable an organising phenomenon to be understood and analysed. These are theories *of* organising. The second purpose is to provide a basis for action. These are theories *for* organising. For example, if we take transformational leadership theory as a theory of organising, there is no doubt that it provides a helpful perspective on the leadership of organisations and institutions. It enables the practice of leadership in those settings to be understood and analysed. The four main themes in transformational leadership of idealised influence, individualised consideration, inspirational motivation and intellectual stimulation (Bass 1996) – the four 'I's – offer a very helpful way of looking at leadership practice. Together they comprise a very useful analytical framework for making sense of leadership actions. However, the four themes may not be so useful in providing a basis for action. The context, the organisational task and the leadership purpose may not be entirely suited to the transformational leadership model. The same can be said of the plethora of leadership models available to educational leaders (see, for example, Davies 2005). Nonetheless, organising is a purposeful action, so those who organise in schools must base their actions on a theory of some kind. Their theory for action provides them with their rationale, their reason and their justification for their actions. Their theory for organising may have elements of an established theory of organising of some kind such as our example, transformational leadership. Their theories of organising and their theories for organising are not, however, likely to be the same. Moreover, whatever theories practitioners are working with are firstly likely to be implicit (at least for much of the time), and secondly to be a 'hybrid' derived from an eclectic mix of, among other things, exposure to some research or theory somewhere at some time, professional 'folklore' learned from other colleagues and personal sense-making.

We argue that for any one actor to slavishly follow the principles of a particular theory of organising is not likely to be appropriate. Firstly, the context for organising is very variable; it changes from setting to setting and from time to time, especially in schools (James and Connolly 2000). It follows therefore that the most appropriate organising action is likely to vary and the rationale for it (the theory for organising) will vary also. Secondly, as Giddens tells us (Giddens 1979) there is an interplay between agency and structure. Actions affect structures and structures affect actions. As a consequence, an organising action of some kind that was appropriate yesterday will not be appropriate today because yesterday's organising actions will have changed the structure. This argument particularly applies to leadership as an organising action. Leadership is widely accepted to be an influencing activity and the outcome successful leadership will thus be a change in the leadership context of some kind. Therefore leadership actions – styles, modes, strategies – have to change continually. Successful leadership is ever-changing and dynamic and needs to be engaged in reflectively to ensure its appropriateness (James and Connolly 2000).

This difference between theories of action and theories for action can present those organising in schools with a difficulty. Frequently, the abstract nature of theories of action makes such theories seem very distant from their everyday school life with its variety, its ever-changing nature and its numerous requirements for instant action. This disjuncture can mean that theories of organising may not help those organising in schools when they are searching for an appropriate theory for organising. But arguably those who have a responsibility for organising schools (the staff) would benefit from understanding what is happening in their institutions. It can be very helpful to have a grasp of 'what might be going on here'. The members of staff, especially those with leadership responsibility, may find it helpful – and indeed educational – to be able to analyse organisational processes. To undertake this kind of analysis, they require analytical frameworks – theories of organising – in order to help them make sense of the workings of their institutions. We argue that the closer the theories of organising and theories for organising are the more useful they are likely to be. Moreover, a single framework that provides both a theory of organising and a theory for organising is likely to be the most helpful. For us, that is one of the strengths of system psychodynamics. It provides both a way of understanding the processes of institutions and a basis for action. It is both a theory *of* action and a theory *for* action.

SYSTEM PSYCHODYNAMICS

System psychodynamics contains a number of linked concepts that come under the headings of psychodynamics and social systems theory (Obholzer and Roberts 1994; Neumann 1999; James and Connolly 2000; Gould, Stapley and Stein 2001). It is a very useful set of ideas that can explain the behaviour of institutions and the people who work in them, provide a rationale on which to base appropriate organising actions and help with managing institutional change.

Psychodynamics

Psychodynamics is concerned primarily with mental processes, their changing nature and their 'movement' within and between individuals and groups. These mental processes and the forces they create are often in conflict within and between individuals. They are both conscious and unconscious. Psychodynamic and psychoanalytical concepts and theories can give important insights into the processes of organising (Kets de Vries 1991; Gabriel 1999). They can furnish a rich understanding of life in the workplace (Hirschhorn 1988) and, when combined with open systems theory, can provide a framework that has considerable interpretive, diagnostic and heuristic value (Obholzer and Roberts 1994).

Using psychodynamic theory to explore the nature of mental forces and the internal struggles and conflicts those forces can create can be highly illuminating. However, while it can reveal problems and give useful organisational diagnoses, psychodynamic theory may not provide a clear solution or an 'organisational cure'. Thus, on its own, the use of psychodynamic theory may not be entirely helpful to those who have a responsibility for organising in institutions. It may not provide the answers they require. This is where social systems theory and 'thinking systemically' can be very useful.

Social systems theory

Social systems theory is a very potent way of exploring and conceptualising the processes, roles, tasks and interrelationships of individuals, groups and institutions. We take a system to be the *"reproduced relations between actors or collectivities, organised as regular social practices"* (Giddens 1979: 66). Social systems involve *"regularised relations between individuals or groups"* and Giddens argues that typically these can best be analysed as *"recurrent social practices"* (Giddens 1979: 65–6). This view of a social system necessitates a boundary, a discontinuity of some kind that distinguishes one set of regular social practices from another. Thus boundaries are fundamental to social systems. From a classical systems theory perspective, these other social systems would be represented by the environment in which any one system worked.

The general idea of systems theory for organisations was developed by Kurt Lewin in the 1940s and has been developed subsequently, particularly during the 1950s and 1960s (Miller and Rice 1967; von Bertalanffy 1968). It is derived from systems in living organisms. In essence, all living organisms survive by being open systems. Figure 3.1 shows an illustration of an open system. The system has a selectively permeable boundary that surrounds the internal processes, the core. It separates the core from the environment. All open systems, at whatever level, require inputs and produce outputs.

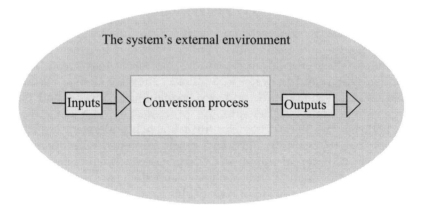

Figure 3.1   A diagrammatic illustration of an open system.

The boundary is a crucial requirement of an open system. It may be socially constructed and can be interpreted in a range of ways as we discuss later. It surrounds the core and separates it from the external environment. Without the boundary, the core merges with its environment and other systems and ceases to exist as a separate entity. Boundary exchanges must be selective so that only designated objects of some kind enter and leave. It follows that the system must manage movement across the boundary in some way.

The system requires various inputs if it is to function properly. The flow of inputs across the boundary and into the system is therefore essential. The system also needs internal processes within the core to do the work and, if it is working properly, the system core will produce outputs. These outputs are the result of the conversion of the inputs by the internal processes of the core. Outputs, by definition, need to cross the boundary and leave the system.

In systems theory in biological settings and particularly in technical settings, where it underpins control theory and cybernetics, the notion of feedback is very important. Feedback is where the level of the output is sensed in some way and signalled to whatever controls the input. Figure 3.2 shows an open system with the feedback loop in place. The

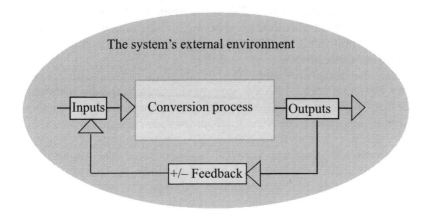

Figure 3.2 An open system with the feedback loop.

level of the output is literally 'fed back' to the controller of the input. If the feedback is negative, that is a high level of output reduces the input, there is a stabilising effect. Hormone systems in mammals and household central heating systems, for example, work in this way. If the feedback is positive, that is a high level of output increases the level of input, then the system becomes unstable. The loud, unexpected and unexplained screech which can be heard occasionally through the speaker system at rock concerts is an example of positive feedback. It happens when the sound produced by the amplification system is picked up by a microphone and then amplified and the microphone picks it up and so on. The output from the amplifier is fed back to the input and the system becomes unstable, hence the screech.

Open systems theory, especially when used creatively and simply, provides a valuable means of understanding individual and institutional behaviour, management practice and leadership actions. There are important limitations, however.

Firstly, systems thinking from scientific settings applied to social systems are simply metaphors and heuristic devices for representing and imaging complex social phenomena. For example, behaviour in social systems is not deterministic in the way that effects in many scientific systems are. People are not caused to act and to respond in the way that technical systems are; they act on the basis of reasons that can have kinds and degrees of validity.

Secondly, the notion of social systems working in an undifferentiated 'environment' is somewhat limiting. The environment of social systems is innumerable other social systems that all have their own properties and purposes. The characteristics of social systems and the ways they carry out their practices – their rules – contribute to the formation of a social structure (Giddens 1979). Taken together, the recurrent practices of social systems, the application of generative rules and resources and the intended and unintended consequences of social systems collectively are a social structuring process.

Thirdly, the purposive activities of social systems both create the structure in which social systems operate and are created by the structure in which they operate. As Giddens illustrates, in social systems there is a duality of structure. The structural properties of social systems – the way they do things and their resources – are the means of creating the social systems and they are also the consequence – the outcome. Thus social systems form structures and structures form social systems. There is a dynamic and recursive interaction between the two. The notion of structuration is concerned with the conditions governing the continuity or, importantly, the transformation of structures.

Fourthly, thinking about social systems in terms of system theory can lead to a somewhat one-dimensional and simplistic way of thinking about systems and can often fail to capture the rich and complex nature of organisational life. It is here that linking psychodynamic theory with social systems theory is significant. The two theory sets are complementary. Psychodynamic theory can help to uncover and clarify organisational processes. Its power is in its diagnostic capability. Social systems theory provides a view of social systems – the individual, the group and/or the institution – and the way they are both created by and create social structure. Its strength is in providing a shape and a view of organisations and institutions, albeit a somewhat uni-dimensional, decontextualised and technical view. The linking of the two gives a very powerful and comprehensive means of explaining organisational phenomena and for deciding on the most appropriate action.

ASPECTS OF THE SYSTEM PSYCHODYNAMICS

In this section, we review some of the key aspects of system psychodynamics.

Unconscious processes

A key aspect of system psychodynamics is that not all our thoughts and feelings are consciously experienced, nor are they accessible to us. Throughout our lives, we unconsciously experience many phenomena and unknowingly we store away aspects of that experience. Unconsciously, we hide hopes, fears, desires, anxieties, urges and terrors, and by definition we are not aware of them. Whether these inaccessible notions are held in 'the unconscious', which is a part of the mind with its own processes and systems as Freud asserted, or whether they are simply accumulated in an unconscious way remains a matter of debate. Nonetheless, there is overwhelming evidence that this repository of ideas and emotions, however and wherever salted away, has a significant influence on our behaviour. Its influence can help to explain why actions that have a surface rationality and validity may have a hidden meaning and significance. The idea of 'unconscious influences' is particularly useful when thinking about people's behaviour in work institutions and the ways in which those institutions operate. There can be little doubt that the conscious actions of those who work in institutions are influenced by their unconscious thoughts and feelings, especially given the social significance of institutions. It would be remarkable if they were not.

We can never gain direct access to unconscious phenomena. So, while it is very helpful to have the emotional terrain or the geography of teaching and educational leadership mapped out in the way that Andy Hargreaves and Brenda Beatty and others have (Hargreaves 1998a, 1998b, 2001; Beatty 2000), such mapping can only be a partial picture of our emotional experience. To continue the earth science metaphor, the emotional geology is at least as important as the emotional geography, if not more so. The emotional geology – the unconscious – has a very significant influence on how we behave generally, how we behave in institutions particularly and how we behave in educational institutions especially (James 2004). Just as the forces under the Earth's crust shape the surface topography, unconscious forces shape people's surface terrain, have colossal and unmanageable power and are impossible to predict. We may have some sense of where it might rupture the surface layer and reveal itself but in everyday life the unconscious is known only from occasional glimpses when it breaks through to the surface and by occasional tremors and eruptions when it lets us know it is there.

The emotional dimensions of work in institutions

It is, of course, stating the obvious to say that all organising actions are imbued with emotion. Fineman (1993) was quite correct when he argued that *"Emotions are not simply excisable from organizational processes, they both characterize them and inform them"* (Fineman 1993: 1). Furthermore, some would argue that institutions, such as schools, are especially infused with emotions (James 1999). However, until relatively recently, emotions have not featured in mainstream accounts of organising, especially in schools. Studies of organising and organisations have tended to view institutions as rather tidy, ordered places where everything is manageable and is managed.

In the last two decades, the study of emotions at work in organisations has come to the fore. Arlie Hochschild's (1983) study of alienation in Delta Airlines is generally viewed as being the starting point and it was taken forward, albeit from a different perspective, by Fineman

(1993). Hochschild's was a largely Marxist analysis whereas Fineman adopted a social constructionist perspective. Since those two substantive contributions, there has been an enormous growth in the field. In education, there has been a significant development of interest in the emotional dimension of the work of schools led by academics such as Hargreaves and Beatty (Hargreaves 1998a, 1998b, 2001, 2004; Beatty 2000; Beatty and Brew 2004), and others, for example Boler (1999). The growth of interest has been such that we may well be seeing the emergence of a new paradigm in organisational research (Barsade, Brief and Spataro 2003). It is certainly the case that researching emotions in organisations requires particular methodological approaches (Gabriel 1999; James 2004) and it raises significant epistemological issues too. New paradigm or not, exploring the emotional aspects of organising in schools certainly has the potential to enrich understandings of schools and the actions of those who work in them.

Hochschild (1983) makes an important distinction between emotional work and emotional labour, although the two are often conflated in the literature. Emotional work is undertaken whenever employees need to control their emotions in undertaking their functions and responsibilities. Arguably, emotional work is a characteristic of many occupations. Emotional labour occurs when employees engage in emotional work as a specific work requirement and when their remuneration depends on it. From Hochschild's perspective, teachers and educational leaders undertake both emotional work *and* emotional labour. They are required to control their emotions as part of their work and, while their remuneration may not directly depend on their emotional labour, it is certainly a condition of employment. Thus both emotional work and emotional labour come with the territory of teaching.

The work of teachers and school leaders is governed by 'feeling rules' (Hochschild 1979) and by 'display rules' (Rafeli and Sutton 1989; Ashforth and Humphrey 1993). Feeling rules are the socially shared guidelines that govern how we want to try to feel and they are often hidden and tacitly agreed. An example of feeling rules in a school would be a teacher trying to motivate and inspire a class while feeling exhausted and lacking in enthusiasm at the end of term. The feeling rules are governing how the teacher wants to feel. Display rules are the underlying rules, which again are often unspoken and covert, that guide which emotions are to be publicly expressed. An example of display rules in practice would be a teacher not expressing her dismay at a colleague's incompetent professional practice while in the presence of pupils. It would be inappropriate to display such emotions with pupils present.

Boler (1999) developed Hochschild's perspectives from a feminist standpoint, in particular exploring emotions as sites of social control specifically in educational practices. She argues that pupils and their teachers are controlled by the various discourses on emotion such as the moral/religious, the scientific/medieval and the rational. Organisational discourse is filled with emotion. Further, many would argue, for example Parkin (1993), that emotions are genderised. They are employed to shore up a male hegemony where male 'rationality' takes precedence over female 'irrationality'. Hearn (1993) views the gendered nature of emotions differently arguing that men are no more immune from emotion than women. He argues that both men and women seek out different 'emotional zones' where emotions can be expressed in a way that is culturally acceptable.

Defences against emotions

The emotional labour and the emotional work of teaching and their costs may result in teachers – indeed all those who work in schools – defending themselves from the emotional experience of their work. They may seek to protect themselves using a range of behaviours known as social defences (Hirschhorn 1988; Gabriel 2000; James and Connolly 2000). Social defences are a group of mental processes and actions aimed at reducing the pain of emotions, most notably anxiety, or eliminating forces that are experienced as threatening a person's mental survival (Gabriel 1999). Arguably, anxiety is the dominant emotion to be defended against because it has a strong physiological basis that initiates a very powerful protection mechanism and because it frequently accompanies other emotions. Social defences may take the form of patterns of behaviour that can be recognised and typified such as covert coalitions, resistance and splitting and projection. James and Connolly (2000) give examples of social defences in action in schools and colleges. We consider splitting and projection in some detail below because of its widespread prevalence and organisational significance. At a different level, those who work in institutions may engage in 'organisational rituals' as a form of emotional protection. These routines then become their taken-for-granted ways of working, which may have no apparent connection to any rational understanding of experience.

When these 'desires to defend' against work-related emotion and anxiety become habitual and rationalised, they can develop into very durable organisational practices. For individuals in any work institution, defensive behaviours of all kinds can give structure, security and a sense of order to a potentially unstructured, insecure and chaotic working life. However, because of their durability and their purpose of protecting against pain, they can be very difficult to change and can inhibit learning and limit creativity.

Emotions and change

Educational change and emotion are inextricably linked (Hargreaves 1998b) and the emotional response to change can be very powerful.

The response may be particularly strong if the change involves altering defensive behaviours, especially when those defensive behaviours are deeply founded (James and Connolly 2000). The reason why changing defensive behaviours is so difficult is as follows. Defensive behaviours are 'ways of going on' that protect individuals and groups from unpleasant, even painful, emotions. The experience of change can bring with it a sense of loss, insecurity and inadequacy, experiences which may carry distressing feelings of dismay, fear and even terror – a whole range of anxieties. Changing defensive behaviours involves changing, which can be associated with difficult feelings and anxieties, those behaviours that are designed to protect against other difficult feelings and anxieties. So, change can bring with it two sets of difficult emotions – a 'double dose of difficult dreads'. It is the 'double whammy' of educational change (James and Connolly 2000).

Emotions and micropolitics

The emotional experience, mental forces and the defences against emotional experience are fundamental to organising in schools and are highly influential in organisational micropolitics in educational institutions. The micropolitics of schools has received some attention by researchers in educational administration, leadership and management, for example Hoyle (1986), Ball (1987), Blase and Anderson (1995), Bennett (1999), Vann (1999) and Busher (2001). Arguably it has not received as much consideration as one might expect given its prevalence and the nature of work in schools. Realist micropolitical perspectives and psycho-dynamic micropolitical perspectives differ. A realist micropolitical perspective sees political behaviour as a complex net of individual explanations and agendas, initiated and constructed by the mobilisation of self-interest (Fineman 2003). The psychodynamic micropolitical perspective sees organisational politics as arising from individual and collective, conscious and unconscious fears about identity, worth and vulnerability. These anxieties can be at the heart of very powerful emotions such as anger and euphoria and can be the basis of more commonplace feelings such as annoyance and happiness. In both the realist and psychodynamic perspectives, symbols and what they represent are important, although from the psychodynamic viewpoint symbols can be especially significant since they may represent *"the visible tips of wholly unconscious processes"* (Gabriel 1999: 309).

Emotions and decision-making

The ever-present nature of emotions means that emotions and rationality cannot exist separately and, moreover, they intertwine. Thus feelings will always play a part in organising actions although organisational actors may seek to de-emotionalise (Fineman 1993) their work, deny their emotional experience by means of social defences (James 1999) and behave rationally.

One important way in which emotions 'interfere' in the process of organising is by creating a disparity between the 'espoused' and the 'in use' theories of organisational actors. It was Argyris and Schön (1974) who first drew attention to these two contrasting theories and the idea was developed and refined in subsequent work, for example Argyris and Schön (1987), Argyris (1987) and Argyris and Schön (1996). Espoused theory is *"the theory of action that is advanced to explain or justify a given pattern of activity"* whereas a theory in use is *"the theory of action which is implicit in the performance of that pattern of activity"* (Argyris 1985: 13). The important distinction here is not between *"theory and action but between two different theories of action"* (Argyris, Putnam and McLain Smith 1985: 82). Argyris (1980) argues that effectiveness is the result of congruence between in use and espoused theories. However, a theory in use may be hidden and impossible to describe because *"individual members who enact it know more than they can say"* (Argyris and Schön 1996: 14). As a result they are unable rather than unwilling to describe the theory embedded in their everyday practice. Further, it may be difficult to discuss because to do so would result in an exposure of the incongruity between the espoused and the in use which could be threatening or embarrassing. The emotional experience of organising in schools can play a significant part in both separating and bringing together the espoused and the in use (James and Vince 2001), which can have significant organisational implications.

Splitting and projection

Splitting and projection is one of the most important social defences (Obholzer and Roberts 1994). It is grounded in object relations theory, which provides an explanation of the way we relate to objects in our environment. Object relations theory was originated by Melanie Klein in the 1930s (Segal 1979; Phillips and Stonebridge 1998; Likierman 2001) and subsequently developed by others such as Fairbairn and Winnicott (Hughes 1989). According to object relations theory, our sense of objects is formed by feelings and unconscious mental representations, known as phantasies. (These unconscious processes contrast with fantasies which are conscious daydreams (Gabriel 1999).) An individual's relationship with objects constantly defines and redefines her or his ego (Gabriel 1999). Individuals may expel feelings about objects into others by projection, may incorporate the expelled feelings of others by introjection and may split feelings into good and bad categories.

Since the 1950s, object relations theory has provided a powerful way of understanding institutional life – see for example, Jacques (1952), Jacques (1955) and Menzies (1960). More recently, other authors such as

Kets de Vries (1991), Obholzer and Roberts (1994), Hirschhorn (1997) and Gabriel (1999) have used it to give a very powerful means of interpreting organisational phenomena such as the relationships between managers and subordinates, dysfunctional working between divisions in large companies and the nature of leadership. They have focused in particular on splitting and projection.

Splitting and projection is a defence against unbearable feelings, particularly contradictory ones that generate painful or threatening internal conflicts (Halton 1994). Individuals and groups may protect themselves from these inner struggles by splitting their feelings into different elements. This process is often accompanied by projection where the problematic feelings are located in other individuals, inanimate objects, groups or institutions (Likierman 2001). The projection of feelings may be supplemented by behaviours that have the purpose of reinforcing the projection. The condition resulting from splitting and projection is known as the 'paranoid-schizoid' position. It contrasts with the so-called 'depressive' position in which the contradictory elements are held together and retained within the individual or group. In this integrated state, the individual or group gives up the security and simplicity achieved through splitting and projection and accepts the confusion, inconsistency and conflict created by contradictory feelings (Likierman 2001).

Splitting and projection can have a number of outcomes. The individual (or group) who projects troublesome feelings may, as a consequence, experience idealisation, acquiring "*an aura of perfection ... stripped of all undesirable and negative qualities*" (Gabriel 1999: 298). Recipients may begin to "*unconsciously identify with the projected feelings*" (Halton 1994: 16) in such a way that their own feelings are affected. This process is known as projective identification. Moreover, the recipients may begin to experience the projected feelings as if they were their own, a process creating a state of mind referred to as counter-transference (Halton 1994). Importantly, they may start using them, perhaps inappropriately, as a basis for action. In organisations, splitting and projection is a frequently encountered organisational behaviour and can be the genesis of blame, bullying and scapegoating (Dunning, James and Jones 2005).

The significance of the boundary

In system psychodynamics, the boundary is a key concept that links psychodynamic theory and open systems theory in a number of ways. The boundary represents structural inconsistency and discontinuity (Lamont and Molnar 2002; Heracleous 2004) and boundaries can be internal as well as external (Hirschhorn 1988; Schneider 1991; Roberts 1994). Gabriel (1999) asserts that "*The first boundary we discover is that which separates us from an external world*" (p. 98) – the boundary of the ego. Later, the ego itself acquires boundaries which separate conscious and unconscious mental activities and other internal entities and the ego becomes co-extensive with the part of the mental personality that stands at the boundary with the external world (Gabriel 1999).

Hernes (2004) argues that organisational boundaries are not incidentally shaped by organisations but are inherent to the organisation itself and indeed to the process of organising. Thus he argues that boundaries are not by-products of organisation but that organisations evolve through the process of boundary setting. From this standpoint, Hernes (2004) is therefore critical of organisational theory that views boundaries as fixed and static entities. They are variable, unclear and, to varying degrees, permeable, a view supported by a number of other studies, for example, Weick (1979, 1995), Perrow (1986) and Scott (1998).

In recent times the 'boundaryless organisation' has been advocated by a number of authors, for example Hirschhorn and Gilmore (1992) and Ashkenas (2000), who argue that reducing boundaries helps to create more vigorous and progressive organisations. Others, for example Paulsen and Hernes (2003), argue that the boundary is not diminishing in such settings but rather is merely mutating, a view which we support. For us, it is difficult to envisage any organisation as boundaryless. The seductiveness of the boundaryless organisation is that it may overcome conflicts that are often associated with boundaries. Czander (1993) argues that all organisational conflicts are boundary issues of some kind. As points of dissimilarity, distinction and interruption (Lamont and Molnar 2002; Heracleous 2004), boundaries will be emotionally charged places of anxiety and tension (Douglas 1966; Hernes 2004). Violations of the boundary are expressed as conflicts and have the potential to escalate into major events, which is why there may be reluctance to protect role boundaries, or indeed a desire to over-protect them (Czander 1993).

Schools as organisations may be viewed as a complex network of interdependent subsystems where boundaries are continually being reinforced and attacked, where boundaries overlie each other and where 'boundary rules' are frequently violated. What is important is not perhaps removing these boundaries but gaining a greater insight into how they are experienced and managed. Many theorists consider the maintenance of boundaries to be critical to organisational success (Czander 1993; Diamond, Allcorn and Stein 2004). Boundaries maintain stability and a boundary perspective may be helpful in working with change processes.

Organisational boundaries are composite, are experienced in a variety of ways and can be analysed from a range of different standpoints (Hernes 2004). Hirschhorn and Gilmore (1992) identify authority, political, task and identity boundaries. Miller and Rice (1967) make the distinction between task and sentient boundaries, Van Maanen and Schein (1979) distinguish between functional, hierarchical and inclusionary boundaries, while Scott (1998) clarifies the distinction between behavioural and normative boundaries. Leach (1976) defines boundaries as spatial, temporal and psychological, an analytical framework supported by Stapley (1996) and Diamond, Allcorn and Stein (2004). Hanna (1997) suggests that within departmental structures there are physical, social, temporal and psychological boundaries.

The management of a system boundary is crucial to organisational success. It preserves what is within the boundary (the core), gives the core the resources necessary to do its work and maintains a continuous interaction with the environment (Czander 1993). Inadequate boundary management may fail to bring in appropriate resources or allow inappropriate ones to enter. It may also allow valuable resources to leave the core or fail to ensure that the system produces resources that are appropriate for its environment. Boundary management involves a full consideration of the system's primary task (see below) so that non-task-related processes within the core are minimised, ensuring that the system has the resources required to perform its primary task and monitoring the primary task so that it remains relevant to the needs of the environment (Obholzer and Roberts 1994; James and Connolly 2000). Crucially, the way the boundaries of the social system are managed is a key structural property. The recreation of the boundaries of a social system and the emotional experience of that process is a central condition controlling structural continuity or radical change – transformation.

The notion of role

The notion of role as the practices that an actor in a social system may engage in is a very valuable heuristic for understanding experience in institutions. It is, however, the subject of much debate by social theorists. Those debates hinge on whether social systems consist of interconnected predetermined roles or whether social systems are made up of practices. From the 'systems as predetermined roles' standpoint, actors are assigned and are expected to conform to a role. Such a view is open to critique for being a normative, deterministic and static view of actions in social systems. Giddens (1979), in seeking to establish a dynamic view of social systems, argued that it is practices that make up social systems, not roles. Practices represent the point of articulation or linkage between actors and structures, rather than roles. As such, practices create structure and are created by structure, not roles.

It is, of course, possible to assign roles as social positions to actors in a social system. Such positions are forms of social identity which carry obligations that the incumbent of the position is expected to fulfil. Roles as practices cannot be assigned in the same way. Those in any particular social position, need to find an appropriate set of practices consistent with the tasks of that position, make up those practices into a coherent set and then they need to carry out those practices – to work on the task (the importance of 'task' is discussed below). In essence, organisational actors need to find, make and take their roles (Reed 2000). As with any social system, these practices – or roles within this conceptualisation – are bounded. For a range of reasons, which we would argue are related to the emotional experience of practice, individuals may be unable to find and make and take an appropriate role (set of practices) for the tasks associated with their social position.

The concept of role straddles both the psychodynamic and open systems dimensions of system psychodynamics and institutional transformation. Individuals in institutions take up both formal and informal roles (Hirschhorn 1985). Formal roles are those specified by the organisation, for example in a school, teacher, caretaker, head of department or bursar. Informal roles, however, such as victim, scapegoat, father figure or protector, are those that an individual may be required to undertake for the organisation, often unconsciously, as a consequence of the emotional-motivational milieu. The prescription of a formal role presupposes the presence of a boundary that distinguishes what is included in the set of practices or behaviours that would be appropriate for the role and what would not. The role boundary and the influences upon it are significant in understanding organisations from a system psychodynamics perspective and working with boundaries can be very important in bringing about institutional transformation.

The primary task

The primary task is the work of the core of the system and for those who work on the primary task it has considerable psychological significance. The notion of the primary task was first developed by Rice (1963) who described it as the task an organisation must perform to survive. That description is not saying that organisations must have an explicit or an agreed primary task or that an organisation should be working on the task it may have been assigned. Rather it is saying that it is the task that the organisation feels – consciously or unconsciously – it needs to undertake if it is to continue, to carry on. Although the concept may seem to be an oversimplification, especially given the complexities faced by many institutions including schools, the primary task is a very valuable heuristic device. The primary task:

> allows us to explore the ordering of multiple activities ... and to construct and compare different organisational models of an enterprise based on different definitions of its primary task.

> (Miller and Rice 1967: 62)

The notion of the primary task was developed further by Lawrence (1977) who described three different kinds: the normative primary task, which is the defined, formal or official task; the existential primary task, which is the task the work group members believe they are undertaking; and the phenomenal primary task, which is the task that can be inferred from work group members' behaviour of which they may or may not be consciously aware. Although these forms of the primary task may be different, arguably they should be the same if the system is to be effective. Furthermore, reflection in action and on action (Schön 1983) by those engaged on the system's primary task should centre directly on optimising the appropriateness of work on the normative primary task and improving work on it. Arguably, reflection can be important in ensuring that there is no dissonance between the normative and existential primary tasks and making sure that the normative primary task and the phenomenal primary task are the same.

For a number of reasons, work on the primary task is always accompanied by anxiety (Obholzer and Roberts 1994). Firstly, working on the primary task carries a risk. Those undertaking the primary task may fail, which may be experienced very negatively and may cause anxiety. Secondly, the task will have been assigned in some way and those working on it may be called to account for their work on it. Their work on it may be deemed to be inadequate and to be found 'wanting' can again be experienced as highly threatening and may engender anxiety. Thirdly, working on the primary task requires a commitment to agency. It obliges individuals and groups working to act. They are required to marshal their resources and to commit themselves to work on the task and to engage with it in a way that makes a difference. Working wholeheartedly on a primary task requires courage, especially if the primary task is both difficult and meaningful.

Defining the primary task of the system is important but also difficult (Roberts 1994). If the definition is too narrow, or is only in terms of the members' needs, the system's survival may be threatened. If it is too broad in terms of the members' resources, they will not know what to do for the best. Defining the primary task in a work organisation can be taxing and may cause conflict. Agreement on the primary task is unlikely to be full and uncontested and those difficulties need to be resolved if the organisation is to begin to improve its effectiveness. Organisations often concentrate on methods rather than aims as a way of avoiding conflicts that might arise if they were to focus on and clarify organisational aims. They may define the task in a way that fails to give priority to one set of activities over another, which is another way of avoiding conflict. Often organisations define their aims in very broad and general terms and as a result members of the organisation are unsure about what should be the focus of their endeavours. Nonetheless, we argue that consideration of the nature of the primary task is very important and it can be very useful in promoting organisational development and in enhancing organisational effectiveness.

The problems associated with an inadequate definition of the primary task have been identified by Roberts (1994) and are as follows.

- *Failing to relate the primary task and thus the outputs of the system core to a changing environment.* This lack of responsiveness can then cause stress and impact negatively on organisational effectiveness.

- *Boundary problems.* If the task is not clear, boundaries come to serve defensive functions instead of facilitating work on the primary task. As a result, boundaries may become impermeable thus preventing the productive interrelationships of subsystems. Moreover, organisation members may engage in 'turf protection' because they are unsure what is their task and what is not. Organisations with impenetrable boundaries become fertile breeding grounds for splitting and projection which may result in a range of organisational malpractices (see above).

- *Inadequate task definition encourages task avoidance strategies.* These strategies are very alluring because they ease the anxieties that come with the primary task. Task avoidance can be particularly significant for those who hold roles as positions. If the task is not clear or if it carries too much anxiety, those responsible for the task may well not engage in working on it. The full repertoire of behaviours associated with a social position – the practices – that might be used to achieve a clearly defined task may not be deployed and over time may well shrink.

Leaders and leadership

In this section, we want to make four brief points about leaders and leadership, firstly about the nature of leadership, secondly to comment on theories of leadership and theories for leadership, thirdly to consider the special place leaders may have in our minds, and fourthly the representational role of leaders.

There is general acceptance that leadership is concerned with bringing about change through influence whereas management is concerned with taking responsibility for maintaining current activities and performance – see, for example, Cuban (1988). Both leadership and management are modes of organising, and organisations are created through leadership and management actions. They may both involve taking responsibility, although managing, because it is more likely to be a formally delegated responsibility, is likely to carry a higher burden of accountability. Motivating others plays a part in both leadership and management.

Because leadership is concerned with influencing others and changing practice, perhaps radically, arguably, motivation plays a larger part in leadership than management. Managers may well disagree of course arguing that high levels of motivation may be required to sustain system efficiency and effectiveness. Because of the intimate link between emotions and motivation (Gabriel 1999) both these organising activities involve engaging the emotions of others.

Leaders may act in a way that reduces organisational effectiveness. Members of the organisation may well influence others to engage in actions that are counter-productive in relation to the normative primary task and that may actively oppose and counteract management work on it. This counter-productive leadership work may be engaged in possibly because of a lack of clarity about the definition of the primary task (what the organisation must do to survive), a lack of agreement on what the normative primary task is and an unrecognised disparity between the normative, existential and phenomenal primary tasks. Institutional leadership is thus closely related to the primary task. James and Connolly (2000), using a system psychodynamics perspective, developed a notion of institutional leadership as a special organisational role, a set of practices that enable others to perform their role in relation to the primary task.

As we have argued earlier, theories of leadership provide a way of looking at and analysing leadership. There is a huge array of different theories of leadership in the leadership literature for this purpose and, indeed, in the educational leadership literature. For example, Leithwood, Jantzi and Steinbach (1999), following a review of the educational leadership research literature, identified the instructional, transformational, transactional, moral, participative and managerial. There are many more – strategic, invitational, ethical, constructivist, poetical, political, emotional, entrepreneurial and sustainable leadership (Davies 2005). Again, as we have argued earlier, these theories of leadership may or may not provide useful bases for action – theories for leadership – although some authors advocate particular theories of leadership as theories for leadership. For example, Leithwood and his colleagues (1999) advocate transformational leadership and Stoll and Fink (1996) advocate invitational leadership. As we have argued earlier, for a variety of reasons, advocating a theory of leadership may not be helpful to those wishing to become good leaders, and adopting one particular leadership model is not likely to be successful.

One of the key issues about leaders and leadership from a system psychodynamics standpoint is what leaders and leadership represent in people's minds, what the notions 'call up' for us and what our expectations of them are. Although definitions of leadership tend to represent it as an organisational property (that possibility is implicit in the definition of James and Connolly (2000) for example), in our minds it is not always represented as such. Arguably, instead, our sense is that leadership 'comes from the top'. We do not often hear people referring to their role, or being referred to in their role, as '*a* leader of the institution'. We are more likely to hear people referring to their role and being referred to as '*the* leader of the institution'.

As a consequence of the special place leaders have in our minds, the role (as position) and the practice of leaders are significant. Leaders may be the target of the projected emotions of others. They may consciously and unconsciously act as 'lightning rods' for the unacceptable feelings of others (Dunning, James and Jones 2005). Leaders may experience problems if they take in those feeling and start acting on the basis of them. Leaders may also be the subject of conscious and unconscious fantasies about who they are and what they might do. People may hope and/or fear that they take on the informal roles of 'the saint', 'the saviour', 'the destroyer', 'the protector', 'the father figure', 'the mother figure', 'the knight', 'the nightmare', 'the devil' and so on. Again, problems for leaders may well come if they unconsciously take up and perform these roles.

A final point about leaders and leadership is the notion of representation. Because of the significance of leaders 'in the mind', the representational role of leaders and leadership is important. In this role, in our minds, leaders embody, symbolise and epitomise their institutions and they stand for, act for and speak for their institutions. This role is arguably the responsibility of the leader – the head – of an institution, but others may take up this role both formally and informally on the leader's behalf. They may all represent their institution in which they have a leadership role.

Group mentalities

Another key theme in system psychodynamics is the concept of group mentalities. The idea of group mentalities is grounded in the work of Wilfrid Bion (1961). Bion's considerable body of work focused on the individual and the group (Armstrong 2005). Bion identified that there are two main tendencies in the way in which groups work: the work group mentality and the basic assumption mentality. In a group with a work group mentality, the group members focus on carrying out a specifiable task – their primary task – and assessing their effectiveness in doing it. Groups with a basic assumption mentality have a propensity to avoid work on the primary task. Their endeavours are focused on meeting the unconscious needs of the group and its individual members. A major need is the reduction of anxiety and internal discord. Eventually, the perpetuation of the group becomes an end in itself.

Bion identified three kinds of basic assumption mentality: dependency, fight and flight, and pairing.

Groups operating with a basic assumption dependency mentality act as if their primary task is to satisfy the needs and desires of their members to feel cared for. The processes also make sure that group members do not have to address difficult issues, solve important problems or make significant and necessary decisions. In this mentality, the group loses its focus on the normative primary task. The group members will look to the leader to collude with their mode of operating and will expect the leaders not to confront them with the problems. If the leader does collude, the group may well become dependent on her or him. If the leader refuses to collude, he or she may be viewed as heartless, unfeeling and insensitive.

In the basic assumption fight and flight mentality, the group generates a threat of some kind which they must either attack or flee from. In order to maintain this position, the danger must always be present. Groups with this predisposition tend to become preoccupied with an external threat or enemy. As a result, a culture of paranoia and aggressive competitiveness may come to dominate, which can bond the group and promote team spirit. Its real benefit, however, is that it allows the group to avoid work on the primary task and to keep clear of the anxiety associated with such work. The group may look to the leader to organise an aggressive and protective (and of course preoccupying) action of some kind. If the leader refuses but instead attempts to focus the group's energies onto the primary task, he or she will be viewed as weak and cowardly.

A group with the basic assumption pairing mentality believes that some future event will save them regardless of their actual problems and needs. The group may focus on the future as a defence against its current difficulties and anxieties. Group members are motivated by a false hope and an erroneous optimism that matters will improve. The group may feel that its salvation lies perhaps in the pairing or coupling of, for example, two members of the group or the leader and a person or entity outside the group. If the leader does not collude in this way but instead attempts to the focus the group's work on the present rather than its fantasies for the future, he or she will have to confront the group with difficult feelings of disillusion and disappointment.

A number of issues arise from the notion of basic assumption tendencies. Firstly, the mentalities are not always fixed positions. They are tendencies, and groups can move from a work group mentality to a basic assumption mentality and between different basic assumption mentalities. Secondly, the 'tendencies' of the group can be used diagnostically to establish the needs of the group. If the group leader then comes to understand the group's needs, he or she can respond appropriately and begin to focus the group's energies onto the primary task. Thirdly, while leaders can use various basic assumption tendencies to their advantage, and leaders frequently do, for example by focusing on an external enemy rather than on pressing internal problems, ultimately they must face the group with the requirement to concentrate on the primary task. Any collusion with the group's tendencies towards basic assumption mentalities should be temporary or the leader will run the risk of supporting the group's efforts to avoid work on the primary task. Furthermore, because the group's basic assumption mentalities are based on fantasies, eventually the leader will come to be seen as not up to the task of delivering the fantasy world of which the group members dream. Fourthly, as we discussed above, work on the primary task always carries anxiety of some kind. Groups with basic assumption tendencies are endeavouring to protect themselves from this anxiety. All three basic assumption tendencies are thus social defences (see above). It is important therefore that those anxieties that are part and parcel of the primary task are contained, held and worked with. This containment of anxiety is an important organisational function.

Emotional containment and control

There is a good case for arguing that the more difficult feelings there are in an organisation, the more likely it is to resort to defensive behaviours (Dunning, James and Jones 2005). Put simply, if there are more difficult feelings around, people are more likely to seek to protect themselves from them. For any institution, that is any established organisation with a social purpose, difficult feelings will be present because of the institution's designated social responsibility. So, it may appear important to minimise or even eradicate the difficult feelings, which will include anxiety, that are associated with the primary task. But there is a paradox here. We know that very high levels of emotion and anxiety inhibit the motivation to act. People and groups become 'paralysed with fear' in such situations. At the other end of the scale, with very low levels of emotion, there is no motivation to act. In those situations people are simply not moved to action. The central issue is that emotions motivate actions and are a prerequisite for acting but they are very difficult to control. An alternative to emotional control is emotional containment.

Containment is the organisational process of providing the conditions that facilitate effective and authentic receptiveness and reflection. The term was first coined by Wilfrid Bion (1961) in the context of psychoanalysis and it describes an environment in which the experience of emotion and anxiety can be held, surfaced and worked with. A containing environment for emotions contrasts with a controlling environment for emotions where feelings are restrained, hidden and not allowed to become apparent. In such controlling environments, emotions and anxieties have to be dealt with in other ways and, because they may be painful, may need to be defended against. Controlling environments may therefore call up social defences against emotional pain. Moreover, 'being controlled' can itself feel very threatening, which may create emotional responses of its own. As a result, a controlling environment may create more difficult feelings than it prevents.

Passion in institutions

The notion of engaging the emotional energies of teachers and educational leaders has recently come to prominence. Day (2004a, 2004b) has drawn attention to the importance of passion in both teaching and in successful school leadership. James (2004) has argued that a key task of educational leaders is to develop passionate schools where energy flows directly and without interruption towards work on the primary task. In this section, we address some of the issues that relate to passion in institutions and attempt to connect passion – strong feelings, fervour and enthusiasm for an object of some kind – with some of the key themes in system psychodynamics and institutional transformation. To confirm, at the heart of our ideas is the notion that institutions are particular organisations that are established for a social purpose of some kind and that passion for the work of institutions such as schools can be an important characteristic of those who work in them and for them. We begin by addressing aspects of the source of passion and explore some important and relevant issues. We then consider ways of working with passion.

Arguably, we are all driven by psychic forces, for which Freud used the term 'libido'. For Freud, these libidinal forces had two basic forms: the life instinct, which he termed 'Eros', and the death instinct, 'Thanatos', which is a desire for death, withdrawal and return. Although Freud used the term 'instinct' to describe these forces, 'drives' may be a better term and the concept of 'drive' has been broadened by other theorists. Drives can be the forces within us that give us ambition, a desire to make some kind of difference or to lead a good life. At a fundamental level, drives underpin behaviours and characteristics such as sexual desire, aggression and rivalry. At a more learned and acquired level, they underpin other desires such as a need to control the behaviours of others, to please people, to be well thought of, to achieve, to be perfect or to repair inner damage and fragmentation through reparation.

Some of these forces are very strong, so strong that we may wish to hide them or to pretend they are not there. They can become pathological and then very dangerous and can combine with other objects and behaviours to become fetishes and other significant psychological disturbances. In a 'civilised society', these forces can be seen as difficult, which can result in a desire to conceal them. They are, however, very important and, arguably, they are the wellspring of passion. Working with passion gives rise to a number of considerations.

Drives, passions and other psychological forces are very significant. They are what push us to do what we do, so recognising them is important and they also need to be worked with, considered and reflected upon. Leaders in institutions need to be aware of them and to be able to handle them – their own and those of others. Arguably, leaders need to enable the institution and its members to become passionate about their work.

Passions and drives are vital but they can become distorted or misdirected or initiate the dominance of action over reflection and other more thoughtful processes. Importantly, passionate energy can be channelled inappropriately into defensive behaviour so that people work harder dissociating themselves from the outside world and their work on the primary task and defending themselves from potential emotional pain than they do engaging with the world and working on the primary task with all their energies.

The energy released by working with colleagues who we like and who we are attracted to is important. It is, however, often underplayed and can 'disappear' as part of the de-emotionalisation of work in institutions. However, when the passion for working on the task with an 'attractive colleague' is directed inappropriately towards the other, the passion for work on the primary task is likely to be dissipated (Hirschhorn 1988).

As we discussed above, work on the primary task, especially if the task is difficult and significant, requires courage. There is a danger that the courageous passion needed to undertake difficult work, especially when the work is undertaken in a selfless way, can transform into aggression that may transmute into a sense of anger and negativity towards others. It is important that such strong feelings remain directed towards the primary task. A reflective stance may also help in monitoring the energy being expended on the primary task and the level of commitment to it.

Rivalry can become a competitive urge that can distort the rationale for achieving the primary task. One interpretation of the term 'rivals' is that it means being equal with or approximately equal with another or others in some kind of endeavour. Rivals can be competitors but competitors are participants in some kind of contest. While the two terms of course overlap in common usage, we argue that they are different. The difference comes from an individual's or group's rationale for its work on the primary task. Does a teacher in a school work hard to be seen to be the best teacher in the school and thereby gain the status he feels he needs? Or does he endeavour to be the best teacher because he wants to do the best possible educational work with his pupils?

Monitoring, checking and 'ensuring that things happen' are important management activities. But if these practices are driven only by a desire to 'control' then the organisation may feel restrained, repressed and held in check. Moreover, an excessive desire to control can make delegation more difficult which may have many unwanted consequences.

The desire to please others, being driven to achieve and the desire for perfection can be very useful but need to reflected on and worked with carefully lest they develop into activities with unwanted consequences (Fisher and Torbert 1995). A desire to please and to be well thought of is of course very useful. Colleagues with such a drive can be very helpful in any institution. But all too often, the desire to please can lead to people taking on too many tasks and lacking focus, which can cause stress and may eventually lead to 'burn out'. A desire to achieve can also be a very valuable quality. However, if 'achieving' becomes the fundamental desire, it can drive out collaborative ways of working and other enabling practices that are arguably essential organising capabilities in institutions. It can also lead to an obsession with acting as opposed to reflecting (and therefore learning). Further, an achievement orientation can narrow the focus of the task at the expense of retaining a sense of proportion and an awareness of the wider context. The desire for perfection can also be very helpful. Wanting work to be done well is very important. However, if the desire for good work becomes an obsession for perfection, then nothing is ever good enough, tasks may never be completed and engagement with the primary task may be prevented because to do it perfectly becomes a monumental and impossible task.

The drive to repair 'inner damage' can be very important. It is 'reparation' work (Hirschhorn 1988) and, as Melanie Klein argued, is concerned with creating an object of beauty to repair internal fragmentation. Klein argued that artists may be driven by such a desire in their work. Reparation may be what pushes leaders of institutions such as schools to undertake the often very difficult work they do (James and Connolly 2000). For example, a headteacher 'turning round' an underperforming school may be driven by a desire for reparation, with the 'Good School' representing the object of beauty that they have created. No one would deny the value of such work or deem the underpinning motivation as unacceptable. However, over-identification by the headteacher with the beautiful object (the Good School) they have created may cause difficulties in succession planning, enabling continual change and initiating further development.

A desire for security can be important and needs to be recognised. If the desire becomes excessive so that much-needed change is blocked, then it becomes unhelpful. Ensuring that the need for security is met can help individuals and groups take the kinds of risks that are often necessary during institutional change.

The pathway of the development of passion may not straightforward. The release of passion in institutions needs to be continually worked with. Arguably, the main inhibitor of passion among those who work in institutions is an anxiety about what might happen if they became fully passionate about their work. They thus seek to defend themselves against becoming fully engaged and committed to their work – and importantly their work on the primary task. It is thus important for leaders to tap into what people really desire and why they desire it; to concentrate on what people want to do and what is meaningful to them and to focus on what they want to become. This process is rarely straightforward. Gutmann (2004) refers to this pathway of development as a series of zigzags, which might take the individual or group sometimes forward to a new place, sometimes backwards in regression or sometimes sideways to a different perspective. The resolution of the distortions of energy and the release of passion can result in a sense of authenticity and the notion of 'flow' that is *"being totally, and positively, absorbed in what one is doing: a deep sense of rightness, goodness, engagement or being"* (Fineman 2003: 23).

CONCLUDING COMMENTS

In this chapter, we have sought to set out some of the main features of a perspective on organisations, which is known as system psychodynamics or, because of its transformatory potential, institutional transformation. The concepts that comprise the theoretical framework will be useful in explaining the work of the schools we studied and, importantly, in beginning to understand the basis of their success. The nature of practice in these schools will in turn enhance, enrich and enliven the abstract concepts we have discussed. In summary, the main concepts in system psychodynamics are as follows.

- *Unconscious processes* may exert a powerful influence on conscious practices. The surface emotional terrain may not be fully understood without some reference to the underlying unconscious emotional geology.

- *The emotions of work in institutions* are in part a consequence of the special social purpose of institutions such as schools. Work in institutions may not be fully understood without a consideration of their social role.

- *Defences against emotions* are rituals, routines and 'ways of going on' that individuals, groups and institutions engage in to protect themselves from emotional pain. Splitting and projection is a very significant and prevalent social defence. Defensive behaviours may have little relevance to the work of the institution and can be very resistant to change. The emotional experience of work affects organisational micropolitics and can affect the difference between espoused and in-use theories of action.

- *Boundaries* are places of structural discontinuity. They are created and reinforced and attacked and destroyed in the process of organising. Boundaries are very important in institutions; they can be the source of organisational conflict and they have to be actively managed.

- *The notion of role* is used in two ways, firstly to describe social positions and secondly as social practices, which relate to work on the primary task.

- *The primary task* is what an individual, group or organisation feels it must do to survive. Clarifying the primary task of a work organisation may be difficult but can be very important in improving organisational effectiveness.

- *Leaders and leadership* are centrally concerned with influencing change. Leadership is a special organisational role in that it is those behaviours that enable others to perform their role in relation to the primary task. Leaders attract considerable conscious and unconscious psychological attention and because of that can have a significant role in 'representing' their institution.

- *Group mentalities* have two forms. A 'work group mentality' is where the group focuses on a specifiable primary task. It contrasts with a 'basic assumption mentality' in which the group avoids primary task-related work and concentrates on meeting its unconscious needs.

- *Emotional containment* is concerned with providing a secure environment within which individual and organisational emotions and anxieties can be expressed, held and reflected upon.

- *Passion* is where energy flows in an uninterrupted and continuous way to the primary task.

4

The research

INTRODUCTION

This book reports the findings of a study which researched the characteristics of high attainment schools in disadvantaged settings. We describe these schools as being very effective. Their pupils reached high levels of attainment in national tests although the pupils in the schools experienced considerable social and economic disadvantage. We use the percentage of pupils in the school entitled to free school meals as a measure of socio-economic disadvantage. The research took place in Wales, UK as part of the Narrowing the Gap Initiative, which is funded jointly by the Welsh Assembly Government and the Welsh Local Government Association.

Our intention in this chapter is to provide some background and context to the research by discussing the key features of the education system in Wales, UK and the central issue the study addresses. Our intention is also to outline how we undertook the research. We thus describe the kind of study we undertook, the schools we studied (the sample), our approach to the data collection, and how we collected and analysed the data.

THE EDUCATION SYSTEM IN WALES

There are approximately 1,630 primary schools in the maintained education sector in Wales, about 230 secondary schools and 45 schools for pupils with special educational needs. A quarter of the schools are Welsh-medium schools where classes are taught in the Welsh language. The Welsh Assembly Government administers education at the national level and 22 local authorities manage the sector locally. Local authorities in Wales have a more prominent role in managing schools than elsewhere in the UK. Wales has its own school inspection service, Estyn, which uses an inspection framework that is different from those in other parts of the UK. The General Teaching Council for Wales gives financial support for a range of individual and whole-school professional development activities. Awdurdod Cymwysterau, Cwricwlwm ac Asesu Cymru (ACCAC) is the principal advisory body to the National Assembly for Wales (NAfW) on the school curriculum, examinations, assessment and vocational qualifications. The National Curriculum in Wales includes Welsh and its content is slightly different in other ways from the National Curriculum in England. Its structure is similar, however, with Key Stage 1 (KS1) for pupils aged 3 to 6+ years, KS2 for pupils aged 7 to 11+ years, KS3 for pupils aged 12 to 14+ years and KS4 for pupils aged 15 to 16+ years. At the time the research was undertaken, there were end-of-KS tests, Standard Assessment Tests (SATs) at the end of KS2 and KS3. End-of-KS1 SATs were in place in the period immediately prior to the research but abolished as the research was undertaken. End-of-KS2 SATs have recently been abolished too, after the research was completed.

THE CENTRAL ISSUE

The educational attainment of primary school pupils in Wales has improved over the last ten years or so (Welsh Assembly Government 2002). The increase in the median percentage of pupils in individual schools who attain the KS2 SAT core subject indicator (at least National Curriculum Level 4 in mathematics, science and English or Welsh) has steadily increased as shown in Figure 4.1. During the same period, the difference between the median percentage for the lower quartile and for the upper quartile has reduced but only slightly. Thus the gap between the attainment of pupils in KS2 SATs in KS2 schools where attainment overall is high and those KS2 schools where attainment overall is low has not narrowed substantially (Welsh Assembly Government 2002).

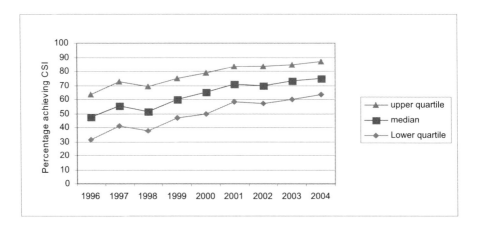

Figure 4.1 The percentage of pupils in a school attaining the Core Subject Indicator (CSI), which is at least National Curriculum Level 4 in mathematics, science and English or Welsh from 1996 to 2004.

In Wales, as is generally the case in many other countries, the socio-economic status of the pupils is one of the main contextual influences on pupil attainment (Teddlie, Stringfield and Reynolds 2000; Welsh Assembly Government 2002). An indication of socio-economic disadvantage in a school may be gained by the percentage of pupils entitled to free school meals (FSM). Pupil attainment in KS2 SATs as indicated by the percentage of pupils in a school attaining the core subject indicator correlates negatively with socio-economic disadvantage as shown in Figure 4.2.

However, despite this overall correlation, in some schools where the percentage of pupils entitled to free school meals is very high, say above 30 per cent, pupil attainment is also very high. Indeed, some of these schools are in the top quartile for pupil attainment. They appear to overcome one of the main reasons for the gap between pupil attainment in schools where pupil attainment was high overall and pupil attainment in schools where it was low. The schools we studied were in this group.

THE KIND OF STUDY WE UNDERTOOK

The overall aim of the research was to analyse the nature of schools in disadvantaged settings where the level of pupil attainment was high. We undertook case studies of 18 such schools and then carried out a cross-case analysis. In each school, we collected and analysed data from a wide range of sources. We then identified prominent themes in all the cases, aggregated those themes into features and then categorised the features into a small number of characteristics.

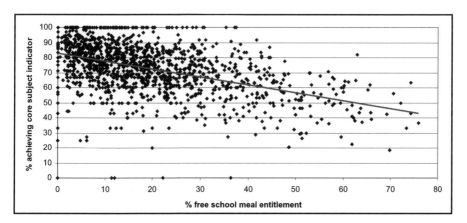

Figure 4.2 The percentage of pupils in a school attaining the Core Subject Indicator (CSI), which is at least National Curriculum Level 4 in mathematics, science and English or Welsh plotted against the percentage of pupils in the school entitled to free school meals.

THE SCHOOLS WE STUDIED

We were interested in characterising schools where the levels of attainment and disadvantage were both high. In the research we have used the terms 'attainment' and 'achievement' in specific ways as they are used in education policies in Wales. Although they may be considered to be broadly similar in meaning, we use the term 'attainment' to indicate the measure of pupils' capabilities at a particular point in time in relation to national norms using tests and examinations such as National Curriculum Standard Assessment Tests (SATs). We use the term 'achievement' to describe pupil progress by reference to some sort of starting point for the pupil concerned. Achievement may relate to any appropriate capability, not simply those measured by SATs.

Our measure of the overall disadvantage experienced by the pupils was the percentage of pupils who were entitled to free school meals (FSM). We recognise that this percentage is only a very approximate measure of disadvantage and has a number of flaws. Firstly, children whose families receive Family Tax Credit because of low income are not entitled to FSM. So, using the FSM percentage may significantly underestimate the extent of disadvantage in the schools (Maden 2001). Secondly, disadvantage can be experienced in a number of ways and may not simply be in those economic forms that would then confer entitlement to FSM. Moreover, the disadvantage may only specifically affect those pupils who are entitled to free school meals and the remainder of the pupils may be wealthy in a socio-economic sense and not at all disadvantaged. For the purposes of this study, we have accepted that these are extreme interpretations and take the view that social disadvantage is typically linked to economic disadvantage and that they both may contribute to educational disadvantage. We have also accepted that the level of FSM entitlement is generally an indicator of wider disadvantage among the pupil population and is not likely to be limited to an atypical group.

The case study schools were chosen on the basis that they met the following criteria.

- *The schools were recommended by their local authority education services as doing well in difficult circumstances.* It was important that the schools we studied were valued and acknowledged as successful by their local educational communities. We considered the recommendation by the schools' local authority education services to be important in validating their educational work.

- *The schools had recently received a favourable inspection report from Estyn.* Again, it was important that the work undertaken by the schools chosen for in-depth study had been validated by a set of criteria broader than the fact that their pupils had reached a particular level of attainment in the end-of-KS2 SATs. A favourable inspection report from Estyn would be an indication that a broad range of appropriate 'in-school processes' were securely in place.

- *The schools had consistently high levels of pupil attainment.* All the schools had consistently been in the upper quartile of all the schools in Wales for the percentage of their pupils attaining the KS1 and/or KS2 core subject indicator in the three years prior to the study. This consistency of performance was considered to be important. We were anxious to identify practices that were reliably and dependably sound and not those which succeed briefly because of their novelty value or because of the Hawthorne effect (Roethlisberger and Dickson 1939).

- *The schools were in the free school meal bands 4 to 6 (13–21 per cent to 35–50 per cent) in the period 2001 to 2003.* Generally, the level of free school meals is set in bands. Band 1 is below 5 per cent of pupils; Band 2 is 5–9 per cent; Band 3 is 9–13 per cent; Band 4 is 13–21 per cent; Band 5 is 21–35 per cent; Band 6 is 35–50 per cent; and Band 7 is above 50 per cent. All the 18 schools selected were consistently in free school meal band 4 or above (see below for details). The consistency of disadvantage is important because it indicates that the school is consistently successful in working with a constant feature of their context. Their apparent success is not the result of a temporary 'statistical blip'.

The 18 schools were geographically spread throughout Wales and were in 12 different local authorities. Two were infant (KS1) schools, two were junior (KS2) and the remainder were primary (KS1 and 2) schools as shown in Table 4.1. Five were Welsh-medium schools.

THE DATA COLLECTION AND ANALYSIS

We were keen to develop a rich and vivid picture of life in these schools. We therefore set out to collect data of various kinds from a range of sources. This approach was not so much to triangulate the data ('The finding must be true because a number of people have said it and it is stated in various documents') as to develop as full a picture as possible ('Particular ways of working are described, confirmed and elaborated upon from a variety of standpoints'). Each data collection visit lasted approximately one day. In setting up the visits, we were keen to establish that the data collection was not 'inspectorial' in nature, that we wanted to have open access to those who were working in the school and that we wanted to speak to parents and members/the chair of the governing body. The data collection was undertaken in the spring and summer terms of 2004.

Table 4.1 The case study schools by local authority and type of school

LEA	Type of school
Blaenau-Gwent	Infant
Bridgend	Primary
	Primary
Caerphilly	Primary
Cardiff	Primary
	Primary
Carmarthenshire	Primary
	Primary
Conwy	Primary
Gwynedd	Primary
	Primary
Merthyr Tydfil	Primary
Neath-Port Talbot	Junior
Pembrokeshire	Primary
Rhondda-Cynon-Taf	Primary
	Primary
	Infant
Swansea	Junior

Data was collected from pupils, parents, support staff, teachers, senior staff, the headteacher and a member/the chair of the governing body and/or a governor. We also collected documentary data of a range of kinds such as policy documents, information sheets and handbooks during visits to the schools. Typically, we spoke to pupils in groups using a range of methods to elicit their individual thoughts about their schools. Teachers with various levels of seniority, a range of experience and with differing responsibilities were interviewed. In addition, we held discussions with groups of staff and often the whole staff about the school. Parents and classroom learning assistants of a range of types were interviewed individually and/or in groups. Some individuals from these two groups were also members of the governing body and we were able to talk to them about that aspect of the school as well. Members/chairs of governing bodies were typically interviewed individually. The headteacher and senior teacher/deputy headteachers were interviewed individually and, usually, more than once.

Key questions which were pursued during the data collection were as follows.

- What is it about this school that enables its pupils to achieve a higher standard than might be expected from its setting?
- Why does the school do it that way?
- What are examples of what the school does to ensure high standards of pupil achievement and attainment?

Spoken data was recorded by means of written notes which were 'written up' immediately after the visit. The whole data set from a school was then analysed and a report written which summarised the analysed data. Following the case study of 12 of the schools, the reports were analysed and emerging themes were identified. These themes helped to shape the data collection in the remaining six schools although the data collection in these schools also sought to reveal other features. When all the data collection visits were complete, significant recurring themes from all 18 reports were identified and all the reports were then reanalysed to develop a full understanding of the ways in which the different themes were represented in the data. The descriptions of the themes were then checked and confirmed by all the members of the project team.

THE CASE STUDY SCHOOLS – THE NATURE OF DISADVANTAGE

All the schools were in the FSM bands 4 to 6 (13–21 per cent to 35–50 per cent) in the years 2001 to 2003. In the descriptions below, where two bands are given it is because they are primary schools and the ranges differ for the infant and junior stages or there has been a change during the three years.

School A

A Welsh-medium school in a town in North Wales (FSM band 6)

The school is located in a slate quarrying area. Some quarries are still operational, but the industry has declined and employment opportunities are limited. The local community is thus 'economically poor' (headteacher). Many families are dependent upon social security benefits. There are sometimes conflicts between families and within families which are 'brought into the school yard' (headteacher) and occasionally into the classroom. Overall there is a 'high level of need' (headteacher) in the community the school serves. One difficulty the school experiences is the high level of 'turnover' in the community it serves with newcomers arriving unexpectedly and leaving suddenly after a short while. The nature of incoming families is often problematic, for example 'one-parent' families; two adults, each with children from at least one former relationship; or families who are 'escaping' from something or somewhere and/or are 'looking for the good life' (headteacher). Many of these families display varying degrees of awareness of the Welsh language and culture. The school has to invest time and effort working with the pupils and their families when they may only be in the area for a matter of weeks in some cases. Increasingly, the families arriving do not speak Welsh and as a consequence the proportion of local Welsh speakers is decreasing.

School B

A Welsh-medium school in a semi-urban setting in North West Wales (FSM band 5–6).

The school is set in a group of small former quarrying villages all located close to each other in a valley. There are no longer any quarries active in the area. It is an area of low incomes and low expectations according to the headteacher. Non-Welsh speaking families who are typically experiencing difficulties arrive often unexpectedly at the school and want their children to attend. Often, when the children have been in the school only a short while, the families typically depart, again sometimes unexpectedly. The 'unexpected arrival, brief stay, unexpected departure' of pupils is particularly challenging. The families *"often expect and sometimes demand that the school should be a replica of the one they have left behind"* (headteacher), particularly in terms of the medium of communication in the school. They may also act out previous home–school conflicts in the school. There is potential divergence and discord between the Welsh speaking and non-Welsh speaking families which the school actively responds to. The management and resourcing of provision in two languages also presents particular challenges.

School C

A Catholic school in a town in North Wales (FSM band 5–6)

The school is located in one of the poorest areas of the town and most of the pupils live locally. Overall though, the school has an exceptionally wide catchment area due to the lack of other Catholic primary schools in this part of North Wales. The headteacher sees a declining interest in Catholic education and there is no nearby Catholic secondary school to which pupils can progress. The school has to convince current and prospective parents of the value of Catholic education at primary level, even though there is no obvious pathway into Catholic secondary education. The main disadvantage issues are low incomes and low levels of employment.

School D

A voluntary controlled Welsh-medium school in a village in West Wales (FSM bands 4–5)

The school serves a community which has a *"transient quality"* (headteacher). There is a substantial and continual influx of non-Welsh-speaking families into rented accommodation who then rapidly move on to seek work and accommodation elsewhere. Pupils *"are continually coming and going"* and *"staying for perhaps only six months"* (headteacher). There is a high dependency on state benefits in the local community as there is considerable unemployment and under-employment.

School E

A bilingual school serving a small village in West Wales (FSM bands 5–6)

The area has suffered economic decline over the last 25 years, with the local colliery closing in the late 1980s. The community the school serves is not prosperous – *"only a very small percentage of children come from professional backgrounds"* (chair of governing body) – and there are some areas of substantial economic disadvantage. About a third of the pupils come from 'broken homes'. There are pockets of social problems. One housing estate where many pupils live experiences particular social problems. There is some in-migration, with families seeking the perceived better life in a semi-rural environment. The families arriving tend not to be Welsh-speaking.

School F

A bilingual school in rural West Wales (FSM bands 4–5)

The community the school serves is not generally disadvantaged but there are pockets with quite severe problems and many severely disadvantaged families. Some parts of the community, for example the farming community, are relatively wealthy. The community is characterised by the rapid influx of families from outside the area many of whom are typically non-Welsh speaking and may even be antipathetic to Welsh-medium education. The school provides two language streams and endeavours to protect and sustain the Welsh ethos and the language of the school. Incoming families frequently have social and economic problems of a range of kinds. Potential discord is exacerbated by the fact that several of the Welsh-speaking pupils come from relatively 'comfortable' backgrounds. Welsh-speaking parents are more active in the school than many of their non-Welsh-speaking counterparts. The school has to balance all these diverse and sometimes conflicting elements to ensure as much harmony as possible.

School G

A large Catholic junior school in a city in South Wales serving a wide area (FSM band 4–5)

The main catchment area of the school is *"town-centre based"* (headteacher), although some pupils travel up to ten miles to attend school. The school serves two major housing estates where there is widespread disadvantage. The proportion of single parents is high and many families live on state benefits. Expectations tend to be low and the children's home life is often impoverished in a variety of ways. *"Many children are not spoken to in their homes, many children have special needs"* (headteacher).

School H

Situated on the outskirts of a large town in South Wales (FSM band 6)

The school's catchment area is largely urban and includes a large council housing estate where there is considerable social and economic disadvantage. Many families on the estate *"have regular contact with social services"* (headteacher). Drug abuse is a problem and the pupils from this estate are *"very knowledgeable about drugs"* (headteacher). A large proportion of the pupils' fathers are unemployed. Some pupils have *"transient fathers"* (headteacher). Many single parents have a number of part-time jobs. There is only one child attending the school who is *"from a professional family"* (headteacher). Birth rates are falling locally and there is considerable movement of families in and out of the community. Those moving in are often attracted by cheap housing. Children from the local women's refuge attend the school. The main disadvantage facing the school is the dependency culture locally. *"They are used to having things done for them. The community has to be dragged along"* (headteacher).

School I

A school close to a large town in South Wales (FSM band 6)

The catchment area is very mixed but predominantly disadvantaged. *"The parents range from convicted drug dealers to hospital doctors – people who are very deprived, very poor working class to others who are prosperous middle class"* (headteacher). The school serves extensive housing association accommodation in the locality which in recent years has been used to house 'problem families' from further afield. Low pay rather than low employment is the issue. A high proportion of the pupils have extended families living around the school and *"there are lots of cousins"* (headteacher) on the pupil roll.

School J

Located in a village at the top end of a chain of former coal-mining communities in a South Wales valley (FSM bands 4–5)

With the closure of the last mine in the area in the 1980s, there are few jobs locally. Most parents work in the local town or further afield but unemployment is having a slow and increasing impact. More children are from families which are poorly paid rather than unemployed. The number of 'broken homes' locally is increasing as is the number of families with difficulties moving into local housing association accommodation. According to the headteacher approximately 25 per cent of pupils are without resident fathers at home or have step parents.

School K

Situated in a 'traditional' mining village in the South Wales valleys (FSM bands 4–5)

Unemployment is high and there are very few employers nearby. Those in work often commute out of the area. Deprivation does have an impact on the people of the area but generally the pupils are protected. *"Families ensure the kids are OK"*, as the headteacher put it. There is a problem with drugs in the locality with evidence of misuse found on the school premises on occasions. Periodically, vandalism is a problem.

School L

A bilingual school located in a built-up area in an 'urban village' in the South Wales valleys (FSM band 5)

Thirty per cent of pupils are bussed in from similar villages nearby. Twenty-five per cent of the children come from areas that are economically disadvantaged where unemployment levels are high. Parts of the catchment area have a drug abuse problem and the school has been targeted by drug sellers outside the school gates.

School M

Situated in a village in the valleys in South Wales (FSM band 5)

The area the school serves is *"economically OK but it's a struggle"* (headteacher). There are numerous cases of *"absent fathers and single mothers"* (headteacher), which results in the pupils experiencing emotional problems and not having limits put on their behaviours. *"Mum is exhausted* [by being the sole carer]; *dad spoils them* [when he visits]", as the headteacher put it. Some parents are unable to afford the school uniform for their children. The children have *"restricted experience"* (headteacher). Children from outside the school's natural catchment area attend a special needs unit in the school.

School N

A school in a former mining village in a South Wales valley community (FSM band 6)

The socio-economic context is *"grim"* (headteacher) with very high levels of deprivation. This deprivation results in a lack of aspiration and ambition. There is very low employment, a high involvement of social services which struggle to cope, extensive social problems, widespread drug abuse (but according to the headteacher not as bad as a few years ago), unstable parent/carer relationships and multi-partner family relationships. *"The traditional family is in the minority"* (headteacher). *"The more successful of our children have left the area; housing is cheap and it attracts a lot of people who already have problems"* (chair of governing body).

School O

Located in a former mining village in the South Wales valleys (FSM band 4)

Most of the pupils come from the village and the similar neighbouring village. There are jobs locally but most pay low wages. *"It's an area of low means rather than low employment"* (headteacher). There is some vandalism in the area but the school is not a target. There are insufficient activities for youngsters in the village and poor transport does not enable them to travel far easily. There are drug abuse problems locally, with conspicuous drug dealing. The proportion of broken homes is high, though the headteacher felt this impacted pupils less than one might expect with most adapting readily.

School P

A school in a village in South East Wales (FSM bands 5–6)

The area served by the school has seen considerable deprivation and unemployment levels have been very high. Employment rates are lower now but *"the rates of pay are pitiful"* (headteacher). Very few parents work in professional occupations and only a few are skilled workers. Many pupils are affected by the high levels of deprivation.

School Q

Located in a large city in South Wales (FSM bands 5–6)

Employment levels are low and there is a high dependency on social security benefits. The pupils are socially and materially disadvantaged.

Many experience continual change in their parents' relationships and/or have young and relatively immature parents.

School R

A school located close to the centre of a large city in South Wales and in the 10 per cent most deprived wards in Wales (FSM band 6)

There are low incomes and high levels of unemployment in the school's catchment community. The key issue for this school is the decline in parenting skills: *"It's taken a dive in the last ten years"*, said the deputy headteacher. Parents lack appropriate discipline techniques and there is little stimulation of the children at home. As a result, some children struggle to speak properly, do not know how to play, may have no pens and paper at home and/or cannot use a knife and fork. Increasingly, parents ask for general advice about parenting and more want reassurance that they are bringing up their children well.

SUMMARY OF THE OUTCOMES

The analysis of the data revealed 91 themes which were aggregated into 21 features that were then grouped into seven characteristics. We considered one characteristic in particular to be central. The remaining six key characteristics contributed to and sustained that central characteristic and themselves contributed to and were sustained by the central characteristic.

The central characteristic

A productive, strong and highly inclusive culture that ensures effective and enriched teaching for learning for all pupils and improving and further enriching teaching for learning for all pupils.

The key characteristics

1   Leadership
2   The mindset
3   The teaching team
4   The engagement and commitment of the pupils and their parents
5   Very efficient and effective organisation and management
6   Mutual support, validation and valuing from all those connected with the school

In the following chapters, we explore each of these characteristics, beginning with the central characteristic and then dealing with the key characteristics in turn.

5

The central characteristic

INTRODUCTION

Perhaps unsurprisingly there was a powerful emphasis in the sample schools on enabling the pupils to attain high scores in national/standard tests, especially Standard Assessment Tests (SATs). Given the way we selected the schools any other outcome would have been remarkable. However, what was somewhat surprising was that the work of the staff centred equally powerfully on ensuring that their teaching was varied, stimulating and engaging. They endeavoured to provide an enriched curriculum. Moreover, the schools worked hard to improve their teaching for learning for all their pupils and to enrich it yet further. With this ensuring learning and improving teaching orientation, the schools' cultures were thus *productive*. The schools also gave a very powerful impression that they worked in ways that were reliable, robust and relentless. As a result, the cultures of the schools were very strong. Furthermore, the schools worked hard to engage everyone connected with them in their work, especially the pupils of course, but not only the pupils. The schools thus had *highly inclusive* cultures.

Our intention in this chapter is to discuss only the main features of this central characteristic and to attempt to create a boundary between it and the key characteristics with which it is interrelated. In this chapter, we therefore focus on the features that make up this central characteristic which are as follows.

- a productive culture;
- a strong culture;
- a highly inclusive culture;
- continuing professional development;
- changes/initiatives;
- extra-curricular activities.

The central characteristic: A productive, strong and highly inclusive culture that focuses on ensuring effective and enriched teaching for learning for all pupils and improving and further enriching teaching for learning for all pupils.

A PRODUCTIVE CULTURE

The central and overriding feature of these schools was their focus on teaching for learning and improving teaching for learning. It was the focus of their energies and their endeavours. Understandably, this feature emerged strongly in the data and linked to many other features and characteristics. It had a number of significant themes.

A passionate focus on teaching for learning

The schools worked passionately to ensure effective teaching for learning. With the same fervour, the schools continually sought to *improve* their teaching for learning. There was thus an emphasis on attaining high scores in SATs but there was an equal emphasis on making sure that the curriculum was broad, balanced and enriched. The teachers' work with their classes was very much the priority. "*It all comes down to teaching in the classroom*" said one of the headteachers when asked why the school was successful. There was a pupil/learning-centred approach. The schools endeavoured to meet every pupil's learning needs. The schools' powerful emphasis on making sure that their teaching brought about pupil learning and making sure their teaching continually improved meant that the cultures were very productive.

Meeting special educational/additional needs was very, very important

The schools worked hard to respond to pupils' special or additional learning needs and deliberately committed resources to this aspect of their work. Early intervention to meet additional learning needs was considered to be crucial. There was a relentless determination to meet the needs of all pupils with learning difficulties. "*We never give up*", said one teacher. In many cases, the way the schools approached meeting special or additional learning needs was simply to view it as part of the process of meeting the individual learning needs of *all* pupils, which was a widespread feature of the schools. In a sense, special educational needs were not considered to be all that 'special'.

An emphasis on the 'basics'

The schools concentrated on literacy and numeracy, which were clearly viewed as important foundations for the pupils' learning. The chair of the governing body in one of the schools expressed a sentiment, which was widespread in many schools, that "*There is an emphasis here on the core business, which is getting the basics right, teaching the children well to ensure they get a good start"*. In many cases, these 'basic subjects' were taught in the morning. A number of the schools had the Basic Skills Quality Mark. The basics of teaching were important as well as the basics of learning. Respondents referred to a range of teaching methods that they considered were part of sound teaching including varying the pupils' learning experience, the appropriate use of questions, regular recaps and reviews during lessons and/or lesson sequences, the use of 'advance organisers' (telling the pupils what was going to happen) and sound pupil–teacher relationships. The teaching was therefore thorough and secure. Creativity in teaching was valued as well.

The arrangement of classes varied but in all cases had been carefully thought through

The schools varied in the way they arranged their classes. There were examples of mixed ability classes across the whole school, setting for mathematics and English, and mixed age classes. There was often variation of teaching arrangements within schools as well. The schools appeared to be ready change the arrangement of classes according to the content of the lesson and the needs of the pupils. So, for example, one school was happy to teach mathematics to a very large group of relatively able pupils in the school hall while smaller groups were being given intensive teaching elsewhere. The key messages here are that: there was no common classroom arrangement across the schools that led to them being very effective, or that one fixed arrangement always worked better than any other regardless of the learning task, or that an upper limit on class sizes will guarantee effectiveness. Ensuring that the arrangement of classes meets the pupils' learning needs was the key. In these schools, the arrangement of classes had been considered carefully to optimise pupil learning.

Thorough, collaborative lesson planning

The planning of lessons and schemes of work was undertaken carefully and methodically. The teachers worked collaboratively in pairs, groups and even as a whole staff in some instances to plan lessons and schemes of work. Lesson planning was considered important but it was not undertaken obsessively. The emphasis was on excellent practice in the classroom, which was where energy should be expended – *"It's what happens in the classroom that counts"* as one headteacher put it. Another headteacher confirmed this point very succinctly, *"It's a question of being prepared for the lesson and then <u>doing it</u> in the classroom"* (his emphasis). His message was clear. Energy should not be wasted with unnecessary planning at the expense of good teaching during lessons.

Regular assessment of pupil progress

The assessment of pupil learning was considered to be very important. In the words of one headteacher, "*Assessment lies at the heart of all teaching and learning*". Typically, there was a plan of regular assessment, an assessment cycle, across a year-group or the whole school. Different tests would be set on a termly or an annual basis. There were instances where the pupils were encouraged to evaluate and assess their own work using the same success criteria as those used by their teachers.

Continuity and progression in teaching for learning were important

The schools sought to ensure that their teaching was continuous and linked and that it progressed in a sequential manner. This approach contributed to the sense of consistency and stability for the pupils and increased their confidence. The teachers did not like skimming through work just to ensure coverage. It was important to make sure that the pupils had learned before they moved on to the next stage.

Differentiation in teaching for learning was important

In many of the schools, there was a wide range of ability among the pupils. The schools responded to this variety with differentiation of teaching for learning. It was considered to be very important. In the words of one headteacher, "*Differentiation of work is crucial*", and he was emphatic: "*It's a planning requirement here*". There were examples of up to four levels of differentiation of learning tasks in one class. Nursery nurses and other classroom assistants were considered to be important in managing differentiated tasks. The teachers and schools appeared to welcome 'difference' in the pupils – it enhanced and added value to their work.

The schools used a wide range of learning activities and experiences

Varying the pupils' learning experience both during lessons and within a lesson sequence was important. It motivated the pupils and stimulated their interest. New technologies were much in evidence, for example interactive whiteboards, and were used extensively to augment learning. In addition, the schools created and took advantage of opportunities to enhance and enrich pupil learning. There were numerous examples of educational visits by the pupils and visitors to the schools such as members of the local community, dance groups, bands and even poets. These activities helped to provide an enriched curriculum which had the dual purpose of compensating for the pupils' possible lack of experiences of this kind outside school and enhancing learning in school.

Target setting for pupils was very important

The setting of learning targets for pupils was a feature of teaching in all the schools. Teachers used school-based tests to help with setting targets. One school had educational improvement plans for all pupils, not just those with special educational needs. Typically, the pupils were engaged fully in setting their own targets.

The pupils were kept busy

There was a work ethic in the schools – *"Not a minute is wasted"*, said one teacher. Homework was set as a matter of routine, which parents in particular valued. The pupils were actively engaged in and committed to their learning.

A STRONG CULTURE

The schools had strong cultures. Their ways of working were unyielding and unrelenting and there was total commitment and enthusiasm for the work. Within this feature there were a number of themes.

The strength of the culture was derived from a range of sources

In different schools, the robustness of the culture was underpinned by one or more strengthening qualities such as the religious ethos of the school, teaching through the medium of Welsh, the ideals, aspirations and drive of the headteacher, and/or the collective passion of the teaching staff to get the best out of everyone involved in the school. In one school, there was a strong desire for 'order', which was lived out in the sense of 'everything being as it should be'. A number of schools had more than one of these strengthening qualities. The deep-rooted culture underpinned the profound commitment to the pupils' educational, moral, spiritual, cultural and social development which was a very significant feature of the schools. This commitment helped to sustain and strengthen the culture.

There was a sense of fairness in the way the schools worked

Parents and pupils appreciated the feeling of justice and even-handedness that pervaded the schools. Those in the schools endeavoured to be fair in the way they operated. It helped to make the schools happy places and strengthened their ways of working.

There was a desire to achieve

All the schools were characterised by a widespread desire for everyone in the schools and all those connected to the schools to do well, to achieve.

Above all, the schools wanted the pupils to do well. They wanted the pupils to do the best they possibly could and then to improve on their previous best. This desire linked with having high aspirations and expectations and considerably strengthened the working culture. The notion of 'doing well' frequently spread throughout the whole school. In the words of one headteacher, "We – the pupils, teachers, the whole school community – want to do well in everything we do". 'Doing well' was an aspiration, an aim and a purpose. It was a key strengthening quality. The term also represented the drive, determination and motivation present in the schools. 'Doing well' might be construed as being competitive, but it was not. 'Winning' from the 'doing well' perspective was used as a measure of achievement, not as an end in itself.

A HIGHLY INCLUSIVE CULTURE

The schools were highly inclusive in the way they worked. They sought to engage the commitment of everyone connected with them. This feature is threaded through many – if not all – the various features and characteristics of the schools. In this section, we focus on three particular aspects: inclusive learning, inclusive organising and inclusive working with all those connected with the schools.

All the pupils were included

The inclusive approach applied especially to the pupils of course. One parent summed it up: "No child is pushed to one side, they all matter and the attitude of the staff is always positive" (his emphasis). The notion of inclusion was not passive though. The schools sought the active engagement and commitment of all the pupils in order to bring about inclusive learning.

There was an inclusive approach to organising the schools

All the staff were included in decision-making about resources and about important policy matters. There was thus inclusive organising. As we discuss in Chapter 7, the way all the staff worked together was a very significant aspect of the work of the schools.

There was inclusive working with all those connected with the schools

The schools worked hard to include everyone connected with them in their work. But more than that, they endeavoured to engage the commitment of everyone connected with them. The pupils' parents were viewed as important members of the team, the members of the governing body were engaged in the life of the school and the school's links with the local authority were strong. They were all actively involved in supporting the schools. Even the schools' connections with Estyn, the school inspection service in Wales, which, given Estyn's significant role in calling schools to account, might have been expected to be problematic, were sound. The schools actively sought – and received in many cases – the support of other agencies such as the General Teaching Council for Wales.

CONTINUING PROFESSIONAL DEVELOPMENT

In line with the schools' commitment to improving their practice, continuing professional development was considered to be very important and there were a number of themes in the data under this heading.

The organisation of training and development was taken very seriously

Typically, professional training and development was considered to be very important. Training and development sessions were typically regular and frequent, for example, one evening each week after school – "*without fail*" as one headteacher put it. These sessions were linked directly to the school development plan and specific initiatives. Sessions were led by staff from within the school, for example, by a subject leader or by an outside expert such as an adviser or an advisory teacher from the local authority. Everyone was involved in school-based sessions, including support staff. When teachers attended external courses, new knowledge was shared effectively, typically at the school-based sessions. Many of the schools had received grants from the General Teaching Council for Wales to support professional development activities.

The school development plan was very important

All the schools had development plans and they were significant in the lives of the schools. They shaped developments and improvement initiatives. "*It is the spine of the school*", said one headteacher.

Performance management had been in place for a long time in one guise or another

The work of the teaching staff was a matter of continual review. In many of the schools, all the staff – not just the teachers – were included in formal performance management processes. Performance management procedures were long-standing in a number of schools. In those schools where this was not the case, performance management had apparently been implemented without difficulty.

The schools were a learning resource for others

The schools were used in a variety of ways to support the professional development of teachers generally. Staff from the schools contributed to local authority courses and the schools were used as a resource for the development of other teachers. In many cases, visitors to the schools' local authorities spent time in the schools to witness good practice. The schools were involved in the education and training of new teachers.

Computers and interactive whiteboards had developed practice

Typically, the schools were well resourced with 'new technologies' of a range of kinds which were in widespread use in the classes. Their use had enhanced teaching and learning, helped to develop collaboration and had facilitated the sharing of good teaching practice.

Professional development frameworks such as 'Investors in People' were used extensively

A number of the schools used professional development schemes of a range of types and a number of them had achieved 'quality marks' of various kinds. These frameworks such as 'Investors in People' had helped the schools to shape their professional development processes.

Teaching and learning were monitored thoroughly

The monitoring of teaching was generally widespread. It was an integral part of the schools' work and was not viewed as threatening.

CHANGES/INITIATIVES

School development initiatives were taken on when the schools thought they could help with specific development needs. The schools felt they were strong enough to resist initiatives that might be detrimental to effective schemes already underway, or that they felt would not be of sufficient benefit to the pupils. The schools were not driven by fads.

The schools were open to ideas to enhance learning, but were not desperate to try new initiatives

The schools were very receptive to innovations to improve their teaching and the pupils' learning but any changes were considered very carefully before they were implemented to ensure they would enhance the pupils' learning. Some schools felt they were quite traditional in their approach. As one headteacher explained, "We're not into things like accelerated learning. No fancy new methods here, the traditional ones work for us".

New initiatives were dovetailed into existing practice

The schools were very good at implementing new ideas and ensuring that any innovative approaches complemented existing good practice.

Implementations were undertaken carefully so that they did not disrupt learning. Staff were trained in preparation for the implementation of new initiatives. In one school, the likely workload of staff involved in a new initiative was logged to help the headteacher to judge whether implementing the proposal would be manageable. The schools were ready to drop schemes that were not working.

There was involvement in international initiatives

Many of the schools were participating in international collaborations and initiatives of a range of kinds. These schemes, such as the Comenius project, broadened perspectives, widened horizons and enriched pupil learning. (Comenius projects are sponsored by the British Council and provide opportunities for schools to undertake development work at pupil and teacher level with schools in Europe.) There were numerous examples of staff and pupils having contact with and visiting countries in Europe and elsewhere through other initiatives.

EXTRA-CURRICULAR ACTIVITIES

In all the schools, there were a large number of extra-curricular clubs, classes and activities. The schools considered them to be important because they enriched the pupils' experience which may have been restricted because of the pupils' disadvantaged circumstances, motivated the pupils in other aspects of their learning, and gave opportunities for the pupils to achieve which enhanced their confidence and self-esteem. Examples of 'clubs' included: a school nutrition action group, a Welsh club, an arts club, a music club, a first aid for pupils club, a computer club, a folk dancing club, a guitar club, a gym club, a golf club, a puppetry club, an internet club, a football club, a gardening club, a library club, a poetry club, a pottery club, a lacrosse club, a chess club, a cartoon club, a dance club, a maths club, an investigative science club, a cycling club, a rugby club, a signing club, a tennis club, choirs, orchestras, a 'light house' club which is based at the local church and a new horizons club where pupils organised the activities and visits they wanted. There were a number of themes within this particular feature.

Extra-curricular activities were used to enrich the children's experience and enhance their learning

These activities were very widespread and were a significant aspect of the life of the school. They were used to enrich the pupils' experience and to compensate for disadvantage resulting from the pupils' circumstances. As one headteacher said, *"We have country dancing, a thriving choir, woodwind, keyboards, guitar and violin. Our view is that if we don't give these opportunities, nobody does, it doesn't happen"*. Many schools had SATs clubs that helped the pupils prepare for SATs, which pupils and parents valued.

Extra-curricular activities were taken seriously

Extra-curricular activities were used educationally and enriched the children's learning by giving them the opportunity to take part in activities that interested them that were not part of the formal curriculum of the school. The boundary between 'curricular' and 'extra-curricular' activities in these schools was therefore blurred.

Parents as well as teachers were engaged in extra-curricular activities

Extra-curricular activities were not just the province of the teachers. Parents were often involved and in some cases took the lead. The various activities and clubs were seen as a way of engaging parents in the life of the school.

COMMENTARY

The features of this central characteristic give rise to a number of considerations. Firstly, an overriding outcome for us is the way the schools focused on ensuring that their teaching for learning was effective and enriched. Very importantly, they also focused on ensuring that the effectiveness of their teaching for learning improved and was enriched yet further. Their work thus had a dual focus and the pre-eminence of this dual-focused task was highly significant. Secondly, the schools were passionate about their work. It was very important, meaningful and significant to them. Their work was a focus for their energy and they were committed to it and were fully engaged in it. This passionate commitment was a very powerful aspect of these schools. Thirdly, the cultures of the schools – they way they do things – was significant. The cultures were *productive* (they focused on the main task), *strong* (their ways of working were relentless and unyielding) and *inclusive* (all those who worked in the schools or who were connected with the schools were all included and were encouraged to actively support the schools' work).

6

Leadership

INTRODUCTION

It is perhaps unsurprising that leadership emerged as a key characteristic of the schools we studied. Leadership is emphasised in the literature on effective schools (see, for example, Sammons, Hillman and Mortimore 1995) and effective organisations generally. What was important was the way in which leadership was configured. The headteachers featured prominently as leaders of the whole institution and they had a significant role in setting, driving and reinforcing the culture. They also worked to increase the amount of leadership, the leadership density, by continually seeking to develop the leadership capability of others. But this development work was not limited to enhancing the leadership capacity of the senior management of their schools and/or those with posts of responsibility such as subject leaders. The headteachers worked to develop leadership capability in all those who worked in the school or were connected with it. In this way, they worked to promote the extent of leadership though the institution, or leadership depth.

Another key aspect of the leadership of the schools was of course the leadership work of the school governing bodies. They are leaders in a legal and statutory sense of course, but in these schools they were also that in practice. The governing bodies undertook important leadership work in the schools and we thus discuss their work in this chapter.

Our aim in this chapter is to describe the leadership processes in the schools. We focus inevitably on the work of the headteacher but we also focus on the leadership capability of others in the school and of those connected with the school. We also explore the work of the governing bodies and, in particular, concentrate on the leadership work of the chairs of the governing bodies.

THE HEADTEACHER

Although the headteachers were very different as people, they shared many professional characteristics and worked in similar ways. Without exception they all recognised and articulated the importance of enabling the pupils to learn and of continually improving teaching in the school. Within the feature, 'The headteacher', there were a number of broad themes that cover the headteachers' experience, authority, educational principles and expertise.

The headteachers had substantial experience in education

The headteachers' professional experience was extensive. Moreover, in many instances, they had been in post for a long time and/or worked in the same school over a long period. In one school, for example, although the headteacher had been in post for only two years, she had joined the staff as a newly qualified teacher over 20 years previously. Interestingly, the headteachers' experience in the same school had not narrowed their educational expertise or restricted their educational vision. They had a sound grasp of educational matters, understood likely policy changes and the possible implications, and were knowledgeable in general terms about good educational practice and developments in teaching and learning.

The headteachers had considerable authority

In very different ways, the headteachers all demonstrated considerable authority in their role. They were thus very powerful but appropriately so. Their authority was derived from a range of sources such as their experience, expertise and/or effort, and was acknowledged and accepted by all those connected with the school. In diverse ways, the headteachers all had an inner strength, an underlying drive and considerable energy. They had a high profile around the school and were a significant presence. The headteachers were well-liked for a range of reasons. They were admired and respected personally, which was readily acknowledged by those we spoke to. For example, one deputy headteacher was clear that the headteacher was *"one of the finest men I've ever met"*. They were also respected professionally. For instance, one deputy headteacher spoke glowingly of the headteacher and of *"her utter dedication"* to the work of the school. They were also admired and respected for their expertise, *"What he knows, he just amazes me"* (teacher). They were also respected by the pupils who referred to them very positively. The headteachers were firm disciplinarians but not in a punitive sense. Their approach to pupil discipline was underpinned by their educational ideals and values.

The headteachers had a modesty about them and were typically very quick to deflect direct positive feedback onto others in the school. For example, they would deny positive comments about them from their colleagues in our presence and offer to return them as fulsome praise to the staff, or they would explain in very generous tones that it was the work of others that was the reason for the school recently receiving a complimentary inspection report. Thus the success of the school was not because of their endeavours but the result of the *"marvellous"* staff and the 'wonderful' way they work together as a team. One headteacher was very clear that she was uncomfortable with direct personal praise – *"I don't like all this fuss and flattery"*.

The headteachers were generally optimistic. Despite any setback, problem or disappointment, they felt that circumstances would improve and/or that the school was capable of improving them. They felt that the school was doing good work which would make a difference. The headteachers made a very significant impact on the prevalent attitude and approach in the school which we discuss in the next chapter.

The headteachers were happy to stand out from the crowd. They were comfortable with being unusual – perhaps even eccentric – and may have even cultivated it. One headteacher, talking passionately about raising expectations and aspirations and his role as the head of the school, said, *"You have to be prepared to stand out from the norm, to be a bit eccentric and to hold out against being sucked into lowering your standards"*. This position enabled them to establish and sustain their sense of difference from others in the institution, and the feeling that they represented and embodied the educational vision of the school.

The headteachers' educational values, beliefs and ideals were very significant

It was clear from the discussions with the headteachers that their work was underpinned by very strong educational values, beliefs and ideals. These principles were the foundation of their high level of educational conviction and commitment. This sense of obligation and responsibility was very powerful. For example, during one interview, one of the headteachers in trying to capture the importance of his work said with considerable force, *"We cannot let these kids down"*. Holding such principles so strongly was widespread among all the headteachers in all the schools. The headteachers coupled their beliefs with very high standards, expectations and aspirations, especially for the pupils. They were ready to praise pupil achievement of a range of different kinds including improvements in behaviour, success in activities outside the school and achievements in 'non-academic' school work. They had a strong desire to enable others – parents and staff and others connected with the school – to achieve and were ready to give praise for such achievement.

The headteachers had considerable leadership expertise

From our observations and discussions with the various members of the school communities, it was clear that the headteachers had significant leadership capability. They had the capacity to respond appropriately to a wide range of situations and incidents and were ready and able to adapt their responses to the very varied situations they encountered. The headteachers displayed a sense of comfort with their work and the context. They thus appeared to be in the right schools for them. The headteachers gave the impression that over time they had adapted themselves to their schools, and/or had adapted their schools to them. They were well-suited to their work.

The headteachers had a range of important leadership capabilities

By all accounts, the headteachers were very good classroom teachers. They were therefore able to model good practice from which others could learn. Their expertise and experience as teachers also gave them the flexibility to take classes in order to give the usual class teachers extra free time for preparation and development work or to cover unexpected teacher absence. The headteachers were good communicators in a variety of ways. They were also excellent organisers, which helped to create a strong culture (see Chapter 5). The headteachers were able to anticipate the consequences of developments and changes, a quality which one teacher described nicely: "*She sees round corners before you do*". They managed the school's budget very effectively. Being "*good with the finances*" in the words of one teacher was highly valued. The headteachers were adept at using financial resources to benefit the school. For example, the financial acumen of one headteacher had "*helped us to maintain staffing levels*" (teacher). The headteachers were adroit at gathering and holding onto resources for their schools. They were ready to fight for resources and actively sought them out. "*The Head will go for any grant going*", as one deputy headteacher put it. This approach was not an illustration of a lack of long-term strategy but a recognition that resources gave flexibility and enhanced the school's capacity to meet the pupils' learning needs.

The headteachers had a grasp of the 'big educational picture' (the educational world generally) and the 'little educational picture' (what was going on in their school). They knew where the work of the school fitted into the wider educational scene and they kept abreast of developments. They also understood their school's work in relation to the community of families whose children attended their school and the local neighbourhood. They filtered information from the world outside the school and were then thoughtful about the educational messages that were passed on to the staff. Thus, in the words of a teacher in one of the schools, "*She prevents us from worrying about the things we are not doing*". The headteachers had an in-depth knowledge of their schools. They knew the pupils, the pupils' families and all the adults who worked in the school. They appeared to know everything that was going on in their schools and attended to detail.

The vignettes in Figures 6.1–6.3 provide pen pictures of three of the headteachers (their names have been changed).

David was appointed to the post of headteacher of the primary school 28 years ago but for the last 18 months has been headteacher of the junior school only (the infant and junior schools share the same site). It's a large school – about 350 pupils. David has appointed the whole staff. He sees his job as easy – "*because of the support from the staff*". 'Self-help' features very strongly in his make-up. In the school, store rooms have been converted into classrooms, cellars dug out to create a music room and parts of the school have been substantially rearranged. David is competitive; he wants the school to be the best and to improve further for the sake of the pupils – "*Children deserve the best*".

David sees himself as hard working which he thinks the parents like. He cares passionately about the school and is ready to reward the staff. He gives them presents, such as a bottle of wine, if they have done something which deserves especial appreciation. David wants the school to be of a standard that would be good enough for his own children – in all aspects. He was appointed to the primary school as an outsider. "*The previous headteacher's brother thought he would get the post and there were five other internal applicants. I had to fight very hard in the early days*". He was very authoritarian then but feels he has developed "*a team school*".

David considers himself to be very self-critical and reflective. By his own accounts, he is never satisfied. He seeks to overcome any lack of ability in any of his own work. For example, he did not let his own lack of expertise in ICT hold back developments in the school. He realised he needed to learn about it if he was to initiate and lead the growth of ICT usage in the school. So he set about doing so and was then able to lead and manage developments in ICT use. Computers and whiteboards are now used extensively in all classrooms. He always wants to "*move to the next level*". David considers that he leads by example – "*If the head can't be bothered, why should you?*"

David is much liked, admired and respected by the staff. The deputy headteacher thought David was 'one of the finest men I've ever come across'. Different members of staff considered that David:

- "*gives direction and leadership, and we're all brought on board*";
- "*provides the impetus to improve*";
- "*provides 'the playing field'*" (on which the staff work as a team);
- "*gives time and commitment, takes trouble, makes an effort*";
- "*provides opportunities*";
- "*knows everything*";
- "*is a disciplinarian*";
- "*knows the children*";
- "*makes sure the school gets good publicity*";
- "*celebrates our successes*";
- "*is mean with the budget – he's always getting good deals*".

Figure 6.1 David

Peter was appointed to his 300-pupil primary school two and a half years ago, following the retirement of a long-serving predecessor. Previously he had worked as an adviser for a neighbouring LEA and, prior to that, as a non-teaching deputy in one of that authority's largest and more challenging primary schools. Though he had gained greatly from his experience as an adviser, he was extremely happy to have returned to a school-based role, "*I love coming to work*". He finds the challenges and rewards inherent in working closely with pupils and teachers highly stimulating.

For Peter, the most important people in the school are not the pupils – important as they are – but the staff. He believes that it is important to treat them with respect: "*to recognise that they have a difficult job; to accept that it's a reasonable assumption that their lives and families come before the job*". Working with the staff in this way was more likely to generate a climate of positive feeling and commitment.

Peter had "*inherited*" most of the members of his staff, though he felt that these colleagues were very much in tune with his own professional philosophy and style. A main underpinning of this approach was "*being up for it*", that is seeking ways of making the work in classrooms exciting, enjoyable and stimulating – for teachers every bit as much as for pupils. This stance was characterised by a willingness to take what he termed "*intelligent risks*". Peter commented on a syndrome he'd encountered as an adviser when he'd visited schools where teachers seemed frightened and insecure about trying anything new and was relieved to be working with colleagues who were professionally confident and curious. He valued teachers who were "*a bit eccentric*", people who were "*if not young, then young at heart*" and who were able to capture children's interest and enthusiasm.

The school has no discipline problems, which, for Peter, was the result of deliberately creating a climate which children found encouraging and sympathetic. As an example, he cited the case of two Year 5/6 boys who had been regarded as major problems in the schools they'd previously attended:

> They were essentially nice kids but the kind who get into trouble readily, very physical, non academic 'into things' kids – the sort a particular kind of teacher comes to regard as a kind of pariah. They were kids whose experience of school in the past was often one of being in the wrong – not for doing things which are really wrong but for being themselves. Here, they've come to know that they're not going to be dropped on from a great height for that and it's generated some really positive attitudes: really significant improvements in their sense of self worth and, consequently, their effort and behaviour.

Figure 6.2   Peter

Sian joined the school as headteacher 18 years ago. She has appointed all the staff currently in post, and staffing has remained remarkably static over several years. Sian has a very modest almost self-effacing approach. In her own words, she is not comfortable with *"fuss and flattery"*, preferring to praise her staff and pupils for the good work in the school rather than singing her own praises. Sian expresses a concern that she might not always encourage and support her staff sufficiently, perhaps surprisingly because, in the words of her staff, she *"is always encouraging and supportive"*, and is *"always there with help or to express an opinion"* (their emphases). Sian, again in the words of her own staff, is 'the head of the team', but she is concerned in case she comes over as being *"too authoritative"*. This anxiety probably stems from Sian's completely unassuming, 'down to earth' nature. She comes over as very honest and ready to give open self-evaluations of her 'growth' and development as a headteacher. Sian very clearly accepts what she can't change and is very keen to improve what she can.

Sian confesses that she has *"had to learn to delegate work"*. Although she knows that delegation is necessary and usually 'a good thing', she has not found it easy as it is not in her nature *"to push extra work on others"*. Sian readily and happily acknowledges the positive results, however, pointing to the *"growth in confidence and stature"* of the staff, and their ability and willingness to take a *"more proactive role"*, as evidence of this success. Specific results in her view have been the blossoming confidence of one member of staff who is now a happy 'stand in' for Sian if need be (during any absence, for example) and the successful completion of the National Professional Qualification for Headship (NPQH) by another member of staff.

The chair of the governing body describes Sian as *"a very good head"*, adding that there is *"a polish and an order"* to all she does. She is the *"clear leader"*, but is always *"very open in discussion"* and always *"provides the governing body with all the information we require"*.

Sian considers that the working culture and 'whole-school' ethos are deeply rooted in certain 'core' values, namely the focus on the pupils' moral, spiritual, cultural and social development and the school's *"unashamed Welshness"*. These features she describes as the *"pillars"* that support the school's culture and overall approach. Coupled with these, she emphasises *"high and fair expectations of everyone"* and *"respect – the foundation on which everything else is built"*.

Figure 6.3   Sian

THE DEVELOPMENT OF LEADERSHIP DENSITY AND DEPTH

This feature illustrates the way in which the 'amount of leadership', the leadership density, and the 'extent of leadership', the leadership depth, were developed in the schools. Given that leadership was widespread, we first discuss the notion of responsibility in the schools, then we describe the way leadership density and depth were developed.

Responsibility for leadership

A significant theme in the data was that the headteachers were the designated leaders of their schools, and they fulfilled their leadership role properly and to its fullest extent. They were responsible for leadership – it was manifest in a whole set of ways as described above – and equally they took their responsibilities very seriously. It was clear, however, that the leadership work in the school was not undertaken solely by the headteacher. Others had leadership roles too. For example, they might have been given a designated leadership role such as a deputy headteacher or a curriculum coordinator for, say, mathematics. These others in designated leadership roles took their responsibilities very seriously. Other members of staff might have a leadership role because of their considerable teaching expertise or because they had taught in the school for a long time. The members of staff in these informal leadership roles also took their leadership work and their 'informally designated' leadership responsibilities very seriously. Given the diversity of the leadership roles and the extent to which the different members of staff were responsible, leadership was acted out in a range of different ways. What was clear, however, was the way in which any leadership responsibilities and practices were taken seriously.

Developing leadership density

There appeared to be a strong desire, demonstrated typically by the headteacher, to develop leadership capability in others. Responsibility for managing and developing aspects of the school – leadership work – was shared. So, there were numerous examples of delegation – although some of the headteachers admitted that delegating to others had not come easily to them. Relationships between the headteachers and deputy headteachers, although configured differently in different settings, were very sound. The relations between the headteachers and the governing bodies were very secure and they had a shared sense of the leadership of the school even though they had very different roles. The governing bodies appeared to take their responsibility for leadership very seriously and all understood the importance of enabling attainment and achievement in the pupils and improving the ways the pupils learned. There was thus a rich pool of leadership expertise within the schools – there was leadership density. Furthermore, the headteachers and others as appropriate worked to increase this leadership density.

Developing leadership depth

Although there was very strong leadership from the headteachers in the schools, there was also leadership throughout the school and indeed part of the headteachers' work appeared to be the development of the leadership capacity of others. There were numerous examples of relatively inexperienced teachers leading important curriculum developments which had the purpose of improving pupil attainment and achievement. Teachers with designated responsibilities, say for special educational needs, also talked lucidly and eloquently about how they led that aspect of the school's work and how it fitted into the overall work of the school in bringing about pupil learning. Classroom teaching assistants displayed considerable authority when explaining how they had influenced improvements in practice in the classrooms where they worked which had helped to improve pupil learning. Leadership thus appeared to be widespread throughout the schools. There was leadership depth, a quality which headteachers and others as appropriate worked to increase.

THE LEADERSHIP WORK OF THE GOVERNING BODIES

The governing bodies were committed, supportive and engaged. The members of the governing bodies had strong and close connections with the schools and positive relationships with the headteacher, with individual members of staff and with each other. There was mutual support and trust between the school and the governing bodies and, interestingly, within the governing bodies. There were two prominent themes in the data on the governing bodies of the schools.

The governing bodies worked

In two senses, the governing bodies performed well. Firstly, they functioned properly according to their designated responsibilities. Secondly, they did all they could for the schools – they worked for their schools. They were fully engaged and committed. The governors clearly enjoyed their work and gained benefit from it. In the words of one governor: *"Being a governor in this school is a very positive experience"*. In the case study schools, the governors:

- were kept informed;
- were encouraged to undertake training and to attend courses;
- provided thoughtful challenge to and validation of the schools' work – especially in promoting pupil attainment and achievement;
- did not have an 'axe to grind';

- typically had specific responsibilities and linked with particular teachers;
- had sound relationships with the teachers;
- had a specific 'curriculum link' in some instances;
- all attended most if not all the meetings of the governing bodies;
- typically cared strongly about their schools. One chair of a governing body, when asked why he felt the governing body worked well, said of the governors, *"All care strongly about the school and its pupils"*.

The chair of the governing body was respected and experienced

Typically, the chair of the governing body was highly valued by the school – especially by the headteacher. The chairs also typically had experience in education and more widely outside education. As a rule, they lived locally and were well known to parents. The chairs were very constructive and supportive. In the view of one headteacher, the chair of the school's governing body was always 'available, and ready and willing to praise'.

COMMENTARY

The headteachers appeared to have a substantial authority, that is power, that was widely sanctioned. They used their authority to set, drive and reinforce the school's culture. Their leadership work helped to strengthen the culture and enabled it to energise the work of the school – enabling and improving learning – in an inclusive way.

To understand the reason for developing leadership density and depth, it is important to consider what we mean by 'leadership'. In their research on schools that had substantially changed their practice in order to improve pupil achievement, James and Connolly (2000) defined leadership as those behaviours that enabled others to take up their role in relation to the institution's main and defined task. Leadership is thus a special organisational role. It is not doing the work as such but enabling others to do their work. In these schools, as we have discussed in Chapter 5, the main or defined task is ensuring effective and enriched teaching for learning for all pupils and improving and further enriching teaching for learning for all pupils. So, in the sample schools, all those who had a leadership role worked to help others achieve this main task. Because there was leadership density and depth, a large number of members of the school community undertook this leadership work enabling others to work on the main task. Thus, for example, the headteacher would endeavour to enable the teachers to work effectively and to continually improve. Teachers collaborating on joint lesson planning would be helping each other to work on the main task. A teacher returning from a local authority course and describing the key messages from the course to her colleagues would be leading the staff, enabling them to undertake further – and perhaps better – work on the main task.

7

The mindset

INTRODUCTION

There is a good case for arguing that one of the features of effective schools that has not been fully addressed in the literature is the overall approach of those who work in such schools. In our analysis of the data, the way of working and the general attitude of the staff and the headteachers in particular emerged as significant. This overall outlook was apparent in how they approached their work. It coloured how they had solved the problems which the schools had faced in the past and those which they continued to face on a daily basis. It was evident in the way they considered the context in which they worked and the resources that were available to them. In all the schools, there were elements of a clearly discernable way of thinking and working – a mindset – which had a number of components. This overall approach was threaded through and underpinned the other various characteristics. In this chapter, our intention is to give a flavour of this mindset. We have grouped all the various themes together into one single characteristic and have not sought to separate them into different features as with the other characteristics.

THE MINDSET

Capturing something like an overall approach or a general attitude is difficult, so we have attempted to provide a sense of it by describing the various aspects. Many of these facets of the mindset overlap and interact; not all of them would be present in all the schools and some would be more evident than others.

Empowered and proactive optimism

Those we spoke to were certainly not downhearted or pessimistic about their work but nor were they naively hopeful or optimistic. There was an empowered and proactive optimism in the way they approached their work. They gave the impression that individually and collectively they were capable of solving the problems they faced, that they were working to improve matters and that in the long term the situation would improve. This approach was strengthened by resilience in the face of setbacks or problems, which, as in all schools, were part of their everyday experience. *"We must keep going"*, said a teacher in a group discussion during one of the data collection visits. Her colleagues fervently agreed.

A high level of reflectivity

All those we spoke to were highly reflective about their work. The teaching staff were keen to ensure that their practice was as good as it could be and their reflections as they worked helped them to do this. They were equally keen to improve their practice over time and their reflections were central to the continuous improvement orientation prevalent in the schools. The schools had various structures, opportunities and processes for reflecting collectively on their teaching and organising in ways that were inclusive and participative.

We heard numerous examples of jointly developed plans to improve the efficiency and effectiveness of the way the schools organised their work, for example in managing assessment, reporting to parents and record-keeping. These improvements were driven by reflections on current practice.

There was also considerable evidence of a reflective approach to teaching in order to ensure and enhance pupil learning. From our discussions and observations, it was clear that the members of the teaching team worked reflectively – individually and collectively – to ensure that their teaching was appropriate. They also reflected, again individually and collectively, on their teaching with a view to improving it in the medium and long term. This reflection happened in informal and formal settings. We witnessed numerous examples of casual conversations and brief discussions in the staffrooms about teaching. Headteachers stressed how the members of the teaching team talked about their work. Time was set aside in staff meetings to discuss teaching and regular professional development sessions, often involving the whole staff, were focused on improving teaching in order to enhance learning. The schools had well-established self-evaluation procedures.

It was eminently clear that the members of the teaching teams were fully aware and understood the social, economic and political influences on their practice and, in particular, on the context of their work. This deep understanding appeared to underpin their high levels of motivation. The teaching staff all worked zealously to overcome the social and economic disadvantage experienced by the pupils. They appeared to be passionately concerned for justice and equity within a wider social context and a key purpose of their work was to enhance the life-chances of the pupils. The schools, particularly through their headteachers, sought to contribute to the development of educational and other social and economic policies at both local and national levels. The work of the members of the teaching teams was clearly very meaningful to them and had deep significance. From our conversations with them, their reflections on the social and economic issues with which the schools were working and the reasons for them seemed to empower them, to give them considerable insight and to motivate them in their work.

An 'accept-and-improve' approach

A key element of the collective mindset of these schools was what we have termed an 'accept-and-improve' approach. This way of thinking and acting held together two positions. The first stance was a grounded acceptance of various 'givens' in a non-judgemental way. The second was a drive to improve matters. The schools' approach to their buildings provided a useful example of this. The buildings varied in age, situation and state of repair. Some of the buildings were old and not in particularly propitious settings, but nonetheless inside they were all tidy, attractively organised and vivid. There were colourful displays everywhere that were informative, celebrated achievement in the school and the community, and promoted pupil learning. *"With the building, you work with what you've got"*, said one headteacher. In many cases, the buildings had been improved significantly and work on them was ongoing. Improving the buildings typically featured in school development plans and the buildings had been adapted over the years to meet the schools' needs. In some instances, the staff, the governors and the parents had undertaken work on the buildings themselves. Very importantly, the buildings were not an excuse for low attainment, low achievement or low expectations.

A 'both-and' mentality

One important underpinning of the ways the schools worked was their ability to hold together apparent opposites without experiencing a sense of contradiction. We have termed this approach a 'both-and' mentality and contrast it with an 'either-or' approach. So, it was considered perfectly possible: to have *both* very strong leadership from the headteacher *and* very strong leadership throughout the school. One did not exclude or prevent the other. There could be *both* an 'unwritten rule' that agreed practices, for example on managing pupil behaviour or marking pupils' work, must be followed *and* a collective intention to be flexible and to continually seek out ways of changing and improving those established ways of working. It was perfectly acceptable for the teaching team to *both* take their work very seriously *and* to have fun doing it. Many of the staff had *both* worked in the schools for a long time *and* retained their vision, broadened their experience and continued to learn and develop. Importantly, it was considered perfectly possible to *both* teach in a way that ensured good results in national tests *and* that was engaging, stimulating and fun for all the pupils.

Motivation by ideals and aspirations for the pupils

The teaching staff in the schools were highly motivated by their own ideals and aspirations for the pupils. They had a collective and relentless determination to do the very best for the pupils and a powerful desire to enhance the pupils' life-chances. These characteristics underpinned their high levels of motivation.

The staff had high expectations of the pupils

The schools expected effort and achievement from all the pupils. These high expectations were coupled with the provision of high levels of learning support. All the pupils were continually motivated to reach a higher standard. Whenever they experienced difficulty, they received additional help. In the words of one deputy headteacher, "*We have high expectations and high standards and we certainly don't accept the 'poor dab' syndrome. We expect our kids to do well*". The 'poor dab syndrome' is a colloquial way of indicating those situations where teachers' feelings of sadness at a pupil's social or economic plight might tempt them to lower their expectations. There was often a sense that there was no limit to what the pupils could attain. One headteacher put it very neatly, "*There are no lids on kids here*". A parent in another school explained the teachers' attitude, "*The teachers never say 'Can't' here, the culture is 'everything is possible'*". We frequently heard the teachers explaining that they wanted to raise aspirations and the awareness of possibilities and potential.

The staff had high expectations of themselves

The teaching staff had high expectations of themselves in helping the pupils to achieve. They, and in particular the headteachers, had similarly high expectations of all those connected with the schools. Thus the notion of 'doing well' frequently spread throughout the whole school. In the words of one headteacher, "*We – the pupils, teachers, the whole school community – want to do well in everything we do*".

A culture of praise

A consistent feature of the schools was that they had what might be termed a 'culture of praise'. They took every opportunity to praise effort, achievement and attainment of any worthwhile kind. It helped to raise the self-esteem of the pupils and all those connected with the school. Many of the schools had reward schemes for pupil effort and achievement. The headteachers in particular had a strong desire to praise achievement and to give credit to others.

A sense of pride

Those connected with the schools were proud of them. *"There is a pride in the school"* said one governor. The schools were proud of every aspect of their work. They expected the pupils to represent the school. Thus high standards of behaviour were not only expected inside the school, but outside as well. *"It is important to uphold the school's name"*, stated one headteacher.

The schools had a powerful 'ethos of care'

All those in the schools, including the pupils, clearly cared for and about each other. The schools, regardless of size, claimed to have a 'family atmosphere', a term used by many of the schools, large and small, to describe the ethos they had created. The schools also cared about the work of the school, the school building and the schools' local communities.

COMMENTARY

There appear to be four key messages about the overall prevailing attitude and way of thinking – the mindset – of the schools. Firstly the general approach of the schools was positive and proactive. As a result, the schools did not come across as hapless victims of their circumstances. Secondly, one of the driving forces in these schools was high expectations, ideals and aspirations. When expectations were met, aspirations were realised and there was progress towards achieving ideals, fulsome praise was generously given and a sense of pride created. Thirdly, they were thoughtful and 'care-full' in their overall approach. Caring about and giving thought to issues indicated that they matter. Being thoughtless and 'care-less' would have indicated that they did not. Fourthly, the holding together of mutual opposites (the both-and approach) was an acceptance of the often contradictory nature of educational practice. Professional actions are often the best option of all those available – not the ideal, but the best. Moreover, deciding on the best option is not helped by denying other possibilities.

8

The teaching team

INTRODUCTION

'The teaching team' is an important key characteristic. It is centrally concerned with the way the teachers, classroom learning assistants and other adults involved in teaching *all* worked together to fully *utilise* their expertise. Very importantly, in the schools we studied, they also *all* worked together to *improve* their expertise. Our intention in this chapter is to describe the main features that make up this characteristic which are the teachers, teamwork and additional classroom support.

THE TEACHERS

The high quality of the teaching staff and the way they focused on teaching for learning was undoubtedly one of the keys to the schools' success, if not *the* key. A chair of one governing body put it very succinctly, *"If the staff are right, the problems are few"*. Across the data set, a number of themes emerged that related to the teaching staff.

The teachers were very capable, hardworking and committed to their work

By all accounts, the teachers all had considerable teaching expertise and experience, worked hard and were devoted to their work. The schools endeavoured to make full use of all the capabilities and specialisms of the teachers. Teaching staff were assigned to classes with great care. There were a number of instances where teachers stayed with a particular pupil age group for a number of years to develop their expertise in working with pupils at that stage and their knowledge of appropriate expectations and standards.

The teachers were dedicated and devoted considerable amounts of energy to their work. *"They invest time"*, said one parent. The teachers had a collective determination to do the very best for the pupils. *"We will not let these children down"*, said a teacher during a group discussion in one of the schools, to the wholehearted agreement of her colleagues.

The teachers appeared to have a special relationship with their work; it clearly meant a lot to them. One teacher expressed this relationship in a way that captured it for her: *"These children bring out the best in you"*.

While the teachers were clearly very good at working on their own in the classroom, they were also equally good at working together as a team (see below). They wanted to collaborate with each other and had the skills to do so.

The teachers' expectations of themselves and each other were high

The teachers had an individual and a collective spirit of wanting to do the best they could and then to do even better. But this approach was not negative. They did not feel that their work was not good enough and that they should do better. It was that they knew that however good their work was, there was always scope to improve. The approach was not burdensome either. The teaching staff did not appear to be worn down by any sense that 'they ought to do better'. They wanted to do better and worked to improve their teaching in a straightforward, planned and matter of fact way.

New teachers were appointed thoughtfully and carefully

A considerable amount of thought and care was put into the appointment of new staff. It was clearly important in all the schools that new staff would fit in as members of the team. A number of teachers had been student teachers on placement in the schools, involved as parent helpers or teaching assistants or nursery nurses in their schools. One headteacher explained the reasoning behind this strategy by saying that *"They had already been seen in action"*. The teachers were familiar with the schools and, importantly, the schools were familiar with them. Newly appointed members of staff were inducted into the school and the ways of working and expectations were clearly explained. Typically, new staff were mentored in that they would work closely with a particular member of staff, and the highly inclusive and collaborative ways of working in these schools meant that there was a 'collective mentoring' of new staff/ inexperienced staff by the teaching team.

The teachers were consistent in their approach

For many of the schools, the teachers working in the same way over time was important. It gave a consistency of approach, which in turn made the pupils feel secure and helped them to learn. There was a high level of agreement and harmony between the teachers in the way they worked. They were consonant in their overall approach. This collaborative attitude was exemplified by instances of joint lesson planning and of the whole teaching staff having adopted a common lesson format.

Many of the teaching staff in the schools had been in post for a long time

In many of the schools, a high proportion of the teaching staff had worked as teachers in the schools for many years. A frequent explanation was that they liked teaching in the school and had no desire to leave. Many referred to the 'extended family relationship' they had with the school. It was important to them and they did not want to let it go. Although they had been in post a long time, they had still retained enthusiasm for their work and, despite their desire to stay, the teachers also had a desire to improve. Furthermore, it was expected that they would develop in their role.

Career progression in the school may have had a long history

Many of the schools had been the location for long-term career progression for the staff. Thus, for many of them, their career progression had taken place in the one school, and during their time at the school they had taken up more senior posts of responsibility. So, in a number of the schools, the teachers had been classroom assistants and/or parent helpers and/or students in their schools, the deputy head had been a teacher and the headteacher had been the deputy head. This 'extended career in one school' did not appear to be the result of a 'gender effect' with female members of staff being unable to move on because of their husbands'/ partners' own work commitments nearby. For many, there were promotion prospects in other easily accessible schools locally. Their attachment to the school appeared to be the reason why they stayed.

Despite their commitment to their schools, the teachers had 'a life outside'

The staff did not appear to be obsessive about their schools or their teaching. They seemed to maintain balance between their work in school and their life outside. Sustaining this balance was important to them. Moreover, in many of the schools, outside activities and achievements were seen as important and were encouraged. They were 'brought into' the schools to enrich the pupils' experience, to provide learning opportunities and to role-model potential and possibility.

Continuity in teaching and in the teaching staff was important

The sense of constancy, stability and longevity in the teaching staff appeared to be very important. It engendered continuity which gave the pupils a sense of security which, in turn, enhanced their confidence as learners. The disruption caused by using supply teachers to cover for absent teachers was minimised. "If a supply teacher is coming in, they are met and there is always a written plan for the day" (headteacher). Typically, the same supply teachers or teachers who had recently retired from the school were used to cover teacher absence.

TEAMWORK

The way the teaching staff worked together as a team was very important. There was a strong feeling of mutual accountability, a high level of trust and a real spirit of collaborative effort among the staff. This notion of teamwork had a number of themes.

Professional authority was enhanced by the staff working together

Collectively, the staff were more than their sum as individuals. *"The staff have a collaborative strength"*, as one headteacher described it. The staff working together enhanced their professional authority.

There was a very high level of trust

The notion of trust emerged strongly in our discussions with the teaching staff when we visited the schools. It was very important, it was a key aspect of teamworking and it was spread throughout the school. There was an expectation of trust from everyone including the pupils. Trust was important in the management of the school. *"With trust you don't need to check"*, said one headteacher. But such was the nature of the leadership in many of these schools, in the words of a teacher in another school, *"The Head trusts us to do it for the pupils but she would know immediately if we hadn't!"*

The teaching team had been built carefully and thoughtfully

Building and sustaining the teaching team was important and was typically done with thought and care. New members of staff were welcomed for the fresh ideas and complementary skills and qualities they brought. Less experienced teachers were often deliberately added to existing maturity and experience to enrich the team. Typically though, staffing was stable and generally the schools were characterised by low staff turnover with only a few changes over the years. Staff did not want to move on to other schools because, as we heard on numerous occasions in different schools, they were so happy where they were. Members of staff were, however, prepared for moving on if they wanted to through appropriate training and development.

Everyone conformed to the school culture

When new teaching staff joined the school, they were expected to fit in. Moreover, everyone was expected to be part of the team. The socialisation process was rigorous, compelling and unyielding. *"The staff are very helpful when you're new but they are uncompromising"*, said a teacher new one of the schools. All the staff were active team members and no one appeared to be excluded in any way. There appeared to be very few 'difficult' teachers. The atmosphere in the school did not create or permit difficult colleagues and the 'right' teachers were recruited. There was a high level of social mixing and no cliques. Problems were 'surfaced' quickly. The schools did not shy away from conflict – far from it – but as we were often told, conflict was always issue-based, never person-based.

The members of the teaching team planned their work together

The collaborative planning of lessons was widespread in the schools. It made the most of the pool of educational expertise and the teaching team working together also ensured consistency and conformity, which in turn enhanced efficiency and effectiveness. However, the culture of conformity was not constraining – quite the opposite. *"The structures in school are not designed to imprison, but to allow creativity"*, said one headteacher. Despite the ethos of conformity, there was flexibility, and creativity was welcomed and valued.

Working relationships were straightforward and secure

The members of the teaching team in the schools were 'open' with each other and knew each other's strengths and weaknesses. Communication appeared to be easy throughout the school. Those who assisted teachers in the class, nursery nurses and classroom teaching assistants were very much included in the team. The continual positive references by all the members of staff we spoke to, to other members of staff at all levels in the school, indicated that there was equal valuing and parity of esteem across the whole staff despite their different roles and responsibilities. There was a high level of sharing and help was given and received easily. Humour appeared to play an important part in building and sustaining the team.

ADDITIONAL CLASSROOM SUPPORT

Teaching assistants, nursery nurses and parents were widely used to provide additional support for learning in the classroom. Their work was highly valued and, typically, it was evident that the schools would welcome more of this kind of resource. This additional support was used with thought and care to help pupils to achieve and was used to meet specific learning needs. The data on the nature of the additional teaching support and the way it was utilised had a number of themes.

Support staff had a professional approach

Those who worked alongside teachers in the classroom shared a professional approach to that of the classroom teachers in the secure and productive way they worked. Support staff were trained and developed. Their relationships with each other and with the teachers were *"professional"* in the words of a teacher in that they upheld the same standards as the teachers in all aspects. Interestingly, the use of support staff seemed to concentrate and elevate teaching efforts. One headteacher felt that having another adult in the class *"challenges staff to maintain standards"*. He went on to explain that teachers had to explain their actions to another colleague so there was a helpful dialogue. They also had to justify their actions to a colleague who might judge them harshly if they let their standards slip.

Parents and grandparents were used to support the pupils' learning in the classroom

There was widespread use of parents – and even grandparents – to support learning in the classroom and their work was highly valued. Indeed one teacher said with considerable enthusiasm and some irony, *"What did we do before parents?!"* Parents were used with thought, especially in the development of important skills such as reading. So, if they did not have the requisite skills to teach pupils to read, they would support the practice of reading skills by listening to pupils reading. If parents were keen, they were used in any way that was appropriate. One headteacher in a particularly disadvantaged setting was very clear, *"We use them whatever skill level they're at and we develop them as well"*. In one example, the school held meetings of parent helpers, which the headteacher felt *"values their contribution"*. The engagement of parents as assistants in the classroom was typically handled carefully. The schools were aware that it was not possible for all parents to help because of other commitments such as work and caring for younger children. Some parents may lack the confidence to volunteer and would need to be invited to help and be supported in the early stages. All informal helpers were vetted by the schools themselves and through their local authority's procedures. In one school, a former headteacher of the school came in voluntarily to help.

The school secretary was a very important member of the team

The school secretaries typically had a pivotal role and were key team members. Typically, they were active in the school and were a first port of call for those arriving at the school, their office was typically a waiting room for visitors, they had close links with the headteacher and the staff, they knew the parents and families, and were usually acquainted with the local community. In one school the secretary was considered to be very important, *"A great help in a small school"* as the headteacher put it, with responsibilities for assisting the headteacher, managing aspects of financial management, for example, book-keeping, acting as clerk to the governors and giving administrative support to the staff, for example photocopying.

COMMENTARY

Of course, many of these findings are unsurprising, especially for example the high level of expertise of the teaching staff and the extent of their experience. But the emergence of two other issues was more unexpected. The first was the very high level of teamworking among the teachers. They worked together as very effective team players and, importantly, it appeared to give them 'collaborative strength'. The second was the very effective way in which additional learning support in the classroom was used and valued, that there was a synergy from their presence (as one of the headteachers said, they appeared to elevate teaching standards) and that they adopted the same professional approach as the teachers even though their practices and responsibilities were different.

9

The pupils and their parents

INTRODUCTION

This chapter explains the key characteristic, 'Pupils and their parents'. In analysing the data, we could have decided to have separate characteristics, one for pupils and one for parents. But as we looked at the data set and reflected upon the schools and how they worked, it seemed more appropriate to put the two features together into one characteristic. It was almost impossible to think about the pupils in the school without considering their parents for three main reasons. Firstly, given the age of the pupils and the strength of their parents' influence upon them, both pupils and parents need to be fully engaged in the pupils' learning if the pupils are to learn successfully. Also, arguably, the care and education of pupils from the age of three years is much more of a joint enterprise, shared between the schools and the parents, than in later phases. Secondly, we were researching the schools in part because of the socio-economic disadvantage experienced by the families. Therefore to separate the pupils from the parents in thinking about the data did not seem appropriate. Thirdly, as we worked with the data, it was clear that these schools went well beyond 'parental involvement in their children's education', which features in many lists of the characteristics of effective schools (see, for example, Sammons, Hillman and Mortimore 1995) to 'the active engagement of parents in their children's education and their commitment to it'. The schools sought to ensure that the parents were fully and closely involved in their children's learning.

Our plan in this chapter is to describe how the pupils viewed the schools, what they liked about their schools, and what it was about the schools that enabled them to learn successfully. We also intend to describe the ways in which the schools worked to bring about parental engagement and commitment.

PUPIL ENGAGEMENT AND COMMITMENT

A powerful impression from all the data collection visits was that the pupils were central. The schools were very much 'their places'. The pupils had a 'voice' which was listened to. They liked their schools and wanted to attend. In the data set on the pupils, there were a number of themes.

School councils were active

Typically, the schools had school councils and the pupils valued them. In many instances, the school councils were involved in policy-making and in making decisions, such as the management of car-parking at the school and the layout of play areas, and the council members enjoyed this responsibility. A number of the school councils met with their headteachers regularly and frequently. The members of the school councils were an important conduit of information on issues such as bullying and pupil matters generally.

The pupils cared for and cared about each other

In talking to the pupils and staff, there was a clear message that the pupils cared for each other. As one Year 6 pupil put it: *"We keep an eye on the little ones"*. All those we spoke to considered that bullying was not a persistent problem in the schools. When there were any incidents of bullying, the general approach appeared to be to deal with them quickly and firmly. One headteacher felt that petty jealousies, which are often the cause of pupil disagreement and conflict, were minimal because everyone was valued and regularly received praise.

Older pupils expressed a sense of responsibility

There were numerous examples of pupils undertaking responsibilities and helping their schools to work efficiently and effectively. In one school, pupils were involved in liaising with Neighbourhood Watch (a locally based crime-prevention scheme) and putting out and collecting in play materials at break times. In another, they helped the lunchtime catering and supervision staff, *"to make sure no one was cheeky to them"* (Year 6 pupil). These kinds of activities *"give responsibility and ownership to pupils"* said one headteacher; *"It then becomes our school and we look after our school"* (her emphasis).

The pupils were happy which helped them to be confident learners

It was clear that the pupils were happy at their schools, which their teaching staff felt increased their confidence as learners. In one school, when we asked a pupil with learning difficulties what made his a good school, he replied that it had *"happy teachers and happy pupils"*. He was also clear that the happiness of the two groups were linked. Another pupil clearly understood that he would be praised for good work but he also knew the consequences (that he would be reprimanded) if his work was not up to standard. The pupils clearly valued being treated fairly. There was an emphasis both on responding to all pupils' individual needs and on developing the schools as children's communities. Motivating pupils to learn by giving them confidence was important: "*If you convince children they can succeed, they can succeed*" (chair of a governing body – his emphasis).

The schools were very inclusive in the way they valued *all* pupils

Across the data set, the valuing of *all* pupils was a strong theme. The schools wanted to help *all* the pupils to achieve, especially those with behavioural and/or learning difficulties, and were capable of working with *all* pupils. "*Inclusion is important*", said one headteacher; "*I know it's a buzz-word but here, we really live it. We have been asked to take in difficult pupils from very difficult backgrounds and we seem to manage them without too many problems*".

The pupils felt safe and cared for

The pupils we spoke to typically gave the impression of feeling secure in their schools. They felt safe and they felt cared for. When we asked one young pupil what she liked about the school she said she felt the school was "*warm and cosy in the winter, not like home*". In a number of cases, the pupils commented on the high quality of food provided by the schools.

Learning was fun

From conversations with pupils, it was clear that learning for them was not a chore, it was something to be enjoyed and it was a source of pleasure. They liked the teachers who made their learning fun and those teachers who made them laugh. Speaking of his teacher, one Year 6 pupil said, "*He's got good sense of humour*", and then added after some thought, "*sort of, at our level*".

PARENTAL ENGAGEMENT AND COMMITMENT

The schools knew and worked with the pupils' immediate and extended families to engage their commitment to the work of the school and to help the pupils to learn. They endeavoured to work closely with parents, to promote contact with them and to involve them fully. Parents' engagement with the schools and their commitment to them were very important. The data on parental engagement and commitment had a number of themes.

The schools' communications with parents was professional, direct and valuing

The schools stressed the importance of communicating with parents in an appropriate and professional manner. It was very important that all communication was clear, straightforward and valuing. The schools tried not to use jargon when communicating with parents. There was open and early contact with parents if there were problems, especially inter-family problems, which the schools then attempted to resolve quickly. *"Staff need to be honest and diplomatic in working with parents"* (teacher). The schools regularly sent newsletters to parents. The ways the school communicated with parents helped to ensure that the roles and responsibilities of parents were clear and were clearly different from those of the staff.

Parents were respected

The respect accorded to parents was lived out in a number of ways. They were treated with sensitivity and in all dealings were made to feel important and valued. The parents we spoke to felt the school was on their side and that they and the school worked together. In the words of one parent, *"The teachers always have time for parents, they never push us out"*. Some schools used questionnaires and focus groups to elicit parents' views on school matters.

The schools endeavoured to work successfully with *all* families

There was a highly inclusive approach and equality of treatment in the ways the schools worked with parents. Teachers endeavoured to be accessible to all parents and to work with every family.

There was a high level of parental support

The schools felt that the level of parental support for their work was generally very high, which they valued. *"Parents are part of the team"*, said one teacher. A teacher in another school felt that some parents may need to be *"won over"* to supporting the work of the school because of their own negative experiences as pupils when they were at school.

Joint learning schemes for both parents and pupils were valued

A number of the schools had operated joint schemes of various kinds to enhance the parents' ability to help with their children's learning. Many of these were joint schemes which involved both children and parents. In many cases, these schemes were very successful. For example, in four different schools, the Family Literacy Scheme, the Family Numeracy Scheme, PALS (the Partnership Accelerates Learning Scheme) and a scheme where pupils and parents learned Welsh together had all worked well. This last scheme in a predominantly Welsh-speaking area had been particularly successful. Those we spoke to when we visited the school considered that the programme was one of the main reasons for the harmony and friendship between Welsh-speaking and non-Welsh-speaking members of the local community.

Teachers valued parents' help in the school

As we indicated in Chapter 8, in many schools, parents worked in the classroom supporting the teachers' work. This form of parental support was highly valued. Parental participation in teaching was generally thoughtfully managed, was very successful and was felt to be beneficial to the pupils.

There were some issues of concern about the parenting of the pupils

The teaching staff we spoke to did express some concerns about the parenting of the pupils. These issues were always articulated as concerns and never as criticisms. There was a concern about some children's lack of experience of practical play and conversation and the lack of stimulus they received from outside the home and the local area. There was also unease about the level of preparedness of some pupils for attendance at nursery school. The disturbance to pupils if there was a breakdown in their parents' relationship was a concern and there was also some uneasiness about the lack of parenting skills in some cases. The rapid influx of families from elsewhere and perhaps their equally rapid departure was particularly challenging for some schools (see Chapters 4 and 11).

Ensuring full attendance by the pupils was a problem in some of the schools. Generally, however, the reason for non-attendance was not truancy in the sense of children leaving home to go to school and not arriving. Typically, the pupils wanted to attend. As one parent put it, "*The children love coming to school*". In many cases, attendance was affected by families taking holidays during school terms, keeping children away from school for birthday celebrations or simply oversleeping. As a rule, poor attendance involved only a small number of families. The schools were aware of the problems and were addressing them in a collaborative and supportive way. "*We are working with them on it*", as one headteacher said (his emphasis).

COMMENTARY

There are a number of important messages in this characteristic. The first is that considering the schools' work with the pupils and their parents together is justified. There are three key players in all pupils' learning in school, the pupils and their parents, and teachers and that is particularly so for pupils in this age group. All three are partners in ensuring the pupils' learning. They have different roles and responsibilities but in ideal circumstances they should have the same shared aim: to ensure pupil learning. The second is the importance of not only involving parents but of securing their active engagement and commitment to their children's learning. Lastly, the schools valued both the parents and the children. They did not judge them negatively, they accepted them and they sought to work with them to bring about pupil achievement and a high level of pupil attainment.

10

Very efficient and effective organisation

INTRODUCTION

The very efficient and effective way the schools managed their affairs emerged early as a significant overarching theme in the data – perhaps unsurprisingly. All the schools were managed very efficiently. They used their resources thoughtfully and with care. The schools were also managed effectively. They ran their affairs in the way they intended to. So, what they set out to do, they actually did.

A number of aspects of the schools contributed to their high levels of efficiency and effectiveness and we describe those themes in this chapter. A significant feature, which was part of the schools' overall efficiency and effectiveness, was the way they managed pupil performance data in order to enhance pupil learning. We have included that feature of their work in this key characteristic. We also address the issue of school size in order to examine the part that the size of these schools might have played in their success. First, though, we deal with the structure of the schools' workings, the way they managed their affairs and the operating systems in the schools.

STRUCTURE, MANAGEMENT AND SYSTEMS

There were a number of themes in the overall structure of the schools, the way the schools were managed and the systems that operated in the schools.

The schools were well organised and structured

The schools ways of doing things – responsibilities, systems and processes – had been thought through, were clearly set out and were always adhered to. There was 'order' and as a result the teachers were able to apply themselves to their work more effectively.

Delegation was important

In Chapter 5, we described how delegation helped to enhance leadership density and depth. Delegation was also important for the way it enhanced efficiency and effectiveness. It also helped to give the headteachers time for strategic management thus enhancing the overall quality of leadership and management in the school. In addition, delegation helped to develop staff. Delegated responsibilities were recognised with a time allowance.

Resources were used with care

Again in Chapter 5, we described how the schools were adept at acquiring resources. Those resources – and indeed all the schools' resources – were used thoughtfully. They were allocated carefully to maximise their impact on pupil achievement. Resource allocation was often decided upon after a whole staff discussion.

Pupil discipline and behaviour management were taken seriously and were priorities

Typically, pupil behaviour was managed consistently across the whole school, the management of pupil behaviour was very important and unacceptable behaviour was addressed immediately. In most cases, there was a behaviour code, which was clearly set out and in a number of instances was on display.

Management structures varied but were secure and worked effectively

The schools varied in the way management responsibilities were structured and specified but, importantly, all the structures were secure and were effective in the way they worked. Generally, the schools had 'flat' management structures with no senior/school management team (SMT). In the words of one headteacher, *"I don't see a real need for an SMT. With just seven teachers it's just as easy to get the whole staff together as it would be an SMT"*. There were exceptions to this arrangement, however, in the larger schools in particular. In those cases, the structure had been very carefully thought through. In some of the schools, the job specification of the deputy headteacher was quite narrow and what might have been the deputy headteacher's responsibilities were widely shared among all the staff. In others, the deputy headteacher had extensive responsibilities. Regardless, without exception, there was a strong, secure and valuing relationship between the headteacher and the deputy headteacher.

THE MANAGEMENT OF PUPIL PERFORMANCE DATA

The management of pupil performance data, that is the collection, collation, analysis and use of data on pupil attainment and achievement, was a high priority and such data was used extensively to enhance learning. A number of themes featured under this heading.

Data was used to inform discussions on pupil progress

Typically, there were regular discussions with individual pupils and data was used to give pupils feedback and to set fresh targets. "*Setting targets is vital for all pupils*", said one special educational needs coordinator (her emphasis). In some cases, pupils set their own targets and thereby had more of a sense of ownership of them. Pupils in those year-groups not taking SATs typically took other standardised tests which helped with target-setting.

Tracking the progress of individual pupils was a priority

Data was used to monitor and track pupil progress. The use of data in this way was considered to be very important. In some instances, pupil tracking extended to the tracking of pupil groups.

Benchmarking was used but not as an excuse for low levels of attainment

The schools wanted to know how the pupils were doing and data from other schools helped them to find out. Very importantly, benchmarking data was not used as an excuse for having low expectations, nor for low pupil attainment or achievement. In many schools, benchmarking was used competitively to provide targets. "*We want to be the best in the authority, on every indicator*", said one headteacher. Another headteacher took a similar line saying very firmly, "*When pupils leave school, no one will be interested in whether their school had lots of pupils who had free school meals. So we've got to make sure they get as good qualifications as everyone else, if not better*".

THE SIZES OF THE SCHOOLS

The schools ranged in size and in several schools, the number of pupils on roll was changing significantly. School size appeared in the data in a number of ways.

The schools were large enough

The schools varied in size, but despite this variation, they all had a sufficiently large pool of expertise to work effectively, enough capacity to undertake the various tasks and responsibilities and an adequate level of resourcing. Many of the schools – but by no means all – attracted pupils from outside their natural catchment area. Often the pupils attending the school who lived outside the schools' natural catchments had special educational needs.

Not all the schools had stable pupil numbers

Some of the schools were experiencing quite rapid changes in the number of pupils on roll. Typically, the schools were not losing pupils to other schools through parental preference but in some cases local demographic effects were reducing pupil numbers. In one school, the number on roll had declined from 249 to 160 in five years due to the falling birth rate locally. In another, there was a gradual decline due in part at least to families moving out of the area to better housing or to be closer to their work. In a small number of schools, there was an increase in pupil numbers resulting from the trend of families – sometimes families experiencing difficulties – moving into the area from elsewhere to take advantage of low-cost housing.

COMMENTARY

Two issues emerge strongly from the data on this characteristic. Firstly, there does not appear to be a best way of structuring the management of the school, except to say that, whatever the structure, it must work. Moreover, it will only work if people fulfil their responsibilities according to what is expected of them and that systems need to be followed if the school is to organise its affairs efficiently and effectively. Secondly, there are no indications in the data that there is an optimal size or a particular way of organising that will bring about success and high levels of pupil attainment. The issue of size is to do with having sufficient resources – for example, financial, teaching and physical resources – which can be an issue in a school of any size.

11

The mutual support, validation and valuing of the community

INTRODUCTION

It was clear during the visits and from our analysis of the data we collected that the schools did not exist in isolation from the community. The world outside the schools enriched their work and the schools sought to enrich the community. The schools and the community mutually supported each other, affirmed and endorsed each other's good work and appreciated and respected each other. A key and perhaps obvious issue to emerge was that in fact the schools worked with a whole range of communities of different kinds, to which they contributed positively and which contributed positively to them.

Our aim in this chapter is to explore the ways the schools interrelated with their various communities beyond the school gates. In particular, the chapter reviews the various themes in the data which included their relationships with their local communities, their wider communities, their local authorities and with the education system.

THE SCHOOLS AND THEIR LOCAL COMMUNITIES

The schools' relationships with their communities were very important indeed and were significant in the lives of the schools. The analysis of the data revealed a number of themes.

The schools' communities were very diverse

As we have discussed in Chapter 4, although the schools were in disadvantaged settings, those settings were very disparate. The communities the schools served, that is those in which the pupils lived, varied considerably. Many schools served quite narrowly defined communities – neighbourhoods – with which they linked in a number of different ways. Others served dispersed populations so their 'communities' were families from very wide and extensive areas. The communities of other schools had elements of both these two community types. In addition, the schools worked with other 'communities', such as the sporting, business and arts communities, and community sub-groups, for example charities, the police and voluntary organisations.

The nature of disadvantage in the schools' communities was varied and complex

Again, as we discussed in Chapter 4, disadvantage in the schools' communities was diverse and complicated. There were no stereotypes of disadvantage. In some communities, the source of disadvantage was low income levels rather than low employment levels. In others, male unemployment was high, and/or there was a dependency culture, and/or there was a high level of change with families moving into the area and then moving on rapidly to seek work elsewhere. Some of those incoming pupils may be disadvantaged socially, economically and linguistically, arriving in the community to attend a Welsh-medium school. There might be a number of aspects of disadvantage at work simultaneously. As a result, 'disadvantage' had a number of diverse and difficult implications for the schools.

Unsurprisingly, low incomes – for whatever reason – were at the heart of the disadvantage in the schools we studied. It was the basis of the criteria for choosing the schools. Low family income, which results from low pay and low levels of employment, is a criterion for entitlement to free school meals. Low levels of pay may result in a dependency culture, where over time, ambitions, aspirations and goals become scaled down. Low employment opportunities may mean that those who want to find work or seek a higher level of income have to leave the community. The 'low income/high dependency' culture may bring with it a number of attendant problems, such as a lack of stimulation and wider experience for the pupils attending the schools. The lack of employment opportunities may depress the price of houses, which may mean that families, perhaps already experiencing difficulties of one kind or another, may arrive to take advantage of relatively cheap accommodation, then being unable to find work may rapidly move on.

The schools viewed the areas in which they were located as a feature of their work not an excuse for low pupil attainment and achievement

In Chapter 7, we discussed the importance of the mindset of the schools – the prevailing attitudes and the overall approach. The accept-and-improve aspect of the mindset was significant and it was very apparent in the way the schools worked with and responded to the disadvantage experienced by their pupils. Any disadvantage in their communities was a 'given', which was accepted. It was not viewed negatively; it was something to be worked with and even turned to advantage. The schools sought to improve on their starting points – the 'givens'. Importantly, the various 'givens' – in this case the disadvantage experienced by the pupils – were not used as an excuse for low pupil attainment and achievement.

The schools liked their local communities and the local communities liked their schools

For many neighbourhood schools, their relationships with their local communities were very strong and there was a deep empathy and understanding. The schools took pride in their communities and celebrated their achievements. Local successes were recognised, valued and applauded. In many instances, the teachers lived close to the schools, had grown up there and had perhaps even attended the schools where they now taught. The schools had a genuine affection for the pupils and the pupils' parents and wider families. They cared about them and did not judge them negatively. One of the best ways of summing up the relationships between the schools and the communities they served, indeed all the communities the schools worked with, is simply to say that 'the schools liked their local communities and the local communities liked their schools'.

The schools were focal points in their communities

The schools had a central role in their communities. The schools were a meeting place for many parents before and after school. The staff would provide advice and guidance on important family matters. The schools helped to resolve inter-family disagreements. There were examples of parents using the teachers as sources of reassurance that their parenting was satisfactory. Some schools provided out-of-school courses and activities for their local communities such as access to the Internet and computer training. The schools were at the heart of their local communities.

The schools worked to compensate for disadvantage

The schools clearly worked to make up for any educational disadvantage that might accompany social and economic disadvantage experienced by the pupils. They worked to enrich the children's experience and they also endeavoured to provide material resources of a range of kinds such as clothes, school uniforms and food.

THE SCHOOLS AND THE WIDER COMMUNITY

As we said in Chapter 5, the schools had productive links with individuals, organisations and institutions in the wider community in the UK and elsewhere to their mutual benefit. These links broadened perspectives and enriched the pupils' and the teachers' experience.

THE SCHOOLS AND THEIR LOCAL AUTHORITIES

In a range of different and important ways, the schools received considerable support for their work through their partnerships with their local authority education services. Indeed, it is difficult to see how the schools could have done as well as they have and as consistently as they have without it. The schools' relationships with their local authority education services had two main themes as follows.

The local authorities worked for the schools

The schools received considerable backing and assistance from their local authority education services and the schools valued this support. Relationships between the schools and their local authorities were constructive and positive. Examples of local authority support that was particularly valued included:

- advice and guidance – *"They help us solve our problems"* (chair of a governing body);
- accessibility – the local authority was easy to contact for help and assistance;
- excellent individual professional support and mentoring – the headteachers in particular found the advice and wise counsel of senior officers and advisers from the local authority to be particularly valuable;
- the provision of benchmarking data – which the schools found to be invaluable in managing their affairs (see Chapter 10);
- the work of advisers and advisory teachers – who often provided valuable support for professional development in the schools;
- the provision of targeted funding – which the schools used very efficiently and effectively to enhance pupil learning.

Colleagues from the local authority education service were also valued for working hard while perhaps not having the resources they would ideally like. The advice of 'non-education' departments in the local authority was also appreciated. Many of the schools had very close and helpful links with the social services and other community services.

The schools had high expectations of their local authorities

The schools' expectations of their local authorities and especially the education services were very high. In that regard, the local authority was viewed in the same way as all those who worked in the schools and/ or who were connected with the schools. It was as though the schools expected that the high standards they set themselves – working hard, doing their very best for the pupils, being efficient and effective, seeking continually to improve – would also be met by their local authorities. Areas where their expectations were not met were generally to do with the occasional lack of transparency on funding decisions, occasional shortages of expertise in subject teaching matters, insufficient support for teaching through the medium of Welsh and a lack of sensitivity over 'the paperwork' required by some local authorities. On this last point, LEAs sometimes set unrealistic deadlines or asked for information at particularly busy times. But as one of the headteachers said, *"They're usually ready to cut me a bit of slack"*. Some schools, at times, experienced a sense of being overwhelmed by different local authority initiatives (see Chapter 5) and very occasionally there were breakdowns in communication.

THE SCHOOLS AND THE EDUCATION SYSTEM

The schools worked closely with their local education community. They were in successful consortia of other local KS1/2 schools and had good relationships with local secondary schools which they valued. They contributed to local authority training courses, were a resource for the development of other teachers and were involved in the education and training of new teachers.

Directly and indirectly, the schools appeared to be supported by the wider educational 'community' – the Welsh Assembly Government, the General Teaching Council for Wales, ACCAC and professional associations and numerous other individuals and agencies. Understandably perhaps, the schools' relationships with Estyn, the school inspection service in Wales, featured prominently in the data.

Responses to Estyn and to school inspection varied as did the schools' views on the impact of inspection on their work. One view was that inspection in some form was important for the system as a whole and was nothing to be feared or concerned about. For schools that expressed this view, inspection was an opportunity to be reassured that they were succeeding, to celebrate success and to validate important aspects of their work. Another view was that inspection was disruptive and unnecessary because of the existing high levels of accountability throughout the system. Some respondents expressed both views. In addition to these views, there were two other themes in the data on inspection.

Inspection provided opportunities to reflect and learn

There was evidence that the schools, and in particular the headteachers, had learned from going through an inspection. They had learned from the process. For example, one headteacher considered he had developed his leadership and management capability by reflecting on how he managed and led the school through the inspection. Another had come to grasp more fully the importance of attending to detail. A more general view was that it gave them a better understanding of the standards required. The outcomes of inspection had also been helpful in making the schools think afresh about aspects of the leadership of the school, for example attendance at governors meetings and the management structure of the school.

The new self-evaluation inspection model was generally welcomed

At the time the study was carried out, the inspection of schools in Wales was moving towards a system based much more on schools' own self-evaluation of their policies and practices. Many of the schools already had extensive self-evaluation procedures in place that were a feature of the continuous improvement culture, which was a dominant and powerful attribute of all the schools. Despite a general welcome for the new inspection procedures, there were some dissenting opinions expressed in the context of seeing inspection as unnecessary and a disruption.

COMMENTARY

There are three main messages from the data on schools and their communities. The first is the complexity of the notion of community. The pupils who attended the schools did not all come from discrete communities around the schools. In many cases, they came from quite widespread areas. The stereotypical image of these schools serving 'disadvantaged neighbourhoods' was not borne out in reality. Furthermore, the schools worked with a whole range of communities of very different kinds. The second message is that the schools both received support for their work from a number of different 'communities' and individuals and groups within those communities, and gave support to them. The schools and their communities mutually supported each other. Thirdly, the schools were not negative or critical in any way about their local communities. They were accepted for what they were, they did not judge them negatively and no feature of the local community was used as an excuse for low levels of achievement or attainment. In the main, the schools were not overly negative about the other communities they worked with – the local authority, for example. Such criticism that there was appeared to be reserved for Estyn, perhaps understandably given its inspectorial role (see Chapter 13) and in many of those cases the criticism was tempered by a positive acceptance. In their daily practice, the schools did not appear prepared to spend a lot of energy and time complaining about matters that were beyond their control.

12

What makes these schools very effective?

INTRODUCTION

In Chapter 2, we reviewed what is already known about effective schools, those schools where the pupils do well. As far as this study is concerned there were a number of significant outcomes from that review. There was a feeling that the lists did not accord sufficient status to learning, that they were largely 'content lists' which conveyed little about the way the various characteristics were undertaken, and that the lists may not fully encompass all the characteristics that are needed if a school is to be effective. There was also a sense of the development and refinement of the characteristics of effective schools over time and also a confirmation of the substantial impact of pupils' social and economic circumstances and their prior capabilities on their subsequent educational attainment. A third and important outcome as far as the schools we studied were concerned was that schools with a high proportion of disadvantaged pupils can experience serious internal management problems which means that for them becoming effective and improving is particularly challenging.

In Chapters 4 to 11, we outlined the research we undertook into schools which have high levels of both pupil disadvantage and pupil attainment, which we have called very effective schools. In this chapter, our aim is to answer the question, 'What makes these schools very effective?' Our overall intention is to review the characteristics of the schools, to understand them more fully and to develop them further. There are thus three main sections in this chapter. In the first section we interpret the findings and attempt to make sense of them, and in the second we consider the outcomes in relation to what is known about the characteristics of effective schools. In the third section, we reflect on particular outcomes, for example the way the schools went about their work, the importance of their focus on ensuring and improving learning, and support for schools from the community.

AN INTERPRETIVE REVIEW OF THE FINDINGS

As we discussed in Chapter 2, research into the characteristics of effective schools has identified what schools do under various headings such as 'Professional leadership', 'Purposeful teaching' and 'A learning organisation'. We have adopted a similar approach and have identified six key characteristics, which are:

- Leadership
- The mindset
- The teaching team
- The engagement of the pupils and their parents
- Very efficient and effective organisation and management
- The mutual support, validation and valuing of the wider community.

We have then described what the schools do under the various headings. Their various activities contribute to and sustain the core of what they do, which is to maintain a productive, strong and highly inclusive culture that focuses on ensuring and improving learning for all pupils. This core work is their central characteristic.

In this section, we review the findings of the research and in particular explore the ways in which the six key characteristics contribute to and sustain the central characteristic. We also explore how the characteristics might work together. But before we do that, we examine what was apparently one of the overriding features of the schools and their main task – ensuring and improving learning for all pupils.

The focus on ensuring and improving learning for all pupils

It was very clear from our study that the staff in the schools concentrated on making sure that the pupils learned as a result of their teaching. This *teaching for learning* was their central concern. The teaching team judged the effectiveness of their teaching on whether the pupils achieved, that is 'Did the pupils improve on their previous best?' and 'Did they attain, that is did the pupils do well in (national) tests and assessments and similar kinds of tests?' If not, the teaching was changed with a view to ensuring that they did. So, the schools did their best to *ensure that their teaching for learning was effective* and they worked to ensure that this was the case *for all pupils*. But more than that, the teaching teams sought to *enrich* their teaching and endeavoured to make sure it was stimulating, motivating and engaging for the pupils. So, the staff in the school were centrally concerned with *ensuring that their teaching for learning was effective and enriched for all pupils*.

In addition, the schools were eager to continually improve their work. The staff were therefore keen to change their practice if it would increase the level of pupil achievement and attainment. They wanted to make it more effective. The teaching staff also wanted to enrich it further and to change their practice to make the pupils' educational experience more stimulating, more motivating and more engaging. And they wanted to do this for all the pupils. So, they were also concerned with *improving and further enriching teaching and learning for all pupils*.

Thus the focus of those who worked in the schools was on *ensuring effective and enriched teaching for learning for all pupils and improving and further enriching teaching for learning for all pupils*. We consider this work to be their main task. It was the schools' central concern and their rationale, and all their efforts were directed towards it. From our interpretation of the data, this task and the way in which the schools concentrated on it was the key to their success. The nature of this main task is summarised in Figure 12.1.

The schools in this study, focused on:

1 *ensuring* (that is, as far as is possible, guaranteeing and securing)
2 *teaching for learning* (thus defining and focusing the purpose of teaching)
3 *for all pupils* (thereby giving a high level of inclusivity)
4 *that is effective* (in that it enables the pupils to reach a high level of achievement and attainment)
5 *and enriched* (in that it is stimulating, motivating and engaging)
6 *and improving* (changing practice to increase the level of achievement and attainment)
7 *and further enriching* (changing practice to make the pupils' educational experience more stimulating, motivating and engaging)
8 *teaching for learning for all pupils*.

Figure 12.1 An explanation of the schools' main task, ensuring and improving learning for all pupils.

In the remainder of this chapter, we summarise this main task as 'Ensuring and improving learning for all pupils'.

The central characteristic

A productive, strong and highly inclusive culture that focuses on ensuring effective and enriched teaching for learning for all pupils and improving and further enriching teaching for learning for all pupils.

The cultures of the schools – what they did by custom and habit – focused on the main task of ensuring and improving learning for all pupils. Their ways of working produced the desired outcomes of ensuring pupil achievement and attainment. Their cultures were thus productive. Moreover, their ways of working focused relentlessly on the main task. This focus was not partial, intermittent or half-hearted. It was complete, continual and committed. Their cultures were strong and, as a result, the levels of pupil achievement and attainment were high and were improving. The schools endeavoured to include everyone in their work. *All* the staff were required to work *together*: to help *all* the pupils achieve and attain; to engage the commitment of *all* the parents; and to engage *all* the members of the wider community in their work. The schools were thus highly inclusive in all aspects of their work. There are of course obvious explanations for this approach that are based perhaps on educational values ('Everyone has a part to play in the education of our young people, including the young people themselves, so we must include them all') or to ensure maximal resource use through widespread engagement ('The more contributions we have towards work on the main task, the better – and that includes the pupils' contribution'). The inclusive approach of the schools we studied appeared to recognise the individuals and groups they worked with on the basis of their needs, positions and responsibilities in relation to the main task. It accorded equal valuing and parity of esteem of the different individuals and groups even though their practice, capabilities, responsibilities and scope to influence varied. They all had a valuable contribution to make to the work on the main task. Seeking their commitment to and engagement in the main task demonstrated this equal valuing and parity of esteem. In effect, it says 'We all need to work on this task and we all need to work together'.

This highly inclusive approach helps to make the boundaries between the various individuals and sub-groups manageable. Through equal valuing and parity of esteem, the institution becomes integrated and cohesive and all the different parts can work together better. With *un*equal valuing and *dis*parity of esteem, different individuals and groups may become split and separated within the institution, and in some cases from the institution. They may then form antagonistic groups, cliques, factions and elites. Organisations and institutions that are characterised by splits and separations are fertile breeding grounds for blame (for example, 'Low attainment is the parents' fault'), an 'us and them' feeling (for instance, 'It's the staff versus the pupils in this school') and eventually 'scapegoating' (for example, 'It's all the fault of the local authority. We'd be better off without them. If they'd just go away and leave us in peace, everything would be fine'). All those dangerous organisational behaviours are avoided by having an inclusive approach. Everyone is 'on board'. Everyone is working together to the same end. Everyone has a valuable contribution to make.

The key characteristics

From our interpretation, the six key characteristics sustain the core culture of the school, the central characteristic. Furthermore, they are sustained by this central characteristic. For us, the central characteristic is 'central' because it is essential and it is what good successful schools must have. It is necessary. The key characteristics, however, are essential but on their own they are not enough. They are necessary but not sufficient. The key characteristics help to build and sustain the central characteristic and in the following sections we explore how they do that.

Leadership

The headteacher. The leadership provided by the headteacher is instrumental in establishing the culture if the existing ways of working are not already productive, strong and inclusive. Once established, the ways of working need to be given energy – they need to be driven. A key part of this energising work is the motivation of all those connected with the school and its work. This energising, motivating work needs to be continual so that the school's ways of working are continually strengthened and reinforced and a sense of relentlessness is created. Further, by being inclusive, everyone connected with the schools is enabled and motivated to work on the main task.

Leadership density and depth. Clearly, the kind of leadership schools require, even small schools – enabling, energising and motivating others – is almost impossible for one person to sustain. Hence the value of developing this kind of capability in others. The headteacher therefore has another key role, that of developing and sustaining leadership in other members of the organisation. There are two dimensions to the headteacher's leadership development work. The first is concerned with developing the *strength* of leadership in others which gives a feeling of leadership *density*. The term 'leadership density' was first used by Thomas Sergiovanni (1987) to describe organisational processes that facilitate the active involvement of members of the organisation in leadership. Distributed, shared and participative models of leadership have largely come from this notion. For us, leadership density indicates the level of active involvement in organisational leadership. A higher level of active involvement indicates a higher level of leadership density.

The second dimension of the headteacher's leadership development work is to build leadership capacity in *everyone* in the school. This work is concerned with developing the extent of leadership in the organisation which gives a feeling of leadership *depth*. The more who are actively involved in leadership work, the greater the leadership depth.

To understand fully how this kind of leadership work contributes to the success of these schools, it is important to understand what leadership is in the sense we are using it. Our view is that leadership is those behaviours that enable others to take up their role in relation to the institution's main task (James and Connolly 2000). So, leadership is not doing work on the main task as such. That is a task role. It is concerned with enabling others to do work on the main task. Leadership is thus a special organisational role, a particular set of practices. For some, such as the headteacher or the chair of the governing body, that role will be a formally assigned responsibility for leadership and they will therefore be expected to undertake a leadership role. For others, such as a relatively inexperienced teacher, the leadership role may not be a formally assigned responsibility but nonetheless they may still undertake leadership work in the form of leadership practices that enable others to do work on the main task. So, when a headteacher is developing leadership capacity in others, he/she is developing their capacity to enable others to undertake their work on the main task.

An ideal outcome of developing leadership capacity in others, an outcome of achieving full leadership density and depth, is that all those in the school (even the pupils) would have a role in enabling everyone else in the school to undertake work on the main task. In terms of the development of leadership depth a key question is therefore, 'How active are members of the organisation in enabling others to take up their role on the main task?' A key question in respect of developing leadership density is, 'How many members of the organisation are actively enabling others to take up their role on the main task?'

Two points about developing leadership density and depth are worthy of comment here. Firstly, in the case study schools, the headteachers' authority, that is the sanctioning of their leadership influence by others, seemed to be enhanced by developing leadership authority in others. One might expect the opposite, a lessening of the headteacher's authority when he or she sought to engender leadership authority in others. It appears therefore that leadership, as the capacity to enable others to undertake their work on the main task, is not finite. It can be built and it can grow. Leadership is not a 'zero sum game'.

Secondly, when leadership is fully engendered in this way, those in the school can come to fully 'represent' the leadership of the school. Their view of the school and its work will signify and correspond to, say, the headteacher's view. They will be able to 'speak for' the headteacher. The headteacher's colleagues in this ideal scenario will of course have their own perspective and perhaps see it from their own task role (as opposed to their leadership role) but, nonetheless, they will be able to represent the cultural imperatives of the school. Those who work in the school do not carry the same responsibilities as the headteacher but they share the vision and the values that underpin that vision and the ways of working that will make the vision a reality. This 'leadership representation' was certainly evident in the schools we studied.

Leadership of the wider community.   An important aspect of the headteachers' leadership work appeared to be attempting to engage everyone connected with the school – the local authority and the local and wider communities, both educational and non-educational – in enabling the school to undertake its work on the main task. In this way, the schools worked to develop leadership for the school. In the sections below, we revisit this idea of leadership *for* schools when we discuss the mutual support, validation and valuing from all those connected with the school.

Leadership by the governing body. Finally, the governing bodies, and in particular, the chairs of the governing bodies, had an important role in providing leadership. In a whole variety of ways, they worked to enable the school to undertake work on the main task. But arguably, the governing bodies and the chairs had another significant leadership role, that of authorising the leadership work in the school. By authorisation, we mean conferring authority on someone to do something, to empower them and to officially sanction their work. By legitimating the in-school leadership work – and in particular the leadership work of the headteacher – the governing bodies considerably strengthened leadership authority in the school and added to the leadership density and depth.

The mindset

The overall attitude and approach of these schools, the mindset, that was present in these schools was very significant. Those we spoke to seemed to be empowered, proactive and optimistic. They gave no impression of being victims of their particular circumstances, which were often very taxing. They had a highly reflective approach. They were very thoughtful about their work – all aspects of it. They were active in considering ways to make the school more efficient and effective, in thinking about ways of improving the suitability of their teaching to their pupils' learning needs, and in reflecting in depth and responding to the social and economic circumstances of the pupils and their families. All this reflective work was undertaken with a view to improving their practice. Those in the schools seemed to have a 'both-and' attitude. So for them, it was possible to both care deeply about their work and to see humorous aspects of it, to understand the pupils' perhaps disadvantaged circumstances and to demand high quality work from them, to value colleagues and yet deal openly with conflicts and differences of opinion. Those in the schools were all willing to praise each other and this willingness to praise was not simply 'top down' with the headteacher praising the teachers and the teachers praising their pupils. The pupils were ready to praise their teachers, and the staff and the pupils were ready to praise the headteachers. There was also a caring attitude – which was widespread and was apparent in many aspects of the schools and their work. Finally, those we spoke to were proud of their schools.

We accept that an overall way of thinking, a prevailing attitude, a way of approaching the main task is difficult to grasp and then describe. And in our interpretation, we are not saying that all the schools had equal amounts of the different facets of the mindset and had them all the time.

There was just a sense of an overall way of thinking and working which we have tried to capture.

The mindset contributed to the central characteristic in a number of ways.

The mindset elevates the status of the main task. Many aspects of the mindset raised the status and meaning of the main task, which helped to ensure and enhance motivation to work on it. A high level of reflectivity ensured that work on the main task was approached thoughtfully. The wide-ranging ethos of care meant that the school's work was considered carefully, learners were cared for as part of the main task, parents were worked with carefully in engaging their commitment to their children's learning, and every aspect of the school and all those connected with it were treated with care. There was an eagerness to acknowledge and praise achievement in relation to the main task, and pride in those who were successful in their work on it. There were high expectations of effort and achievement from everyone who worked on the main task and all those connected with the school, which again elevated its status. The notion of expectations extended to deeply held ambitions, aspirations and ideals – especially for the learners. Thus work on the main task was Good Work.

The mindset optimises the energy brought to the primary task. The 'accept and improve' approach allowed energy to be fully assigned to the main task and not diverted into other activities which were either not related to the task or which actually worked against it. So, for example, energy was not expended complaining how little the children knew about the wider world outside their local community; it was channelled into broadening the pupils' experience. Resources were not wasted by withdrawing from the task of teaching. It was accepted that teaching could be difficult – and maybe would be difficult – and energy was expended working out how to teach successfully in these difficult circumstances.

The mindset allows full authority to be brought to work on the main task. The 'both-and' mentality ensured that those involved in the main task of the school brought their full authority to their endeavours, which, in turn, enhanced their work on the main task and their contribution to building and sustaining the culture. A both-and mentality enables opposing and conflicting thoughts and feelings to be held together in the mind. It integrates and combines the apparently contradictory experiences, feelings, thoughts and desires that are part of everyday life, especially in schools, as these examples illustrate.

1   A headteacher with a 'both-and' mentality will be able to hold together *both* her aim and desire to engage all parents in their children's

learning *and* the almost certain knowledge that she will fail to achieve his aim.

2   A teacher will be able to hold together in his mind *both* a view that the local authority should provide all the resources a school needs (and may have said as much to the local councillor) *and* still be eager to help all day Saturday at the school fete to raise money for the school.

3   Pupils may *both* dislike their teachers for telling them to get on with their work *and* know that their teachers are 'doing the right thing' (which may actually be something they like).

The problem with this 'both-and' approach is that it is a contradictory standpoint and can lead to feelings of confusion and paradox and therefore be difficult to sustain. The opposite stance, an 'either-or' approach, splits and separates these internal contradictions (as we explain in Chapter 3). Thus one of the opposing views might be ignored in the interests of easing the difficulty the integrated both-and stance poses, or the difficult feelings associated with one particular view might be projected elsewhere. The following scenarios are what might happen in the examples above if the both-and approach is dispensed with.

1   If the headteacher ignores or denies the notion that she may never achieve her aim, she may appear to be naive, somewhat out of touch with the real world and committing her resources in a rather pointless way. Her authority as a headteacher would be undermined.

2   The teacher might choose not to take part in the school fete, voicing the view that the local authority was to blame for the lack of resources. He had made that view clear and he will therefore have nothing to do with the whole event. As a result, he might lose out on all the benefits that communal endeavour can bring, would miss an opportunity to indicate in a tangible way to parents, pupils and others their commitment to the school, and would pass up an opportunity to enrich the pupils' education. His authority as a teacher would be undermined.

3   If the pupils simply accepted their teacher's instructions, they may be denying the important feelings that come from a dislike of being controlled by others, may simply become passive in the learning process and might not be fully committed and engaged in their learning. Their authority as pupils would be undermined.

With the both-and attitude, the comforting simplicity of a one-dimensional singular view of the world is relinquished and given up. The multidimensional, paradoxical and contradictory nature of the world is accepted.

The mindset can help to sustain a focus on the primary task. The high level of empowered and proactive optimism helped to maintain a focus on the main task. So, for example, the members of a teaching team would not withdraw from work on the main task in order to satisfy their own unmet needs. As a group they would be empowered and assertive (they would have 'collaborative strength' as one of the headteachers so neatly put it) and would not be 'needy', desiring a greater sense of esteem, self-worth and status. They would keep clearly focused on the main task. Further, this high level of proactivity appeared to stop those who worked in the schools from becoming dispirited at the difficulties they faced and it seemed to prevent them from becoming demoralised. The mindset also seemed to stop them from being motivated only by envy or competition. Instead, they wanted to do well and success in the main task was an indication of that. It would show that they were doing Good Work. The mindset, especially the high level of empowered and proactive optimism, also prevented them from becoming victims of their circumstances, passively hoping that matters will somehow improve sometime in the future.

The teaching team

It came as no surprise that the quality of the teachers was a key contributor to the success of these schools. What was a little more surprising was the very strong emphasis on the teachers working together as a team. 'The teaching *team*' was a very important characteristic of these schools and was one of the keys to their success. All the adults who worked in the classroom and who were in different ways engaged in teaching for learning were included in the team, which helped to give the culture an inclusive feel. As well as the members of the teaching team *all* working together to fully utilise their expertise, they all worked together to improve their capabilities. The data also indicated that the work of the teaching team was consistent, powerful and continuous which helped to make the culture strong.

We have characterised the very extensive and very high level of team working as collaborative practice, a concept that we develop more fully in the next chapter. In essence, collaborative practice has three main components: (1) collaboration, (2) reflective practice and (3) a focus on the main task. Collaboration captures the notion of joint working; reflective practice, encompasses a key aspect of the mindset, being reflective in order to ensure that practice is as good as it can be and improves; and the main task focuses on ensuring and improving learning for all pupils.

One important outcome of all three elements being present is the potentially highly motivating and energising nature of collaborative practice especially if the main task is significant and meaningful. With such a main task, collaborative practice becomes, in effect, undertaking Good Work collectively with a group of like-minded colleagues to the best of one's abilities and then seeking to do even better. This view of collaboration represents a compelling shared vision in practice. We develop the idea of collaborative practice further in Chapter 13.

The pupils and their parents

In the introduction to Chapter 9, 'The pupils and their parents', we explained the rationale for considering these two important groups together, an approach that we consider was justified by the outcome of the analysis. The education of young people has to be a three-way endeavour between the pupils, their parents and the school, and it certainly was in the schools we studied. All three groups have different roles and responsibilities, but all three groups have very important parts to play.

From the data, it was clear that the schools did all they could to engage the commitment of both pupils and parents to the pupils' learning. Working with parents was not limited simply to involvement; achieving active engagement was the aim. Endeavouring to gain the pupils' and parents' active engagement with the main task, and securing their commitment to it helped to ensure pupil achievement and attainment. It helped to make the cultures productive. By their consistent and continual efforts to engage the pupils and parents, the schools helped to make the cultures strong. It was also abundantly clear that the schools attempted to engage *all* pupils and *all* parents, which helped to make the cultures inclusive.

Very efficient and effective organisation

Chapter 10 outlined the very efficient and effective way the schools managed their affairs including and especially in the way they managed pupil performance data. Their efficiency and effectiveness was not a function of school size. That is, whether they were large or small or whether their pupil numbers were stable, rising or falling, they were still efficient and effective in the way they worked. Their efficient and effective ways of working enabled the schools to focus on the main task. Functions and responsibilities in relation to the main task were clear, so everyone knew what they were supposed to do and, importantly, they did it. Efficient ways of working ensured that energy which could be expended on the main task was not wasted unnecessarily. The way the schools organised their affairs was very important in strengthening the culture. There was an expectation that the efficient and effective ways of working would be followed consistently. The ways of working were routinised and 'grooved in'. This approach helped to make the cultures strong. Everyone was expected to conform to the established ways of working which enhanced the sense of inclusion.

The mutual support, validation and valuing of the community

These schools had very sound relationships with their various communities 'beyond the school gates'. The world outside the schools enriched their work and the schools sought to enrich their communities. The schools and their local communities mutually supported each other, mutually affirmed and endorsed their endeavours and they appreciated and respected each other. This interrelationship supported the schools' work on their main task. Thus the schools' communities valued the schools' efforts in enabling the pupils to achieve and attain. They also valued the schools' work in enriching the pupils' learning and were ready to add enrichment. The schools also linked with individuals, organisations and institutions in the wider community in the UK and elsewhere to their mutual benefit.

The wider educational community, for example the local authority, the General Teaching Council for Wales and the Welsh Assembly Government, also helped the schools to improve their teaching (and thus the pupils' learning). The community in its broadest sense was a source of further and continual enrichment of the teaching in the school. The validation of the schools' work and their ways of working helped to strengthen the culture of the schools. The schools were more certain that their ways of working were appropriate. The schools sought to engage everyone's support – all the various members of the community – which helped to make the cultures inclusive.

Figure 12.2 illustrates the key characteristics, their link with the central characteristic, its relationship with the main task and the outcome of the schools' work on this main task.

THE CHARACTERISTICS OF THE CASE STUDY SCHOOLS IN COMPARISON WITH THE CHARACTERISTICS OF EFFECTIVE SCHOOLS

In attempting to understand the nature of these schools and why they were successful, we have compared our findings with the outcomes of the comprehensive review of the literature on the characteristics of effective schools by Sammons, Hillman and Mortimore (1995). Their list of characteristics remains one of the most complete, still informs thinking about 'what schools should be like' and underpins other important aspects of educational work such as school inspection. It therefore provides a robust and valid way of comparing the schools in our study with effective schools.

Not unexpectedly, there is broad overlap in the headings set out by Sammons, Hillman and Mortimore and the characteristics we have identified. It would be very remarkable if that were not the case. Table

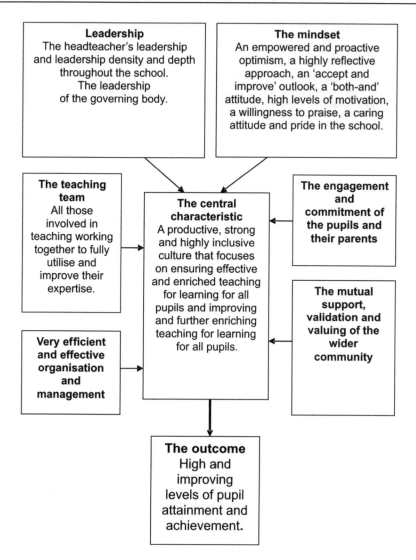

Figure 12.2 A diagrammatic representation of the central characteristic and the key characteristics of the schools in the study together with the outcome.

12.1 sets out the characteristics of effective schools identified by Sammons, Hillman and Mortimore and, alongside that list, we have depicted those characteristics in the schools we studied.

The characteristics of the schools we studied differ in two important ways. Firstly, we have identified a number of additional characteristics which come under the general headings of 'The school and the community' and 'The mindset'. Secondly, the way the characteristics of the schools we studied are described is different and illustrates the passionate and

Table 12.1 The characteristics of the schools in the study in comparison with the characteristics of effective schools identified by Sammons, Hillman and Mortimore (1995).

Characteristics of effective schools identified by Sammons, Hillman and Mortimore (1995)	The characteristics of high attainment primary schools in disadvantaged settings
Professional leadership	
• Firm and purposeful	The headteachers were highly motivated to bring about and improve pupil attainment and achievement. They had considerable authority, a high profile and a significant presence. The headteachers set and maintained productive, strong and highly inclusive ways of working. The governing bodies and in particular the chairs of the governing bodies functioned effectively.
• A participative approach particularly to decision-making	The headteachers sought to develop leadership capability in everyone in the school and there was wide involvement in decision-making, which enhanced leadership depth. They also sought to develop leadership capability fully in others, which created a sense of leadership density. The schools were highly inclusive and wanted to engage *all* stakeholders in their work.
• The leading professional	The headteachers were very good teachers, had very high standards and were respected by their colleagues for their educational expertise. They were motivated by very high professional ideals and aspirations.
Shared vision and goals	
• Unity of purpose	Throughout the schools, there was total and resolute commitment to ensuring effective and enriched teaching for learning for all pupils and improving and enriching further teaching for learning for all pupils. This work was their main task.
• Consistency of practice	There was widespread collaborative planning and development and the prevalent discourse, the extensive team working and the highly inclusive ways of working ensured that practice was consistent. Practice was also consonant – there was a large measure of agreement.
• Collegiality and collaboration	There was extensive and intensive joint working, high levels of trust and a powerful sense of mutual accountability. Everyone was required to be a team player and conform.

Table 12.1 continues

Table 12.1 continued

Characteristics of effective schools identified by Sammons, Hillman and Mortimore (1995)	The characteristics of high attainment primary schools in disadvantaged settings
A learning environment	
• An orderly atmosphere	There was order in the schools. Standards of pupil behaviour were high. The schools were efficiently and effectively organised.
• An attractive working environment	There were vivid educational displays around the school and in every room. The schools were warm and comfortable places in which to learn; the pupils liked them.
Concentration on teaching and learning	
• Maximisation of learning time	The pupils were busy and worked hard. Lessons were efficiently organised and well prepared.
• Academic emphasis	There was a very strong focus on teaching for learning but with creativity and enrichment in all aspects. There was an emphasis on literacy and numeracy.
• Focus on achievement	The schools focused on ensuring optimal attainment (pupils gaining the best possible scores in national tests) and achievement (pupils improving in relation to their previous best in all aspects of their learning).
Purposeful teaching	
• Efficient organisation	Classes were arranged to optimise learning. Collaborative planning made the most of expertise and improved efficiency. Teachers were well prepared and there was a strong emphasis on very high quality teaching. Other adults supported the work of the teachers in the classroom and were highly valued.
• Clarity of purpose	Ensuring effective and enriched teaching for learning was the priority.
• Structured lessons	Lessons were well structured with varied learning activities. A similar lesson format was often used throughout the school.
• Adaptive practice	The teachers worked very hard to meet the individual learning needs of *all* pupils. There was extensive differentiation of learning tasks and widespread and appropriate use of information and communication technologies. Creativity was highly valued.

Table 12.1 continues

Table 12.1 continued

Characteristics of effective schools identified by Sammons, Hillman and Mortimore (1995)	The characteristics of high attainment primary schools in disadvantaged settings
High expectations	
• High expectations all round	The schools had very high, almost limitless, expectations and worked hard to raise aspirations and the awareness of possibilities and potential. There was an expectation that all those connected with the school would do their best.
• Communicating expectations	There was a relentless continuous improvement culture in the schools. Everyone was encouraged to improve but not in ways that were burdensome or created stress.
• Providing intellectual challenge	There was a very high degree of challenge in all aspects and at all levels of ability. The challenge was broad, not just intellectual, and was closely coupled to very high levels of support for everyone.
Positive reinforcement	
• Clear and fair discipline	There were very high standards of discipline with an enforced code of conduct. Bullying was rare and was dealt with very promptly.
• Feedback	Everyone connected with the schools received large amounts of honest feedback. Praise was given to all those who achieved – especially the pupils.
Monitoring progress	
• Monitoring pupil performance	Pupil progress was very closely monitored. There was pupil tracking, group tracking and target-setting for all pupils. Pupils were assessed regularly.
• Evaluating school performance	There was continual reflection and review and an unyielding continuous improvement culture. The schools wanted to do the very best they could for their pupils and then do even better.
Pupil rights and responsibilities	
• Raising pupil self-esteem	Continuous and considerable efforts were made to raise pupil self-esteem and confidence.
• Positions of responsibility	Pupils were expected to contribute to the working of the schools and were involved in decision-making. School councils worked well.
• Control of work	High levels of learner autonomy and responsibility were emphasised. Pupils were involved in target-setting and 'owned' their targets. Pupils enjoyed learning and wanted to learn.

Table 12.1 continues

Table 12.1 continued

Characteristics of effective schools identified by Sammons, Hillman and Mortimore (1995)	The characteristics of high attainment primary schools in disadvantaged settings
Home–school partnership • Parental involvement in their children's learning	The schools actively sought to engage the commitment of the parents to their children's learning. There were close, respectful and 'professional' relationships between parents and teachers and high levels of reciprocal appreciation between parents and the schools.
A learning organisation • School-based staff development (*supplemented by attendance at appropriate external training courses*)	There were regular and frequent school-based staff development sessions that were typically led by subject leaders from the school or advisory teachers from the local authority. These were linked to the school development plan or to particular initiatives to improve pupil achievement. All the teaching staff (including classroom assistants of various kinds) were involved. Learning from external courses was shared efficiently and effectively.

motivated way the schools went about their work. In the following sections, we explore these three main differences: 'The school and the community', 'The mindset' and 'The very high level of commitment and engagement'.

The school and the community

The community

By the use of the term 'community' we do not just mean the neighbourhood in the immediate vicinity of the schools or the community where the pupils lived. Nor do we simply mean the 'education community', that is, the local authority education service, other schools, the National Assembly for Wales, the Welsh Assembly Government, Estyn, ACCAC, the General Teaching Council for Wales, the teacher and headteacher unions, and higher and further education. The community is both these various groupings so it includes: the pupils' families, not just their parents but their extended families as well; those pupils who have attended the schools in the past and their families; and the members of all the different groups in the schools' local communities in all their various guises – members of the local neighbourhood, the local media, local councillors, the police, charities and so on. Given the wide range of individuals, groups, organisations and institutions that have an interest in schools, and given that everyone is required to attend school, almost everyone is part of a school community in some sense. Many of the schools had extensive links with schools and communities further afield in the UK, in other parts of Europe and beyond. Viewed in this way the schools are part of a much wider system of relationships of various kinds. We develop this systemic view further in the sections below.

The mutual support, validation and valuing of the community

The schools we studied appeared to receive considerable support, validation and valuing for their work from the various communities of which they were a part. A key aspect of the support, and the endorsement and appreciation of effort and achievement, was the way it appeared to be mutual. So, in relation to the local community near to the school for example, there was mutual assistance, approval and gratitude. The communities valued the schools' endeavours and achievements and, very importantly, the schools valued the endeavours and achievements of members of the local community. The schools were a resource that added to their local communities and the communities were a resource that enriched the work of the schools. The schools appeared to have similar relationships with their local authorities. Support, affirmation and respect from the local authority were very important to the work of the schools and the schools were a source of expertise and good practice for the local authorities to draw upon as they worked on their own main task. Support from the other parts of the community was also important. In very different ways, the schools received support from a range of different agencies and groups and importantly these organisations benefited from their work with the schools.

Some parts of the community, such as the local authority, will have a formal responsibility to support, validate and value the work of the schools and they may have designated responsibilities for doing so. Some will have direct leverage in this working for schools, for example the General Teaching Council for Wales in the grants it awards for professional development. Some of this support from the wider community will help the schools' work on their main task in a general way; some will give assistance and positive feedback directly to help the schools work on the main task. And here is an important issue: supporting, valuing and validating a school's work on its main task is a form of leadership as we have described it earlier. It is about the wider system enabling the school to take up its role on the main task. We call this leadership 'systemic leadership for schools'.

Systemic leadership for schools

A school's 'system' is the very complex set of relationships among all those connected with it. All schools are part of a system and, by definition, they cannot separate themselves from it. The system includes all the various members of the community, past and present, that we described above as 'the community'. The schools we studied were enabled to work on their main task of ensuring and improving learning for all pupils by the system. It provided leadership for the schools. This leadership *for* schools is different from the leadership *of* schools for which particular individuals and groups such as headteachers and governing bodies have a designated responsibility. Leadership for schools is the work of the wider system. This notion of systemic leadership for schools gives rise to a number of considerations.

Firstly, what is the nature of the systemic leadership for schools? It will of course vary according to the different individuals, groups and institutions offering leadership, and their authority and resources. Systemic leadership for schools may be relatively passive and intangible where perhaps appreciating and speaking well of the school confirms its good work. Leadership for schools in this form might come from parents, relatives of pupils, past pupils and members of the local neighbourhood. It may, however, be more active and tangible. Systemic leadership of this kind could, for example, explicitly validate and value the work of the school thus providing additional motivation to engage on the main task. This kind of leadership for schools might come from the local authority and other agencies that have a formal designated interest in and responsibility for schools. It may involve active engagement and a commitment of resources of some kind which can bring about a higher level of endeavour and activity. Both passive and active support, validation and valuing from the wider system are still leadership acts that enable schools to undertake work on their main task.

The second issue is that the kinds of practices we are talking about appeared to be mutual, certainly in the schools we studied. The wider system provided leadership for the schools and the schools in their turn provided leadership for the different parts of the wider system. Thus the schools, by working with the wider system, helped those various individuals groups and organisations of various kinds to work on their main task.

Thirdly, the notion of systemic leadership has policy implications. Policies for enhancing quality in education that are grounded in market forces, policies of the kind that were prevalent in the late 1980s and 1990s, are likely to restrict systemic support and systemic leadership for schools. Competitive pressures are likely to fragment the system into antagonistic subsystems. The different parts of the system will be set against each other. In an education market, individual schools and those connected with them have much to gain from undermining the work of other schools. Of course, the desire to compete is always likely to be present in schools as in other organisations and institutions. There is, however, a strong case for arguing that other ways of motivating those who undertake Good Work for their pupils and engaging wide (systemic) support for that work is likely to be more productive than encouraging explicit competition.

The final point is that in considering the importance of systemic leadership for schools, we concluded that it could be focused, sharpened and made more explicit. There was scope for more 'leadership *for* schools' from this wider community to give more support to the leadership *of* schools, which was present in abundance within the schools we studied. The need was captured by one headteacher who expressed her wish that the local authority provide the kind of leadership and motivation she needed: "*All the inspiration for improvement seems to come from the schools. We need more inspirational, charismatic leadership from the local authority*". Of course, this statement could be interpreted in a number of ways and there may be a variety of reasons for it. Nonetheless, it raises the important issue of where in the system leadership for schools might be initiated if it is lacking, and who might explicitly encourage it. Local authorities may indeed be well-placed to undertake this task of instigating and activating 'leadership for schools'. They already have a central role in managing schools and the education service. Local authorities have a particularly important role in Wales, although the role may not be so prominent in other parts of the UK. Local authorities have substantial expertise and experience in the work of schools. They also have close links with schools' local communities. There is thus a strong case for local authorities taking up the leadership for schools task more fully and perhaps more creatively than at present. In this work, they could, among other things, remind schools and the various communities they serve and all those connected with schools of the very important work schools undertake, praise them for their substantial efforts and actively encourage them to do even better.

The mindset

As we have already stated, the overall attitude of the staff in the schools was extremely important. We have attempted to capture its nature but as we have said already, doing that is difficult. Nonetheless we are clear that the overall approach, 'the mindset', is an additional characteristic and an important one. To gain a sense of its significance, consider what the opposite attitude might be like.

1 Instead of having an empowered and proactive optimism, the schools would lack authority, would feel they had no capacity to act and would be pessimistic. They would become victims of their circumstances.
2 Rather than having a highly reflective approach, they would be thoughtless and careless about their work. The schools would simply 'do as they were told', even if what they were told to do was inappropriate. The staff would not be able to learn and develop

as professionals, and would not understand the full meaning and significance of their work.

3 In place of an 'accept-and-improve' outlook, the schools would have a 'refuse/reject-and-do-nothing' approach. They would waste energy refusing to accept what they could not change and rejecting those things they were obliged to do, yet they would not be prepared to do anything about it. They might indulge themselves by playing the familiar game of 'Ain't it awful' where moaning about how bad things are becomes a satisfying activity in its own right.

4 As an alternative to the 'both-and' attitude, there would be an 'either-or' approach where options would be narrowed, possibilities would be limited and scope for action would be restricted. Importantly, through this way of working their authority would be undermined and dangerous organisational splits and separations might develop.

5 Aspirations, ideals and expectations would be low and as a result the pupils would not be motivated to achieve. Ambitions would be depressed and the principles and standards on which the school was based would be scaled down.

6 Instead of a willingness to praise, there would be an inclination to criticise.

7 A caring attitude would be supplanted by an approach characterised by a lack of care, a 'can't be bothered' outlook and a thoughtless and inconsiderate approach to others.

8 There would be no sense of pride, satisfaction and pleasure in the school's achievements and the self-respect of all those connected with the school would be lowered.

It is clear that without the right overall approach, the schools would become very unpleasant and, importantly, very 'anti-educational' places. The overall mindset is thus very important.

The very high level of commitment and engagement

It was very apparent from the data that the staff in the schools were fully committed to and engaged in the main task and they endeavoured to engender a similar approach in all those connected with them. This approach explains an important difference between the characteristics of these schools and the characteristics outlined by various researchers, including the wide-ranging list set out by Sammons, Hillman and Mortimore (1995). The difference in essence is that the schools had many if not all of the characteristics in full measure and they engaged with all the various characteristics with passion. It was present in all aspects of their work. They had a powerful desire to engage fully in their work and to engage others in a similar way.

Passion typically refers to strong emotions and feelings. It is usually directed towards an object which is the focus for feelings such as desire, enthusiasm or affection. In many ways it is a flow of energy – libido – towards something. The problem is that, as Freud tells us, this flow can become distorted and misdirected. Importantly, it can become inappropriately channelled both in individuals and in whole institutions. The interesting feature of these schools is that the energies appeared to be concentrated on the main task and seemed to flow directly towards it without interruption.

This passion for the main task and all the various activities that contributed directly to achieving it was a crucial underpinning to the work of the schools we studied. It seemed to create an 'amplifying effect' that increased the energy given to all the characteristics. So the various features and characteristics were engaged with at 'full volume' – with full commitment. What the schools did was important but the way they did it was equally so.

The additional characteristics of the successful schools

The additional characteristics we have identified are shown in Table 12.2. The characteristics relate to 'The school and the community' and 'The overall approach'. Under 'The school and the community' we have focused on 'The school and its local communities', 'The school and its wider community', 'The local authority' and 'The education system'. We are conscious that schools work with a range of groups and organisations – different 'communities' in their locality. Some schools also seek to enrich their work by having links with others in the wider community much further afield – even overseas. We have separated out the schools' relationships with their local authorities because of the particular and especial relationship the schools had with them. They were important working partners. We have included the education community because it was clear that the schools were connected with a number of individuals, groups and institutions within the education community, which they both benefited and gained benefit from.

Under 'The overall approach' we have identified 'The mindset' and 'A very high level of commitment and engagement'. The mindset was a particularly important feature of the schools and the way the schools engaged passionately with their work was a very significant feature. As we have said on page 145 the way all the characteristics of these schools are described exemplifies the very high level of energy and commitment in the way they worked. This characteristic 'threads though' all the others.

WHY WERE THESE SCHOOLS VERY EFFECTIVE?

In the previous sections, we have discussed what the various features and characteristics offer and have considered the contribution they each make to the success of the schools. In this section, we take the exploration of why these schools were successful a stage further.

Table 12.2 Characteristics of schools in Wales, UK in which the overall levels of pupil attainment and socio-economic disadvantage are high additional to those identified by Sammons, Hillman and Mortimore (1995).

Characteristics additional to those identified by Sammons, Hillman and Mortimore (1995)	Descriptions of the additional characteristics
The school and the community	
• The school and its local communities	There were high levels of mutual support, validation and valuing by the schools and their local communities. The communities felt the schools were doing good work and valued the schools' endeavours and achievements, and vice versa. The schools were a resource for their local communities, which were in turn a resource that enriched the work of the schools.
• The school and the wider community	The schools linked with individuals, organisations and institutions in the wider community in the UK and elsewhere to their mutual benefit.
• The local authority	There was mutual support, validation and valuing by the schools and their local authorities. The schools were a resource of expertise and good practice for their local authorities.
• The education system	Support and appreciation from other schools, the National Assembly for Wales, the Welsh Assembly Government, Estyn, ACCAC, the General Teaching Council Wales, the teacher and headteacher unions, and higher education institutions which educate and train teachers and school leaders were important.
The overall approach	
• The mindset	The schools had a particular mindset – an empowered and proactive optimism, a highly reflective approach, an 'accept-and-improve' outlook, a 'both-and' attitude, very high aspirations, ideals and expectations, a willingness to praise, a caring attitude and pride in the school.
• A very high level of commitment and engagement	The staff were fully committed to and engaged in the work of the schools and they endeavoured to bring about a similar approach in all those connected with them.

It is clear that the schools we studied had many of the features that we expect of good schools. That is evident when we compare our findings with those of Sammons, Hillman and Mortimore (1995). So why were these schools as successful as they were? How did the features of these schools collectively contribute to the schools' success? Why were these schools very effective? In this section, we raise a number of possible answers to these questions. Some of the answers may appear to be self-evident but they are worth stating nonetheless.

The features were present, fully and consistently

The most straightforward explanation of why the schools were successful is that they had the characteristics in some form or other in large measure and for most, if not all, of the time. The characteristics took different forms in the different schools, but they were nonetheless in place. In none of the schools was a feature absent. So, firstly, the features were *present*. Secondly, most of the schools had most of the features *fully*. That is, they had them thoroughly, substantially and in large measure. Thirdly, the schools had the features *consistently* – the features and characteristics were present in a sustained and continuous way. The schools we studied would probably not have been as effective as they have been if the features had been only intermittently or temporarily present.

Schools which have a particular feature or characteristic fully and consistently will be more successful than those that do not. For example, schools that have high quality professional development sessions consistently and regularly will be more effective than those that don't. The converse is also true. Schools that have low quality professional development sessions inconsistently and irregularly or perhaps don't have them at all will not be as effective as those that do.

There is a good case for arguing that this 'present, fully and consistently' model applies to all the various features and this explains the schools' success. Moreover, there is also a good case for arguing that schools generally will become increasingly effective when more of the characteristics we have identified are present, more fully and more consistently.

The importance of passionate engagement and commitment

As we have made clear earlier, all those who worked in the schools were highly motivated to work on all the characteristics with passionate engagement and commitment. Further, all those who had an interest in the schools – the wider system – appeared to be highly motivated to work hard for the schools and to provide support (or systemic leadership as we have called it) for them. The high level of motivation in these schools was crucial. The schools were very effective not only because of what they did but because of the way they did it.

The more features the better

In considering the various features and characteristics, we have come to a number of other suppositions all of which relate to the importance of having as many features as possible.

- *The summative effect*. The features of these schools added together in a simple summative way. They combined together, so quite literally it was a case of the more features the better. As a result, the schools were very good at what they were doing and very good at improving what they were doing. The schools were both effective and able to improve.

- *The counterbalancing effect*. The characteristics seem to merge and blend in a very productive way. Many of them counterbalanced, qualified and mediated themselves and each other. So, for example, an authoritative headteacher might produce a dependent culture if part of her or his role wasn't to develop leadership capacity in others and a focus on the main task. A very empowered and cohesive teaching team could come to dominate if they did not strive to actively engage the commitment of the pupils and parents in the pupils' learning and to work with both pupils and parents in an inclusive and valuing way. Ensuring that the work of the school was always efficient and effective could create a very rigid and constraining culture if the staff weren't continually reflective about the way they worked.

- *The synergy effect*. One of the reasons why it is important for schools to have as many of the features as possible as fully as possible and for as much of the time as possible is that so many of them mutually support and add to each other. They operate in synergy. As a result, the more features a school has, the better the features will work. For example, good pupil data management is likely to work better in a school that is already well organised and structured than one that isn't. The work of the teaching team will be enhanced if the pupils and their parents are fully engaged and committed to bringing about pupil learning. The leadership of the school by the governing body, the headteacher and the staff will be easier if there is good leadership for the school from the wider system.

- *Schools are likely to become more successful by ensuring that all the characteristics are present than by improving those that are already in place.* Because of the summative, counterbalancing and synergy effects, schools are likely to become more successful if they concentrate on ensuring that all the various features and characteristics are present rather than improving the ones that are already in place. Working in a highly motivated way on the particular characteristics will be effort wasted if other characteristics are not present. It is better to put effort into ensuring that all the characteristics are in place.

CONCLUDING COMMENTS

In this chapter, we have firstly reviewed the findings of our research on schools that are successful in disadvantaged settings and, in particular, we have explored the ways in which the six key characteristics contribute to and sustain the central characteristic. The main point to emerge is that each characteristic contributes to establishing and sustaining the school culture. This culture is thus productive, strong and highly inclusive. It is focused on the main task of ensuring effective and enriched teaching for learning and on improving and further enriching teaching for learning. The importance of concentrating on the main task cannot be overemphasised. In our view, the schools' focus on the main task was the key to their success. Secondly, we have also considered the outcomes of our research in relation to what is known about the characteristics of effective schools. In particular, we have reviewed the findings in relation to the characteristics of effective schools identified by Sammons, Hillman and Mortimore (1995). An important outcome from that comparison has been the identification of two important additional features, 'The school and the community' and 'The overall approach'. One of the key aspects of the 'The overall approach' is 'A high level of commitment and engagement' which we consider to be very significant. The level of motivation in these schools was very high and it was this motivation that underpinned this characteristic. It generated and drove the passionate dedication of those who worked in the schools. Thirdly, in this chapter we have looked at the way in which the different characteristics and features might operate together to bring about the success of the schools.

13

Interpreting the outcomes

INTRODUCTION

In this chapter, our intention is to gain a further understanding of the characteristics of the schools we studied, to take the ideas we developed in the previous chapter a stage further, and to interpret them and to theorise them. This process will involve abstracting the findings away from the observed and the experienced to a much more theoretical view. We recognise that understanding the work of schools from this kind of theoretical standpoint does not interest everyone. It can be more than sufficient to know 'what works' – schools are of course understandable at that level. Not everyone is interested in 'why it works' in a theoretical sense though we would argue that to know why something works can help in the transfer of those successful practices to other settings.

In the chapter, we draw on the ideas outlined in Chapter 3 where we discussed the concepts underpinning system psychodynamics, or institutional transformation as we have also termed it. In that chapter, we outlined the key theoretical themes in system psychodynamics and explored some key concepts within that overall perspective including: unconscious processes, the emotional dimensions of work in institutions, defences against emotions, emotions and change, emotions and micropolitics, emotions and 'the espoused' and 'the in use', the significance of the boundary, the notion of role, the primary task, group mentalities, the transformation of anxiety and emotion into creativity and passion in institutions.

In this chapter, we investigate some of those concepts further and seek to theorise the nature of the schools we researched. Our purpose is twofold. Firstly, it is to gain a fuller understanding of the schools and why they were successful. Secondly, we want to enrich the way the various notions in system psychodynamics and institutional transformation are conceptualised, thus developing understandings of them and their usefulness.

THE PRIMARY TASK

In our view, a consideration of the primary task is essential in understanding the work of any organisation or institution including, and perhaps especially, schools. For that reason we deal with the notion of the primary task first. To recap, the concept of the primary task was first developed by Rice (1963). It is the task that the organisation feels – consciously or unconsciously – it needs to undertake if it is to continue and to survive. An exploration of the primary task and how it is defined is a useful analytical tool for understanding organising processes (Miller and Rice 1967). The central issue is that the primary task, especially in institutions, may be highly significant and meaningful – again consciously and unconsciously – to those who undertake work on it. So, working on the primary task may at a conscious level be a burdensome responsibility that brings with it stresses and anxieties. At an unconscious level, the same primary task may bring terrors and panics and these painful emotions are likely to be defended against through various task-avoidance strategies. On the other hand, the primary task may be experienced as 'Good Work' that touches both conscious and unconscious desires and may be engaged with passionately and creatively.

One of the key outcomes of the study was the way in which the schools focused their work onto ensuring and improving learning. As we have said in Chapter 12, this main task was their central concern – it was where they concentrated their energies, and it was where they directed their efforts. We have established this main task in full as: *ensuring effective and enriched teaching for learning for all pupils and improving and further enriching teaching for learning for all pupils*.

From a system psychodynamics standpoint, we call this main task the primary task. More importantly, we would argue that it was the task that had been assigned, authenticated and recognised by all those who had an interest in the schools. It was thus the normative primary task (Lawrence 1977). From the discussions during our data collection visits with those who worked in the schools and those who were connected with the schools, the task was the one the schools thought they were undertaking. It was thus the existential primary task. Moreover, it was the task that could be inferred from our observations and the accounts of their behaviours. It was also therefore the phenomenal primary task. We contend that the congruence of the normative, the existential and the phenomenal primary tasks was one of the main reasons why the schools were successful.

The nature of the primary task is also worthy of consideration. Importantly, it was in two parts. One was concerned with ensuring that practice was optimal, that it was the best that it could be in the circumstances. Thus the schools concentrated on ensuring that teaching for learning for all pupils was effective and enriched. But there was a second part that was concerned with improvement. So those in the schools also worked on improving and further enriching teaching for learning for all pupils. Their work was thus fully grounded in reflective practice (Schön 1983). They reflected on their actions and used these reflections to improve and enhance their teaching. Their reflections in action ensured that their actions were optimal in the moment of acting and their reflections on action ensured that their practice continually improved. It was thus a reflective primary task. This reflective primary task has normative, existential and phenomenal dimensions as indicated in Table 13.1.

The way the schools elevated the status of and the normative primary task focused their energies on it was significant. The mindset was particularly significant in this regard. As we argued in Chapter 12, it elevated the status of the primary task, ensured that energy now brought to the primary task, allowed full authority to be brought to work on the primary task, and helped to sustain a focus on the primary task. Arguably, the main benefit of 'The mindset' is the effect it has on the way the primary task is viewed.

Table 13.1 The normative, existential and phenomenal dimensions of a school's reflective primary task and key questions relating to the various dimensions

| Aspect of the reflective primary task | The school's view of the primary task | | |
	The normative primary task	*The existential primary task*	*The phenomenal primary task*
To ensure effective and enriched teaching for learning for all pupils	*The school's defined and designated task* Key question: *How does the school work to ensure effective and enriched teaching for learning for all pupils?*	*The task the school thinks it is undertaking* Key question: *Does the school think it is working to ensure effective and enriched teaching for learning for all pupils and how does it know?*	*From observations, the task the school is actually undertaking* Key question: *Does the school appear to be working to ensure effective and enriched teaching for learning for all pupils and how does it know?*
To improve and further enrich teaching for learning for all pupils	*The defined and designated task* Key question: *How does the school work to improve and further enrich teaching for learning for all pupils and how does it know?*	*The task the school thinks it is undertaking* Key question: *Does the school think it is working to improve and further enrich teaching for learning for all pupils and how does it know?*	*From observations, the task it is actually undertaking* Key question: *Does the school appear to be working to improve and further enrich teaching for learning for all pupils and how does it know?*

GROUP MENTALITIES

One important feature of these schools was their explicit work group mentality. In a group with such a mentality, the group members focus on carrying out a specifiable task – their primary task – and assessing their effectiveness in doing it (Bion 1961; Obholzer and Roberts 1994; James and Connolly 2000). There was very little evidence of basic assumption mentalities – 'dependency', 'fight and flight' or 'pairing' – in the ways the schools worked.

The schools did not appear to be dependent cultures. There was very little sign that the schools had regressed to working simply and solely on meeting their conscious and unconscious needs and reducing anxiety and internal discord at the expense of working on the primary task. Arguably, their work on the primary task, which was highly meaningful to them, met a deep-seated need in those who worked in the schools. Other needs such as a need for affiliation was met by the very extensive collaborative working (see below) which was prevalent in the schools. Further, the schools had a very powerful caring ethos. They both cared for each other and focused on the primary task. Moreover, this collaborative working and the very efficient and effective organisation of the schools will have helped to contain the anxieties associated with the primary task (again, see below).

The schools did not seem to have a fight and flight basic assumption tendency. They were not focused on some external 'enemy' or concern. In the main, their focus was not on trying to 'beat the SATs score of the pupils in the school down the road'. Rather, they simply wanted their pupils to do the best they could and worked to achieve that aim. They did not work hard just to ensure they received a good Estyn report next time around, they simply endeavoured to undertake Good Work, which for them was work on the primary task.

There was very little evidence of a basic assumption pairing tendency in the ways the schools worked. For example, the culture was not one where the schools were wistfully and longingly hoping matters would improve at some point in the future. They did not think their situation would improve if only the school could link up with another school just down the road. They did not hold the view, for example, that the school's work would be better if only a small group of staff would get on better with each other. The basic assumption pairing was thus not evident. Of course, the schools looked to the future, they did actively seek ways of improving and indeed recognised that improvement could well result from amalgamating with or at least collaborating more closely with another school or resolving an organisational conflict, but those strategies would have been pursued actively and with the purpose of directly improving the school's work on the primary task. They would not be worked on instead of the primary task.

One powerful outcome of a school developing and retaining a work group mentality and eschewing basic assumption tendencies is the effect on the authority of the schools as institutions. If they undertake work on the defined and given primary task, their activities are legitimated. Thus undertaking work on the primary task and having a work group mentality enhances the legitimacy of schools as institutions.

ESPOUSED THEORIES AND IN USE THEORIES

To reiterate, espoused theories are those that are used to explain or justify an activity, whereas theories that are in use are those that are implicit in the activity (Argyris and Schön 1974, 1978, 1996). The emotional experience of organising can bring those theories together so they correspond and it can separate them and make them incongruent (James and Vince 2001). In the data collection in this study, we used a wide range of data sources and we checked and rechecked the data we collected during our visits. There was little evidence of a lack of congruity between the ways the schools explained and rationalised their various activities and the explanations for the various aspects of practice we saw and for which there was evidence. Throughout the data collection, explanations of practice were matched by the practice in evidence.

This congruence between the espoused and the in use no doubt contributed to the schools' effectiveness as it does in other work organisations (Argyris 1980). This assertion then raises the question as to how this congruence is brought about. We would argue that the espoused and the in use were held together in two main ways. Firstly, the schools were highly reflective about their work. They actively and thoroughly considered the ways they worked, reviewed how effective they were and sought ways to improve. This continual reflection and review enabled disparities between the espoused and the in use to emerge. Secondly, the emotions that accompany organising in any institution were contained in these schools. Thus emotions were not allowed to run wild. There were containing structures, for example the strong culture, the efficient and effective organisation and the high level of collaboration, that allowed emotions to be experienced and surfaced within the organisation but within a secure way of working (see below).

LEADERSHIP

James and Connolly (2000), following the study of improving schools, concluded that leadership was a special organisational role that was concerned with enabling others to take up their role in relation to the primary task. This current study of successful schools in disadvantaged settings has enabled us to develop that way of thinking about leadership. We explain and discuss those ideas in this section.

Firstly, it is important to distinguish between roles as social *positions* with assigned responsibilities and roles as organisational *practices* in which an actor in a social system engages. Examples of roles-as-positions would be 'headteacher', 'chair of the governing body' or 'classroom learning assistant'. These are designated social positions. Examples of roles-as-practices might be a teacher teaching a group of pupils how to spell particular words, a headteacher reminding a teacher of the importance of having a punctual start to the lesson and that he should make sure he arrives for the start of the lesson on time, or a classroom learning assistant working effectively with a group of pupils with special educational needs. These roles-as-practices relate to roles-as-positions but they need to be 'found' by the actor. They need to be acquired in some way. Once found, appropriate practices need to be made into a coherent set, that is a group of practices that are rational, sound and consistent with each other. They then need to be performed, that is they need to be practised. Thus roles-as-practices need to be found, made and performed. Reed (2000) uses a similar model in role analysis, although he uses the term 'take' instead of perform. There will be an interplay between the individual and the organisation in the process of an individual creating an appropriate role-as-practice. Importantly, roles-as-practices cannot be assigned in the way that roles-as-positions can. Roles-as-practices require agency on the part of those finding, making and performing them.

Secondly, roles-as-practices may be task-related or leadership-related. Task roles-as-practices contribute directly to the achievement of the primary task. The examples of the teacher and the classroom learning assistant in the preceding paragraph undertaking teaching work would be examples of roles-as-practices that are directly related to the primary task. Leadership roles-as-practices are the practices that enable others to undertake work on the primary task. They are concerned with enabling others to find, make and perform their role-as-practice. The headteacher in the example in the preceding paragraph explaining the importance of punctuality to a colleague is an example of an aspect of the headteacher's leadership role-as-practice. The headteacher is enabling the teacher to find, make and perform his role.

Thirdly, in ideal circumstances, there should be a congruence of some kind between roles-as-practices and roles-as-positions. Practices should conform to the responsibilities assigned to the position. Such a view implies that there should be a boundary around appropriate practices associated with a particular role-as-position that distinguishes them from inappropriate practices for a particular role as position. Similarly, there should be a boundary around the responsibilities assigned to a particular role-as-position.

Fourthly, roles of both kinds are under both conscious and unconscious influence. Roles-as-practices may be consciously and unconsciously found, made and performed. Roles-as-positions may be consciously and unconsciously assigned and they can also be formally or informally assigned. An example of the conscious assigning and performing of both kinds of role would be a teacher being appointed to a teaching post (an assigned role-as-position) and then, over time, getting to know the pupils in her class, understanding fully how she needs to work with the group and then teaching them in an effective and enriched way (she has found, made and performed her role-as-practice). Unconscious and informal assigning and performing, or 'acting out' as it is sometimes known, would be the staff of a school in which pupil behaviour is poor unknowingly and informally assigning the newly appointed headteacher the role-as-position of 'saviour'. They unconsciously and, obviously, informally assign him the responsibility for 'saving them from the terrible stresses that teaching in this awful school creates for them'. The new headteacher may then begin to behave, unconsciously, as their 'saviour' and as a 'knight in shining armour', rescuing and liberating the staff from their woes. Unconsciously, he finds, makes and performs a role-as-practice which conforms to this unconsciously assigned informal role-as-position. Similar processes operate in organisational scapegoating (Dunning, James and Jones 2005) where individuals or groups split, separate and project unbearable and unacceptable feelings which are taken in by the potential scapegoat. Having unconsciously accepted the role-as-position (scapegoat) and having started to act out the projected negative feelings as their role-as-practice, they may eventually 'agree' to leave the organisation in true scapegoat manner, taking the difficult and unbearable feelings of the organisation with them.

This interpretation of roles and leadership has a number of consequences and implications. Firstly, in this study, the headteachers had clearly been assigned to their roles-as-positions and had found, made and performed appropriate roles-as-practices. A key aspect of both these kinds of roles was to designate roles-as-positions that related directly to work on the primary task to other colleagues through delegation. Some of the headteachers said that it had taken time for them to find, make and perform this particular role as practice. A second important aspect was to enable those colleagues to find, make and perform roles-as-practices that were appropriate to the delegated roles-as-positions. They appeared to have done this successfully and we would argue this made a significant contribution to the efficiency and effectiveness of the schools.

Secondly, leadership roles-as-practices were not restricted only to the headteacher or others in formally designated leadership positions, such as the deputy headteacher or the chair of governors. Leadership roles-as-positions were widely spread throughout the institution as were leadership roles-as-practices. These leadership roles that accompanied task-related roles-as-positions and roles-as-practices were widespread, which gave the sense of leadership density (Sergiovanni 1987) and depth we described in Chapter 12. The benefits of this way of working are obvious. All those in the organisation engage in leadership practices that are appropriate to their responsibilities, which help others to find, make and perform their task-related positions and practices. Or, put very simply, everyone plays a part in helping others to work on the primary task.

Thirdly, the leadership practices were not directed only towards the staff of the schools. The schools undertook leadership work to enable all those connected with them to find, make and perform appropriate roles-as-practices that directly focused on the primary task. For example, the pupils and their parents were enabled to perform their roles – as positions and practices – in relation to the primary task. Various individuals, groups and agencies beyond the bounds of the institution in the community were also influenced to work on the primary task. Leadership practices generated from within the school helped to enable those in the community to undertake appropriate roles-as-practices to enable the school's work on the primary task that related to their role-as-position. In this way, members of the school's communities, regardless of their role-as-position were encouraged to take up the leadership roles-as-practices enabling the school's work on the primary task. Of course, some of those in the school's community such as advisers and advisory teachers from the local authority would be able to exert considerable leadership influence on the school. Others, such as members of the local neighbourhood who did not have children attending the school, would perhaps have less influence. Nonetheless, the schools would attempt to engage them all as appropriate in the school's work. The schools attempted to enable them to find, make and then to perform appropriate roles-as-practices. Interestingly, the schools themselves, in a variety of ways, sought to contribute to the work of these individuals, groups and institutions in the community, to accept a role-as-responsibility and perform an appropriate role-as-practice in relation to *their* work and primary tasks. There was a thus a mutuality and a reciprocality to the leadership work.

Exploring schools and their interrelationship with their communities in this way is a systemic perspective on the work of schools. The schools we studied did not work in isolation – and of course no school ever does. The schools were part of a wider system, which *"is concerned with the key relationships that influence behaviour over time"* (Senge 1990: 44). Because these relationships are concerned with leadership as we are conceptualising it, we refer to the performing of these leadership roles-as-practices as 'systemic leadership'. It is the influence of those in the wider system – individuals, groups, organisations and institutions – through their various positions and practices enabling the school to undertake appropriate practices in relation to its primary task.

Fourthly, leadership as we are viewing it is a particular form of structuration (Giddens 1979). It is not the kind of structuration that occurs as a result of task-related practices. An example of task-related structuration would be the way a classroom learning assistant's work affects the properties of the social system of a school – and of course vice versa. Work in schools (whether or not it bears directly on the primary task) structures and is structured by the school. Leadership practices as we are viewing them are a particular kind of structuration process where actions are not directly task-related but are concerned with enabling others to undertake work on the primary task. This enabling activity is an important structuring process.

BOUNDARIES

Boundaries of social systems represent structural inconsistencies and discontinuities (Lamont and Molnar 2002; Heracleous 2004). As we argued in Chapter 3, they are a key feature of organisations. Boundaries are shaped by organising and organising is shaped by boundaries (Hernes 2004). As a consequence, the boundaries of social systems are thus potentially continually being created and continually being destroyed.

One of the features of the schools in this study was that the organisational boundaries were securely constructed, sustained and managed by the organising processes of the schools. Designated responsibilities – roles-as-positions – were defined, that is bounded, accepted and undertaken, and appropriate roles-as-practices found, made and performed. Processes and procedures were well known, widely accepted and always adhered to. Unpredictable, inappropriate and idiosyncratic practices which would inevitably threaten boundaries were not tolerated. As a consequence, the institutions felt secure. At the same time, while the schools and those who worked in them both had established and secure boundaries, they also had the potential to change and rework those boundaries. Thus the boundaries around particular roles-as-positions held by individuals, groups and even the whole institution and the boundaries around the associated roles-as-practices did not then become unmanageable barriers to change.

The boundary management work of the headteachers was significant in particular. One of their key tasks was in shaping the organisation by creating and sustaining boundaries. Our supposition is that they worked to ensure that internal boundaries did not become barriers with resulting organisational splits and separations which can then become very favourable locations for splitting and projection (Dunning, James and Jones 2005). Conflicts, which are inevitably 'boundary issues' (Czander 1993) were resolved promptly. Through this boundary management work, the schools would have encouraged internal institutional integration.

One important feature of the headteachers' work as far as we could ascertain was the management of the institution's boundary. The headteachers ensured and secured the resources of the school, made sure the resources of the school focused on the primary task and made certain that the resources of the school were not wasted inappropriately. As well as looking inwards to the workings of the system core, the headteachers looked outwards too. They understood the nature and the expectations of the wider environment in which the school was located. Importantly, they managed the flow of information from that wider environment into the system core in order to minimise its disruptive effects. They thus protected the system core. They also ensured, through the schools' work on the primary task, that the schools met the needs of the environment. These three actions are key aspects of the management of organisational boundaries (Czander 1993).

Importantly, the institutional boundary was not a barrier, it was a managed boundary. As with the internal boundaries the institutional boundary was not a barrier which encouraged splitting and projection. As a consequence, there appeared to be no or at least very few 'bad objects' in the institutions' environments that became the target of the projection of negative feelings. Thus splitting and projection were not engaged in as a way of relieving the discomfort and difficult experiences of their work.

DEFENSIVE BEHAVIOURS

One of the key aspects of the schools was the absence of 'obstructions' in the ways they worked. Insurmountable obstacles, stumbling blocks and hindrances did not feature significantly in the data we collected and have reported in Chapters 5 to 11. There seemed to be a 'flow' to their work. Thus explanations and accounts were not conditional – 'Things would be a lot better if it wasn't for …' Statements were not typically qualified – 'Of course what we want to do is … *but* …' Accounts of actions were not restricted or constrained – 'One thing we might get around to is …' We interpreted the absence of statements of this kind as an indication of the absence of social defences.

Unearthing social defences in organisations can be difficult, so it would not be appropriate for us to say that in these schools defensive behaviour was not a feature of the way they worked. As in most organisations, if not all, defences will be present if only in the form of rituals and routines. But these did not appear to be places where defensive behaviours prevailed and such behaviours were not evident in the accounts of the schools' work that we heard from the various respondents. In the following sub-sections, we explore various potential defences (Hirschhorn 1988; James 1999; James and Connolly 2000).

Resistance

There appeared to be no explicit desire to maintain the status quo by stubbornly opposing *any* change. Imperatives to change were worked with and incorporated into the schools' work in a way that matched their needs. There was a sense that if the schools had no authority to resist, changes were accepted.

Repression

These schools appeared to be 'open places' where feelings – both difficult and pleasant – were expressed and worked with. We did not sense that feelings were repressed or that the schools were repressing places. Difficult feelings appeared to be allowed to surface, and even encouraged to do so, as the schools worked.

Regression

The schools were very mature places in the ways they worked with their circumstances. They had not regressed into haplessness, dependency or child-like behaviour in dealing with the challenges they faced. There was some evidence of covert coalitions, which is a form of regression in which members of an institution may make recourse to familiar relationships that have protected them from anxiety and emotional pain in the past (Hirschhorn 1988). The phrase 'family atmosphere', repeated often to us by respondents seeking to describe the atmosphere in the school, gave an indication of how the school was represented in their thoughts. This 'organisation in the mind' (Armstrong 2005) is the image of the school people hold internally in their minds and it will, at some level, have affected the nature of their working relationships. But such a way of thinking appeared to be countered by working relationships and practices that focused on the work of the school. 'Colleague to colleague' relationships appeared to be the norm. No one referred to the headteacher being the father or mother figure although those archetypes may have been present 'in their minds'. Younger members of staff were simply that and were treated as such and not as sons and daughters.

Identification

The defence of identification is where individuals seek to limit the anxiety associated with enacting their own behaviours by identifying with others. In these schools, there was a very high level of agreement with the educational principles and ideals of the headteacher. But the purpose of the conformity did not appear to be to find a respite from the anxieties of working in very difficult circumstances but appeared to be born of a shared desire to undertake good educational work. It was not about protection, it was about shared endeavour.

Denial

Individuals and groups who reject, disallow and put aside unacceptable aspects of their experience are engaging in the social defence of denial.

These schools could have slipped very easily into this form of social defence. They could have denied their circumstances and the problems the school context brought by saying, for example, that 'These parents may be on low wages but that makes no difference', or 'Inspection by Estyn doesn't make any difference to us, we just carry on as normal', or 'The pupils are just the same as children from better off homes'. They did not, though. All the features of the schools – good or bad – appeared to be acknowledged, surfaced and worked with. They were not denied.

Organisational rituals

The term 'ritual' is used to describe an established procedure or aspect of practice that has no, or very little, apparent connection to a rational understanding of experience. These schools were places of routines and regularised working. But the routines were worked with reflectively to ensure they served an efficient and meaningful purpose. As a result, the routines did not become obstacles and sources of resistance to change.

Splitting and projection

As we discussed in Chapter 3, splitting and projection is a very common defence in individuals and organisations. To recap, in splitting and projection, difficult feelings, most notably the dissonance between internal and external realities that give rise to internal conflicts, are split into their differentiated elements. The process of splitting is often accompanied by projection where difficult elements are located in other individuals and objects rather than in the individuals themselves. This condition resulting from splitting and projection is known as the paranoid-schizoid position. It contrasts with the alternative state, the integrated or depressive position, in which the individual/group forgoes the security and simplicity achieved through splitting and projection and faces the confusion, paradox, inconsistency, incongruity and conflict created by conflicting feelings (Obholzer and Roberts 1994; James 1999; James and Connolly 2000; Dunning, James and Jones 2005).

Very importantly, splitting and projection appeared to be absent in these schools. It surfaced in a minority of schools where those we spoke to expressed some hostile feeling about inspection which they projected to Estyn. But even this view of inspection, which is acknowledged to be an especially 'bad object' for those who work in schools generally, was expressed by only a small number of respondents. The social defence of reaction formation, which is related to splitting and projection, is where protection from the anxieties caused by the contradictions and unresolvable paradoxes is sought by overemphasising one of the pair of contradictory characteristics rather than holding them all in balance. These characteristics are then embodied. So, for example, we might have heard those we spoke to saying, 'The children are fantastic, it's the parents that are the problem', but we didn't. Or in a Welsh-speaking school, we might have heard teachers saying, 'We have no problem with the Welsh speakers, it's those that don't speak Welsh that cause us all our difficulties'. These schools repeatedly expressed a view of the world that was characterised by equanimity. In these successful schools, difficult feelings were held and worked with, which had important consequences.

One way in which the schools worked with difficult feelings was by being highly inclusive in all their practices. In this way, no individual, group or institution, such as a particular colleague, the governors, the local authority, Estyn, the Welsh Assembly Government or part of the local community, became the repository of difficult emotions, the recipient of negative feelings. Within the schools, everyone was expected to be a member of 'the team'. This expectation of team participation did not appear to be negotiable; it was a requirement. Thus there were no outliers, fringe members or solo workers. As a result, the potential for someone being assigned the role of 'bad object', performing that role and then becoming a potential scapegoat was reduced. Furthermore, all those connected with the schools, not just those who worked in the school on a daily basis, were included and their commitment to the work of the school was sought. The schools thus placed themselves *in the system* (see above) and acknowledged and respected the roles that others had in their work. They cultivated this systemic leadership for their school. They wanted others to support them in their work on the primary task, to enable them to find, make and perform appropriate roles-as-practices that would help them with their work. They sought to engender systemic leadership.

CONTAINMENT AND THE TRANSFORMATION OF ANXIETY AND EMOTION INTO CREATIVITY

In Chapter 3, we discussed the notion of emotional containment in organisations. The term containment, a term first coined by Wilfrid Bion, is essentially concerned with providing a secure environment within which individual and organisational emotions and anxieties can be readily surfaced, held and worked with.

The organisation of the schools in this study created a containing environment in a number of ways. Firstly, the way they were organised provided a secure and stable environment. The systems and procedures in the schools and the ways they were consistently adhered to were impressively secure. Their ways of doing things were very robust. The staff and the pupils and all those connected with the schools knew how to 'go on'. Secondly, the highly inclusive collaborative culture provided a containing device which held *everyone* together. No one was permitted to 'act out' the group's emotions on their own or to become the focus for difficult emotions. Collaborative working in this way allows difficult emotions to be collectively held and worked with. They may then be 'returned' to those who expressed them in an acceptable form and reintegrated (Obholzer and Roberts 1994). Emotions were not 'shot straight back from whence they came with a little edge added for good measure' but were understood, their meaning recognised and their origins appreciated and grasped. If expressed emotions are 'batted straight back' they are likely simply to fly back and forth, creating turmoil – an emotional whirlwind. The powerful caring ethos of the schools will have underpinned this process of expressing emotions, accepting them, reworking them into an acceptable form and then returning them so they can be reintegrated. Thirdly, a containing environment was created by joint working on the primary task in a reflective way, work that was meaningful and of paramount importance. The work group mentality was thus sustained and the emotional needs of the group were met, in part at least, through the undertaking of 'Good Work'.

The key issue is that in an environment where anxiety and emotion are contained, social defences, which prevent contact with reality, are minimised and the institution and those who work in it will be aware when change is required. They will also be more ready to work, and to come to understand and reflect upon the consequences of actions. Very importantly, they will be ready to learn and to develop new ways of working that challenge and improve existing practices. They will thus become creative.

WORKING WITH PASSION

In addition to being places of creativity, these successful schools were also places of passion. The strength of the culture, the absence of defensive behaviours and the desire to undertake 'Good Work' all appeared to enable an uninterrupted flow of energy onto the primary task. Their passion to do good work did not appear to be disrupted or misplaced in the ways that we discussed in Chapter 3. Their desires were focused onto ensuring and enriching teaching for learning for all pupils and improving and further enriching teaching for learning for all pupils. The energies of those who worked in the schools were not dissipated in social defences and defensive routines and were not be focused on 'side issues', but were concentrated directly onto undertaking 'Good Work'.

COLLABORATION

One of the outcomes of the study was the importance accorded to joint working with colleagues by all those we spoke to. Collaborative working was espoused and, from our sense of the ways the schools operated, it was in use as well. Joint working was extensive – it was widespread among the staff and, by all accounts, it was intensive. The staff worked together closely in all aspects of their work. The attention to joint working in schools is a relatively recent phenomenon and it takes a number of forms, for example as partnership (Bennett, Harvey and Anderson 2004), federation (DfES 2003) and collaboration (Glatter 2003). We use the term 'collaboration' because of its original etymological connection with 'joint working' (Harper 2001).

Collaboration and its importance in schools has been recognised by a number of authors who have emphasised it as an aspect of work within schools and between schools, for example Nias, Southworth and Yeomans (1989), Lieberman (1990), Smyth (1991), Wallace and Hall (1994), Lomax and Darley (1995), Bridges and Husbands (1996) and Quicke (2000). The idea of schools as 'professional communities' (Louis, Kruse and Bryk 1995; Halverson 2003) and 'professional learning communities' (Dufour and Baker 1998; Roberts and Pruitt 2003) is underpinned by the essentially collaborative nature of educational work.

The collective dimension of practice in work organisations generally has been conceptualised by Lave and Wenger as 'communities of practice' (Lave and Wenger 1991; Lave 1998; Wenger 1998). They define a community of practice as *"a set of relations among persons, activity and world over time and in relation with each other"* (Lave and Wenger 1991: 98). Such communities have three dimensions: firstly, 'What it is about'; secondly 'How it functions'; and thirdly 'What capability is produced'. The production of capability through learning is an important aspect of a community of practice. *"Learning is an integral part of generative social practice in the lived in world"* and *"engagement in a social practice entails learning as an essential constituent"* (Lave and Wenger 1991: 34). Lave and Wenger see reflection on action as an action in itself that plays a significant part in learning, echoing the work of Schön (1983) and Kolb (1984). The dimension of 'What it is about' (Wenger 1998) relates to the task of the community of practice but, arguably, Lave and Wenger do not accord the primary task sufficient status. As we have argued above and in Chapter 3, the primary task and a work group's relationship to it is significant given the inclination of groups to avoid work on the primary task, especially if it is meaningful and significant (Bion 1961; Turquet 1974; Obholzer and Roberts 1994).

Arguably, reflective practice is one aspect of collaboration in educational settings that is not given sufficient attention. If reflective practice is important to and an integral part of individual professional practice, and indeed many conceptualise it that way, then it must be integral to collaborative professional working. Moreover, collaborators in professional work need to engage in collaboration reflectively to ensure that their collaborative actions are optimally appropriate through reflection in action, and to reflect on their practice of collaboration so as to learn from their experience of collaboration and improve the way they collaborate.

The joint working of the schools in this study and a consideration of some of the key concepts, most notably the primary task and its reflective nature in these schools, reflective practice and the extensive and deep collaboration, leads us to suggest a perspective on the work of schools which we term 'collaborative practice'.

Collaborative practice as we are conceptualising it has three interlinked aspects: collaboration, reflective practice and a focus on the reflective primary task. We have illustrated the relationship between the three aspects in Figure 13.1 as a Borromean knot (Lacan 1975: 112).

The three rings represent reflective practice, collaboration and a focus on the primary task. Where they all overlap in the centre represents collaborative practice. The way the circles are arranged in the knot conveys both the sense of overlapping 'sets' and the importance of all three elements being present. In a Borromean knot, the interlocking rings are so arranged and intertwined that when any one of the rings is cut or removed, the remaining two separate and fall apart. Each third ring holds the other two together. The different elements, reflective practice, collaboration and a focus on the primary task, contribute to collaborative practice in the following ways.

Figure 13.1 A Borromean knot diagram showing the three elements of collaborative practice: collaboration, reflective practice and a focus on the primary task.

- *Collaboration* gives opportunities for enhanced reflection through dialogue and discussion and provides cultural norms of situated knowledge through shared practice that frame reflection in action and reflection on action. Collaboration also enlarges the pool of expertise and other resources (Connolly and James 2006).

- *The focus on the primary task* in the schools we studied ensures effective and enriched teaching for learning for all pupils and improves and enriches teaching for learning for all pupils. Because the primary task has the two elements, in essence optimising current practice and reflecting on current practice to improve it, it is a reflective primary task. The focus on the primary task also provides a purpose for collaboration and reflection. Collaboration enhances the quality of work on the primary task by bringing additional resources and enhancing the legitimacy of those who are collaborating. Similarly the purpose of reflection is to enhance the quality of work on the primary task.

- *Reflective practice*, undertaken both individually and collectively, ensures that practice is optimally appropriate and improves. Reflective practice can work at a number of levels: the technical, the practical and the emancipatory level (Van Manen 1977; Zeichner and Gore 1995; Clarke, James and Kelly 1996; Leitch and Day 2000). At the technical level the purpose of reflection is to improve efficiency and effectiveness in terms of practical skill. Reflection at the practical level has the purpose of improving practice in relation to the immediate context of practice – the 'lifeworld'. Leitch and Day (2000) argue that outcomes of reflection at this level may enhance the practitioners' capacity to identify relevant problems, to make practical and moral judgements, and as a result of the reflective process to improve their capacity to self-evaluate. Reflection at the emancipatory level has the purpose of enhancing understandings of the social, economic and political influences on practice. Such improved understandings and the insights gained may result in enhanced practitioner empowerment, authority and autonomy.

Collaboration and reflective practice which do not focus on the primary task may result in anti-task behaviour (Turquet 1974), where work on the primary task is avoided or even actively undermined, and the collaborating group may adopt basic assumption tendencies (Bion 1961). If there is a collaborative focus on the primary task but without reflection, practice both in relation to the primary task and to collaboration may not be appropriate and is not likely to improve. If work is undertaken on the primary task individually without collaboration, the scope and capacity for reflection will be limited. There will be no reference points for reflection, no institutionally set norms to shape reflection, and the limits and controls will be restricted. Importantly, the potential for creativity will be reduced because the containing environment for emotions, which is created by collaboration, will not be present. Finally, we argue that the term 'collaboration' should dominate in a descriptive title of this way of working because collaborative practice is joint working, on a reflective primary task, in a reflective way.

One important outcome of all three elements being present is the potentially highly motivating and energising nature of collaborative practice especially if the primary task is significant and meaningful. Collaborative practice, as we have conceptualised it becomes undertaking 'Good Work', collectively with a group of like-minded colleagues to the best of one's abilities, and then seeking to do even better. This view of collaboration represents in practice a compelling shared vision (Senge 1990) that becomes "*a force in people's hearts, a force of impressive power*" (p. 206).

14

Concluding comments

INTRODUCTION

This book has been about very effective primary schools – those schools in disadvantaged settings where the pupils do well. We have defined success by the proportion of the pupils who reach a high standard in Key Stage assessments and disadvantage by the proportion of the pupils who attend the schools who are entitled to free school meals. In all the schools we studied, the levels of attainment in national assessments and disadvantage were both high.

In this chapter, we look back at and reflect on the research and the outcomes, and raise some issues that we consider to be important.

REFLECTIONS ON THE RESEARCH AND THE OUTCOMES

'Good Educational Work'

Our first thought is that it was a great privilege to visit these schools. These are some of the best schools. It was a pleasure to visit them, to speak to those who work in them and to research their practice. They confirmed what 'Good Educational Work' is and they exemplify the kind of schools all pupils should be able to attend.

Was it all down to luck?

In reviewing the findings of the project and the work of the schools, it has been interesting to consider to what extent good fortune played a part in their success. Are the schools successful by chance? Have the right teachers come together with the right headteacher in the right setting simply by happenstance? To what extent is it possible to control and manage the factors that contribute to the success of the school we studied?

There is no doubt that good fortune plays a part in the success of all these schools as it does in so many aspects of life, and it is difficult to establish what part random influences play. The unconscious may affect events and actions, both individual and collective, and the wider system in unknown ways. We would argue that the mindset – the general attitude, approach and orientation of these schools – is a significant consideration here. It's not that the schools 'made their own luck' or that they saw 'every setback as an opportunity'. It's just that in the face of unexpected, unfortunate and undesirable incidents, the school sought to make the best of things, to adapt accordingly and to move forward. Moreover, as the golfer Jack Nicklaus once famously remarked, he found it interesting that the more he practised the luckier he got. Excellence in schools is not based solely on luck (though Fortuna may play her part) but requires hard work and commitment, and that does not come cheap.

The matter of culture

We have used the notion of culture to explain how these schools worked and we have suggested that the schools (all of which are in some sense successful) have strong cultures. We do not wish this assertion to be misunderstood. The inference is not that the way to success is to generate a strong culture. As we explained in Chapter 2, many of the organisations that were used as exemplars of strong cultures when the link between 'strong cultures' and 'success' was proposed have since come to grief. Also, strong cultures are associated with failure as much as success. The literature has numerous references to schools that have grown complacent and are gradually failing. One imagines the headteachers of such schools, perhaps newly appointed, recognising the situation and seeking to bring about change but meeting resistance, much of which is around the argument 'but that is not our way' – or in other words 'that is not our culture'. Further, it is not clear to us whether the organisational culture is a dependent or an independent variable, or, to put it another way, 'Is the culture we observed the result of success or the creator of success?' We suspect the answer is both, and indeed the way we have set out the central characteristics has that duality within it. There is the question of how culture is created and sustained. The literature which suggests that the role of leaders is crucial in these culture-related activities makes a powerful point, especially so in relation to the leader's influence on the culture of small organisations such as primary and infant schools. But other factors play their part. These include other members of the school staff, professional ethics and history. Writers on culture emphasise the slipperiness of the concept and the difficulty, if not the impossibility, of managing culture so as to create the desired version of it.

The problem with imitation

The key point, which we make in Chapter 2 in the book, is that simple and uncritical imitation of the characteristics of effective schools may well be the road to frustration and failure. The processes necessary to complete the journey to success is almost certain to vary according to the starting point. The headteacher of the 'complacent schools' we discussed in the previous paragraph, for example, may have to take an approach to leadership different from that of established heads in one of the successful schools described in our research. However, while the outcomes of the research offer headteachers and others reasonably reliable indicators of the kinds of practices, values and goals that are likely to be successful, as John Gray cautions (Gray 1990), these should not be viewed as a foolproof blueprint which, if followed, would guarantee success in all circumstances. Thus, while we recommend that those seeking to create or maintain effective schools establish as many close parallels as possible with the model of good practice explicit in this book, they are also likely to have to address additional, distinctive and perhaps unexpected issues.

Boundaries

The second major issue worthy of further comment is the management of boundaries. The organisational model we have used – the open systems model – emphasises the importance of boundaries, their permeability and their frailty. We have argued therefore that the management of boundaries is crucial. This boundary management would appear to be particularly important in understanding the relationship between schools and their communities. The paradox we have described is of an organisation serving its community, interacting closely with it, responding to its needs, and yet preserving and managing the school-community boundary. It appeared to us that the community wished the school to preserve this boundary, to remain a special place – an island – but with very close links and easy communication with the community – the mainland.

One of the outcomes of the study has been to reveal the importance of a school's wider system – the different part of a school's 'community' – in helping it to be successful. The fact is schools do not exist in isolation and, importantly, they are unlikely to do 'Good Educational Work' if they try to do it on their own. A vast array of individuals, groups, organisations and institutions have an interest – a stake – in schools. In a sense, all those in the system 'stand behind' every teacher and every pupil in every classroom. Schools need that network of relationships – 'the system' – to be supportive. There will always be tensions within the system, of course. Conflicts may well occur, for example, and there may well be competitive feelings among the best of collaborative intentions, but there is no doubt that the schools in this study courted and benefited from wholehearted systemic support. Very importantly, they would probably benefit from receiving more of it and so would many – probably all – other schools.

The normative nature of effectiveness

The third point to make is to emphasise the normative character of defining effectiveness. The focus of school effectiveness has of late been on Key Stage assessments and tests, GCSEs and A Levels. Many in education, while accepting these measures, have other values, including providing a fulfilling and enriched experience for children or imparting a set of values. The schools we studied were generally happy places where pupils were motivated to learn but not by fear, suggesting that generating high levels of anxiety in pupils may not be the best way to motivate them to learn. Moreover, happy educational experiences may persuade students that, whatever their current success, returning to education at a later stage may be worthwhile. This 'readiness to return to learning' is not an inconsiderable factor in an age of rapid technological change where jobs may become redundant and career change essential. This notion also illustrates the difference between outputs and outcomes in evaluation systems. The long-term outcome ('a readiness to return to learning') may prove difficult to measure and may lose out to the more easily measured outputs ('high levels of attainment'), but these effects should not be neglected.

The importance of the main/primary task

A consideration of the outcomes and outputs of these schools leads to a key feature of the schools and our interpretation of how they worked, their focus on the main or primary task. A crucial question is, of course, 'Who determines the main/primary task?' because that is what performance measurement should focus on. Government policy has sought through a range of initiatives to increasingly influence this, in part by measurement and inspection. But schools have opportunities to operate within some policy space to influence the determination of the primary task and leadership is in part about interpreting the environment to determine the nature of this policy space. But it is interesting that the community's role in this exercise is limited to being supportive of others' choices. These communities generally had a very functional view of education – the tradition of valuing education as 'a way out of here' remains strong, if declining, in Wales. They weren't interested in debating the nature of education but in how their children could be helped to 'do well'. They were lucky to have schools with committed teachers, heads and governors to enable them to do that. What they could do if that situation changed and they perhaps had more influence in determining the primary task is interesting to reflect on.

One important outcome of this research was the confirmation of the importance of the main/primary task and the recognition that organisations and institutions cannot really succeed unless they have a clear sense of it. There is an extensive literature on the importance of the task in group settings. But this research has re-convinced us that a discussion of 'what we are meant to be doing' and then focusing efforts upon whatever that task is can be very helpful in achieving organisational success. It can help members of the organisation to know where to concentrate their energies, it can guide all the various practices and the kind of organisation that is created as a result, and, importantly, it can provide a very helpful 'signpost' if the way forward is not entirely clear. At all times, and particularly in the event of a serious setback of any kind, a focus on the main/primary task can guide action. It can help to shape all kinds of organisational processes – 'Do our processes enable us to work on the main/primary task?'

Socialisation and culture

In Chapter 3, we acknowledged Giddens's assertion that organisational life is a recursive phenomenon. That is to say, engagement in the tasks and relationships which characterise an organisation's day-to-day operation determines the nature of future tasks and relationships. These, in turn, similarly influence people's interactive engagement in further tasks and relationships. We need to gain clearer insights into the nature of these recursive processes because they are almost certainly highly influential in shaping the culture of schools. They also probably represent a significant influence upon the nature of organisational socialisation pressures. We also need to determine more precisely those recursive processes which promote effectiveness, those which help schools become effective and those which impede effectiveness. Such understandings should help the endeavours of improvement-oriented practitioners.

Closely allied to this requirement to understand the way in which recursive processes affect the development of culture is the need to understand how leaders of effective schools construct 'positive organisational cultures'. Our research was not of sufficient scope to identify clearly which cultural features of the schools were inherited legacies created by previous leaders or which were traits cultivated by their current leaders. We were also not able to gain a full understanding of the processes of building a shared vision although, arguably, we did gain some insights into the philosophical and political underpinnings of the educational vision prevalent in the schools and the way it contributes to their success. There is more research to be done on this topic.

Long-standing headteachers and staff

Many of the headteachers and staff in the sample schools had been in post for a considerable time or had spent very long careers in their schools. This prolonged experience in one school did not appear to have narrowed their education vision, dulled their motivation or stultified their development. The schools had thus been the locus for the long-term professional development of those who worked there. This counters a widespread orthodoxy, that to stay in one school means that teachers and headteachers will inevitably become stale, cynical and narrow in their range of expertise. It also counters the deterministic 'life-cycle' view for all teachers and especially headteachers which argues for continual 'moving on'. This notion of the length of career in one school takes us back to the idea of 're-creating the new' (James and Connolly 2000) where headteachers (and teachers for that matter) need the capacity to continually regenerate and re-create themselves in their role so they do not become trapped and constrained by their own limitations and by the projected expectations of others. Those are the reasons for staleness and may even unconsciously encourage headteachers and teachers to move on.

Effective teaching and enriched teaching

The schools we studied demonstrated quite clearly that it was possible to have high levels of attainment – success in formal tests of various kinds – and also to have a rich, varied and stimulating curriculum. It is not a matter of having *either* good results *or* an enriched curriculum. It is perfectly possible to have both. It is a classic example of the both-and mentality that was prevalent in these schools. Furthermore, from our experience as teachers in schools it is highly desirable to have both.

The research reinforces the importance of having a 'high demand-high provision' way of working at a school. The teaching staff demanded a lot of themselves and they demanded a lot of the pupils despite, in so many cases, the pupils' disadvantaged circumstances. That approach works because the demand is made in the context of high levels of provision – in helping the pupils to learn, and in providing resources, support, positive feedback and appreciation. There's no doubt that this 'high demand-high provision' approach is very important.

Passion for the work

One of the most striking outcomes of the study was the way in which those who worked in the school all had a passion for their work. It was particularly evident and apparently important in the headteachers. They clearly possessed a whole range of qualities, but underlying all of them was this high level of commitment to undertaking 'Good Work' as we have called it. The education community needs to find new ways of thinking about the qualities required for successful headship that go beyond competencies and perhaps beyond how we currently view this key role. This passionate and fully engaged commitment to the work is a key attribute.

But the high level of motivation was spread across all those who worked in these schools. It was present in everyone, not just the headteacher. They were passionate about their work; it was highly motivating and it meant a lot to them. The importance of motivation and passionate engagement with the work of teaching and organising in schools tends to be neglected in discussions about, for example, inspection criteria, the development of new policies and performance management.

Engendering high levels of motivation is not always easy and it is difficult to capture in policy terms. The levers that are usually pulled to motivate are typically to do with high salaries and improved conditions of service. But as Hertzberg tells us, although these 'hygiene factors' may prevent dissatisfaction they are probably not motivators. Of course, teachers and headteachers deserve to have excellent conditions of service and to be well paid for the difficult work they do, but good pay and conditions does not necessarily bring about the kind of motivation that is required to do 'Good Educational Work'. One way of enhancing motivation might be to provide all those who work in schools with more of a different kind of feedback. In Chapter 3, we discussed the importance of negative feedback in controlling the system and keeping it stable. There is a good case for arguing that there is too much negative feedback in the education system. For example, inspection and calling to account, the frequent negative images and opinions of schools and teachers in the media, the way policies to improve practice in schools so often seem to start from a basis of 'schools are not doing enough to …', all are forms of negative feedback to schools and teachers. Perhaps what might help schools to be more successful is to affirm that the work they do is good and important, to thank them for their efforts and to encourage them to do even better.

A thought about the mindset

One important feature of these schools, which we have tried to capture in 'The mindset' key characteristic and which is threaded through other characteristics, was the 'level of urgency' in the schools. These schools were not frenetic, driven places, but neither were they low-energy, complacent places. The energy level was sufficient to keep the school moving forward at a pace which it could cope with. Of course, the external challenges the schools faced were a strong driving force but these were complemented by internal drives for change that did not become heavy and burdensome.

Welsh-medium education

The Welsh-medium schools in the study were of particular interest. One of their particularly significant features was the way the schools sought to be inclusive in the ways they worked. The Welsh language may have been the medium of communication and teaching in the schools, but it was used in an 'including and inclusive' manner. There was a very positive approach to developing Welsh language capability in all those who attended the schools and it became a way of working that helped pull the whole community together.

NEW RESEARCH ISSUES

As with any educational research, the outcomes give rise to further sets of questions. Some of those that are of interest to us are as follows.

Culture and the nature of work in the schools

- How do the staff formulate and negotiate changes in their practices?
- How do they work through changes in the culture of their schools?
- How do they address and resolve differences in the values, assumptions, political stances and philosophical beliefs which shape the organisational underpinnings of the school culture?
- What is the 'fine grain' of the experience of teaching in these schools and what do these schools do to 'make good teachers'?

Leadership and management

- To what extent are new school leaders able to generate school improvement and establish the kind of good practice evident in the schools we studied and what obstacles do new school leaders face in undertaking such work?
- How does the evidence emerging from our research help new headteachers to negotiate the early stages of their work most productively?
- What is the detail of the daily practice of the headteachers and what exactly is the nature of the way they work that makes such a difference?
- What is it precisely that the chair of the governing body does that means the governing body contributes positively to the success of these schools?

The nature of the characteristics

- Is there evidence of a hierarchy among the key characteristics identified by the study and/or constituent factors of these characteristics and what is the nature of any hierarchies?
- What is the interplay between the characteristics and between the features within the characteristics?
- To what extent are the characteristics defined by the study equally applicable to a wide range of settings/educational institutions?
- Are particular characteristics especially effective in offsetting certain socio-economic or other adverse input factors?

The nature of the settings of the schools

- How is the work of schools in disadvantaged settings affected by different kinds of disadvantage?
- What is the influence of the educational achievements of parents and other adult carers in disadvantaged settings on the work of schools?
- How is the work of schools affected by the size and structure of family groups of which their pupils are a part?
- How are schools affected by the extent to which catchment areas feature long-established or relatively itinerant communities?

Classroom processes

- Which particular modes of teaching are especially important in securing high levels of pupil attainment in schools in disadvantaged settings?
- What are the rationales underpinning teachers' use of particular forms of differentiation of learning activities?
- What is the balance between teachers' promotion of subject-specific skills and generic skills, knowledge and understanding, and how does this balance affect pupil learning?

Epistemologies of practice

- What is an appropriate epistemology for the rich and dynamic nature of practice in schools that are very effective in disadvantaged settings?
- How are emotions experienced and worked with, what practices do they initiate and what part does emotional experience play in the organising and structuring of very effective schools?
- Is there an 'affective paradigm' with particular assumptions about organising, epistemologies to describe the forms of organisational practice, new perspectives on human nature and new methodologies for the study of organising in schools, and if so what is its nature and how might this paradigm be characterised?

MESSAGES FOR ALL SCHOOLS

The work of these schools was 'extraordinary'. By definition, they were places where many of the pupils experienced high levels of disadvantage and yet the pupils reached high levels of attainment, which is unusual. On this basis we have described them as being very effective. But at the same time, in so many ways, much of their practice was 'ordinary' in that the schools were working in much the same way as many good schools have always worked. This idea was reinforced by the comment of one of the headteachers when we rang up to arrange a data collection visit: "*You won't find anything special here. We're just an ordinary school"*. These schools were well managed, the teaching was sound and the schools continually sought to do better. In that regard, many of the schools had a rather 'traditional' feel about them. It was not that the changes of the last 20 years or so had passed them by but that they had accommodated them and incorporated the changes into essentially sound ways of working. They had, in fact, made sense of the changes, and had implemented them in a way that best suited their individual schools. The basics – *all* the basics – were attended to consistently and properly and, as appropriate, changed to improve the pupils' learning. And that is what seemed to count.

VERY EFFECTIVE SCHOOLS ARE WHAT ALL CHILDREN DESERVE

Finally, in reflecting on the excellent practice we have reported in this book, we are reminded of the shameful fact that over 100 million children around the world do not attend a school of any kind, let alone a very effective one. The reasons for that must be addressed. All children deserve the kind of education provided in the schools attended by the more fortunate. It is not right for one group of children to experience high quality education and for others not to. All children everywhere deserve to attend a very effective school.

References

Allaire, Y. and Firsirotu, M. (1984) 'Theories of organisation culture', *Organisation Studies*, 5 (3): 193–226.

Alvesson, M. (2002) *Understanding Organizational Culture*. London: Sage.

Argyris, C. (1980) *Inner Contradictions of Rigorous Research*. New York: Academic Press.

Argyris, C. (1985) *Strategy, Change and Defensive Routines*. Boston: Pitman.

Argyris, C. (1987) 'Reasoning, action strategies, and defensive routines: the case of OD practitioners', in R. A. Woodman and A. A. Pasmore (eds), *Research in Organisational Change and Development*, Vol. 1. Greenwich, CT: JAI Press, pp. 89–128.

Argyris, C. and Schön, D. (1974) *Theory in Practice: Increasing Professional Effectiveness*. San Francisco: Jossey-Bass.

Argyris, C. and Schön, D. (1978) *Organisational Learning: A Theory of Action Perspective*. Reading, MA: Addison-Wesley.

Argyris, C. and Schön, D. (1996) *Organisational Learning II*. New York: Addison-Wesley.

Argyris, C., Putnam, R. and McLain Smith, D. (1985) *Action Science: Concepts, Methods and Skills for Research and Intervention*. San Francisco: Jossey-Bass.

Armstrong, D. (2005) *Organisation in the Mind: Psychoanalysis, Group Relations, and Organisational Consultancy*. London: Karnac.

Ashforth, B. E. and Humphrey, R. H. (1993) 'Emotional labour in service roles', *Academy of Management Review*, 18: 88–115.

Ashkenas, R. (2000) 'How to loosen organisational boundaries', *Journal of Business Strategy*, March/April: 11–12.

Ball, S. (1987) *The Micro-politics of the School*. London: Methuen.

Barsade, S. G., Brief, A. P. and Spataro, S. E. (2003) 'The affective revolution in organisational behaviour: the emergence of a paradigm', in J. Greenberg (ed.), *Organizational Behavior: The State of the Science*. Hillsdale, NJ: Erlbaum.

Bass, B. M. (1996) *Handbook of Leadership: A Survey of Theory and Research*. New York: Free Press.

Bate, P. (1994) *Strategies for Cultural Change*. Oxford: Butterworth-Heinemann.

Beatty, B. R. (2000) 'The emotions of educational leadership: breaking the silence', *International Journal of Leadership in Education*, 3 (4): 331–57.

Beatty, B. R. and Brew, C. R. (2004) 'Trusting relationships and emotional epistemologies: a foundational leadership issue', *School Leadership and Management*, 24 (4): 329–56.

Bennett, J. (1999) 'Micropolitics in the Tasmanian context of school reform', *School Leadership and Management*, 19: 197–200.

Bennett, N., Harvey, J. A. and Anderson, L. (2004) 'Control, autonomy and partnership in local education: views from six chief education officers', *Educational Management, Administration and Leadership*, 32: 217–35.

Bion, W. R. (1961) *Experiences in Groups and Other Papers*. London: Tavistock.

Blase, J. and Anderson, G. (1995) *The Micropolitics of Educational Leadership: From Control to Empowerment*. London: Cassell.

Blase, J. and Blase, J. (1999) 'Implementation of shared governance for instructional improvement: principals' perspectives', *Journal of Educational Administration*, 37: 476–500.

Boler, M. (1999) *Feeling Power*. London: Routledge.

Bridges, D. and Husbands, C. (eds) (1996) *Consorting and Collaborating in the Education Marketplace*. London: Falmer.

Brookover, W., Beady, C., Flood, P., Schweitzer, J. and Weisenbaker, J. (1979) *School Social Systems and Student Achievement: Schools Can Make a Difference*. New York: Praeger.

Busher, H. (2001) 'The micropolitics of change, improvement and effectiveness in schools', in N. Bennett and A. Harris (eds), *School Effectiveness and School Improvement: Searching for the Elusive Partnership*. London: Cassell, pp. 75–97.

Clarke, B. A., James, C. R. and Kelly, J. (1996) 'Reflective practice: reviewing and refocusing the debate', *International Journal of Nursing Studies*, 33: 171–80.

Cohen, M. (1983) 'Instructional management and social conditions in effective schools', in A. O. Webb and L. D. Webb (eds), *School Finance and School Improvement: Linkages in the 1980s*. Cambridge, MA: Ballinger.

Coleman, J. S., Campbell, E., Hobson, C., McPartland, J., Mood, A., Weinfield, F. and York, R. (1966) *Equality of Educational Opportunity*. Washington, DC: US Government Printing Office.

Coleman, P., Collinge J. and Tabin, Y. (1994) *Improving Schools from the Inside Out: A Progress Report on the Coproduction of Learning Projects in British Columbia, Canada*. Burnaby, BC, Canada: Faculty of Education, Simon Fraser University.

Connolly, M. and James, C. R. (2006) 'Collaboration for school improvement: resource dependency and institutional frameworks of analysis', *Educational Management, Administration and Leadership*, 34 (1): 69–87.

Creemers, B. P. M. (1994a) 'The history value and purpose of school effectiveness studies', in D. Reynolds, B. P. M. Creemers, P. S. Nesselradt, E. C. Schaffer, S. Stringfield and C. Teddlie (eds), *Advances in School Effectiveness Research and Practice*. Oxford: Pergamon.

Creemers, B. P. M. (1994b) *The Effective Classroom*. London: Cassell.

Cuban, L. (1988) *The Managerial Imperative and the Practice of Leadership in Schools*. Albany, NY: State University of New York Press.

Cuttance, P. (1988) 'Intra-system variation in the effectiveness of schooling', *Research Papers in Education*, 3: 183–219.

Czander, W. (1993) *The Psychodynamics of Work and Organisations*. New York: Guilford Press.

Daly, P. (1991) 'How large are secondary school effects in Northern Ireland?', *School Effectiveness and School Improvement*, 2 (4): 305–23.

Davies, B. (ed.) (2005) *The Essentials of School Leadership*. London: Paul Chapman.

Day, C. (2004a) *A Passion for Teaching*. London: Falmer.

Day, C. (2004b) 'The passion of successful leadership', *School Leadership and Management*, 24 (4): 425–38.

DfES (2003) *A New Specialist System: Transforming Secondary Education*. London: DfES.

Diamond, M., Allcorn, S. and Stein, H. (2004) 'The surface of organisational boundaries: a view from psychoanalytic object relations theory', *Human Relations*, 57 (1): 31–53.

Douglas, M. (1966) *Purity and Danger*. London: Routledge.

Dufour, R. and Baker, R. E. (1998) *Professional Learning Communities at Work: Best Practices for Enhancing Student Achievement*. Bloomington, IN: National Education Service.

Dunning, G., James, C. and Jones, N. (2005) 'Splitting and projection at work in schools', *Journal of Educational Administration*, 43 (3): 244–59.

Fineman, S. (1993) *Emotions in Organisations*, 1st edn. London: Sage.

Fineman, S. (2000) *Emotions in Organisations*, 2nd edn. London: Sage.

Fineman, S. (2003) *Understanding Emotion at Work*. London: Sage.

Fisher, D. and Torbert, W. R. (1995) *Personal and Organisational Transformations*. London: McGraw-Hill.

Freeman, J. and Teddlie, C. (1997) *A Phenomenological Examination of 'Naturally Occurring' School Improvement: Implications for Democratization of Schools*. Paper presented at the annual meeting of the American Educational Research Association, New York.

Frost, P. J., Moore, L. F., Louis, M. R., Lundberg, C. C. and Martin, J. (eds) (1985) *Organisational Culture*. London: Sage.

Gabriel, Y. (1999) *Organizations in Depth*. London: Sage.

Giddens, A. (1979) *Central Problems in Social Theory: Action, Structure and Contradiction in Social Analysis*. London: Macmillan.

Glatter, R. (2003) *Collaboration, Collaboration, Collaboration: The Origins and Implications of Policy*. Paper presented at the Annual Conference of the British Educational Leadership, Management and Administration Society, Kent's Hill, Milton Keynes.

Goldstein, H. and Sammons, P. (1997) 'The influence of secondary and junior schools on sixteen year examination performance: a cross-classified multi-level analysis', *School Effectiveness and School Improvement*, 8 (2): 219–30.

Gould, L. J., Stapley, L. F. and Stein, M. (eds) (2001) *The Systems Psychodynamics of Organisations: Integrating the Groups Relations Approach, Psychoanalytic and Open Systems Perspective. Contributions in Honour of Eric J. Miller*. London: Karnac Books.

Gray, J. (1990) 'The quality of schooling: frameworks for judgement', *British Journal of Education Studies*, 38 (3): 204–33.

Gray, J. (1993) 'Review of J. Scheerens (1992) Effective schooling: research theory and practice', *School Effectiveness and School Improvement*, 4 (23): 230–5.

Gronn, P. (2000) 'Distributed properties: a new architecture for leadership', *Educational Management and Administration*, 28: 317–38.

Gutmann, D. (2003) *Psychoanalysis and Management: The Transformation*. London: Karnac Books.

Hallinger, P. and Heck, R. (1998) 'Exploring the principal's contribution to school effectiveness: 1980–1995', *School Effectiveness and School Improvement*, 9: 157–91.

Hallinger, P. and Heck, R. (1999) 'Can leadership enhance school effectiveness?', in T. Bush, L. Bell, R. Bolam, R. Glatter and P. Ribbins (eds), *Educational Management: Redefining Theory, Policy and Practice*. London: Paul Chapman.

Hallinger, P. and Murphy, J. (1986) 'The social context of effective schools', *American Journal of Education*, 94 (3): 328–55.

Halton, W. (1994) 'Some unconscious aspects of organisational life', in A. Obholzer and V. Z. Roberts (eds), *The Unconscious at Work*. London: Routledge, pp. 11–18.

Halverson, R. R. (2003) 'Systems of practice: how leaders use artefacts to create professional community in schools', *Education Policy Analysis Archives*, 11 (37). Retrieved 2004 from: http://epaa.asu.edu/epaa/v11n37/.

Hanna, D. (1997) 'The organisation as an open system', in A. Harris, N. Bennett and M. Preedy (eds), *Organisational Effectiveness and Improvement in Education*. Buckingham: Open University Press.

Hargreaves, A. (1998a) 'The emotional practice of teaching', *Teaching and Teacher Education*, 14 (8): 835–54.

Hargreaves, A. (1998b) 'The emotions of teaching and educational change', in A. Hargreaves, A. Lieberman, M. Fullan and D. Hopkins (eds), *The International Handbook of Educational Change*. London: Kluwer Academic, pp. 558–75.

Hargreaves, A. (2001) 'The emotional geographies of teaching', *Teachers College Record*, 103 (6): 1056–80.

Hargreaves, A. (2004) 'Inclusive and exclusive educational change: emotional responses of teachers and implications for leadership', *School Leadership and Management*, 24 (3): 287–310.

Hargreaves, D. H. (2001) 'A capital theory of school effectiveness and improvement', *British Educational Research Journal*, 27 (4): 487–503.

Harper, D. (2001) *On-line Etymological Dictionary*. Retrieved from: http://www.etymonline.com/index.php?term=collaborate.

Harris, A. and Chapman, C. (2002) *Effective Leadership of Schools Facing Challenging Circumstances*. Nottingham: National College for School Leadership.

Hearn, J. (1993) 'Emotive subjects: organisational man, organisational masculinities and the (de)construction of emotions', in S. Fineman (ed.), *Emotions in Organisations*, 1st edn. London: Sage.

Heracleous, L. (2004) 'Boundaries in the study of organisations', *Human Relations*, 57 (1): 95–103.

Hernes, T. (2004) 'Studying composite boundaries: a framework of analysis', *Human Relations*, 57 (1): 9–29.

Hirschhorn, L. (1985) 'The psychodynamics of taking a role', in A. Coleman and M. H. Geller (eds), *Group Relations Reader 2*. Washington, DC: A. K. Rice Institute.

Hirschhorn, L. (1988) *The Workplace Within: Psychodynamics of Organisational Life*. Cambridge, MA: MIT Press.

Hirschhorn, L. (1997) *Re-working Authority: Leading and Following in the Post-modern Organisation*. Cambridge, MA: Cambridge University Press.

Hirschhorn, L. and Gilmore, T. (1992) 'The new boundaries of the "boundaryless" company', *Harvard Business Review*, May/June: 104–15.

Hochschild, A. R. (1979) 'Emotion work, feeling rules and social structure', *American Journal of Sociology*, 85: 551–75.

Hochschild, A. R. (1983) *The Managed Heart: Commercialisation of Human Feeling.* Berkeley, CA: University of California Press.

Hoyle, E. (1986) *The Politics of School Management.* London: Hodder & Stoughton.

Hughes, J. (1989) *Reshaping the Psychoanalytic Domain: The Work of W. R. D. Fairbairn and D. W. Winnicott.* Berkeley, CA: University of California Press.

Jacques, E. (1952) *The Changing Culture of the Factory.* London: Tavistock.

Jacques, E. (1955) 'Social systems as a defence against persecutory and depressive anxiety', in M. Klein, P. Heimann and R. E. Money Kyrle (eds), *New Directions in Psychoanalysis.* London: Tavistock.

James, C. R. (1999) 'Institutional transformation and educational management', in T. Bush, L. Bell, R. Bolam, R. Glatter and P. Ribbins (eds), *Educational Management: Redefining Theory, Policy and Practice.* London: Paul Chapman/ Sage, pp. 142–54.

James, C. R. (2004) 'The work of educational leaders in building creative and passionate schools and colleges', in H. Tomlinson (ed.), *Educational Management: Major Themes in Education.* London: Taylor & Francis.

James, C. R. and Connolly, U. (2000) *Effective Change in Schools.* London: Routledge Falmer.

James, C. R. and Vince, R. (2001) 'Developing the leadership capability of headteachers', *Educational Management and Administration,* 29 (1): 307–17.

Jencks, C., Smith, M., Ackland, H., Bane, M. J., Cohen, D., Gintis, H., Heyns, B. and Michelson, S. (1972) *Inequality: A Reassessment of the Effects of Family and Schooling in America.* New York: Basic Books.

Kets de Vries, M. F. R. (1991) *Organisations on the Couch: Clinical Perspectives on Organisational Behaviour.* San Francisco: Jossey-Bass.

Keys, W., Sharp, C., Greene, K. and Grayson, H. (2003) *Successful Leadership of Schools in Urban and Challenging Contexts: A Review of the Literature.* Nottingham: National College for School Leadership.

Kolb, D. (1984) *Experiential Learning: Experience as a Source of Learning and Development.* Englewood Cliffs, NJ: Prentice Hall.

Lacan, J. (1975) *Encore.* Paris: Editions de Seuil.

Lamont, M. and Molnar, V. (2002) 'The study of boundaries in the social sciences', *Annual Review of Sociology,* 28: 167–95.

Lauder, H., Robinson, T. and Thrupp, M. (2002) 'School composition and peer effects', *International Journal of Educational Research,* 37 (5): 483–504.

Lave, J. (1998) 'Situated learning in communities of practice', in L. B. Resnick, J. Levine and S. D. Teasley (eds), *Socially Shared Cognition.* Washington, DC: American Psychology Association.

Lave, J. and Wenger, E. (1991) *Situated Learning: Legitimate Peripheral Participation.* Cambridge: Cambridge University Press.

Lawrence, G. ([1977] 1985) 'Management development ... some ideals, images and realities', in A. D. Coleman and M. H. Geller (eds), *Group Relations Reader 2.* Washington, DC: A. K. Rice Institute.

Leach, E. (1976) *Culture and Communication.* Cambridge: Cambridge University Press.

Lee, R. and Lawrence, P. (1985) *Organisational Behaviour.* London: Hutchinson.

Leitch, R. and Day, C. (2000) 'Action research and reflective practice: towards a holistic view', *Educational Action Research,* 8: 179–93.

Leithwood, K., Jantzi, D. and Steinbach, R. (1999) *Changing Leadership for Changing Times*. Buckingham: Open University Press.

Levine, D. U. and Lezotte, L. W. (1990) *Unusually Effective Schools: A Review and Analysis of Research and Practice*. Madison, WI: National Center for Effective Schools Research and Development.

Lieberman, A. (1990) *Schools as Collaborative Cultures: Creating the Future Now*. Falmer: London.

Likierman, M. (2001) *Melanie Klein: Her Work in Context*. London: Continuum.

Lomax, P. and Darley, J. (1995) 'Inter-school links, liaison and networking: collaboration or competition?', *Educational Management and Administration*, 23: 148–61.

Louis, K. S., Kruse, S. D. and Bryk, A. S. (1995) 'Professionalism and community: what is it and why is it important in urban schools?', in K. S. Louis and S. D. Kruse (eds), *Professionalism and Community: Perspectives on Reforming Urban Schools*. Thousand Oaks, CA: Sage.

Macbeath, J. (1994) *Making Schools More Effective: A Role for Parents in School Self Evaluation and Development Planning*. Paper presented to the Annual Conference of the American Education Research Association, New Orleans, 4–8 April.

MacGilchrist, B., Myers, K. and Reed, J. (1997) *The Intelligent School*. London: Paul Chapman.

Maden, M. (ed.) (2001) *Success Against the Odds, Five Years On: Revisiting Effective Schools in Disadvantaged Areas*. London: RoutledgeFalmer.

Martin, J. (2002) *Organizational Culture*. London: Sage.

Menzies, I. (1960) 'A case study in functioning of social systems as a defence against anxiety', *Human Relations*, 13: 95–121.

Metcalfe, L. and Richards, S. (1984) 'The impact of the efficiency strategy: political clout or cultural change?', *Public Administration*, 62 (4): 439–54.

Metcalfe, L. and Richards, S. (1990) *Improving Public Management*. London: Sage.

Meyerson, D. and Martin, J. (1987) 'Cultural change: an integration of three views', *Journal of Management Studies*, 24: 623–47.

Miller, E. and Rice, A. K. (1967) 'Systems of organisation', in A. D. Coleman and W. H. Bexton (eds), *Group Relations Reader 1*. Jupiter, FL: A. K. Rice Institute, pp. 43–68.

Mortimore, P. (1991) 'The nature and findings of school effectiveness research in the primary sector', in S. Riddell and S. Brown (eds), *School Effectiveness Research: Its Messages for School Improvement*. London: HMSO.

Mortimore, P. (1993) School effectiveness and the management of effective learning and teaching', *School Effectiveness and School Improvement*, 4 (4): 290–310.

Mortimore, P., Sammons, P., Stoll, L., Lewis, D. and Ecob, R. (1988) *School Matters: The Junior Years*. Wells: Open Books.

Muijs, D., Harris, A., Chapman, C., Stoll, L. and Russ, J. (2004) 'Improving schools in socio-economically disadvantaged areas: a review of the research', *School Effectiveness and Improvement*, 15 (2): 149–75.

Murnane, R. J. (1981) 'Interpreting the evidence on school effectiveness', *Teachers College Record*, 83: 19–35.

NCE (1995) *Success Against the Odds*. London: Routledge.

Neumann, J. E. (1999) *Systems Psychodynamics in the Service of a Political Organisational Change*. Oxford: Oxford University Press.

Newman, J. (1996) *Shaping Organisational Cultures in Local Government*. London: Pitman.

Nias, J., Southworth, G. and Yeomans, R. (1989) *Staff Relationships in the Primary School: A Study of Organisational Cultures*. London: Cassell.

Obholzer, A. and Roberts, V. Z. (eds) (1994) *The Unconscious at Work*. London: Routledge.

Parkin, W. (1993) 'The public and the private: gender, sexuality and emotion', in S. Fineman (ed.), *Emotions in Organisations*, 1st edn. London: Sage.

Paulsen, N. and Hernes, T. (2003) *Managing Boundaries in Organisations: Multiple Perspectives*. Basingstoke: Palgrave Macmillan.

Perrow, C. (1986) *Complex Organisations – A Critical Essay*, 3rd edn. New York: McGraw-Hill.

Peters, T. and Waterman, R. (1982) *In Search of Excellence*. London: Harper & Row.

Phillips, J. and Stonebridge, L. (eds) (1998) *Reading Melanie Klein*. London: RoutledgeFalmer.

Portin, B. S. (1998) 'Compounding roles: a study of Washington's principals', *International Journal of Educational Research*, 29: 381–91.

Quicke, J. (2000) 'Teaching assistants: students or servants?', *Forum*, 45: 71.

Rafeli, A. and Sutton, M. (1989) 'The expression of emotion in organisational life', in L. L. Cummings and B. L. Straw (eds), *Research in Organisational Behaviour*, Vol. 11. Greenwich, CT: JAI Press.

Reed, B. (2000) *An Explanation of Role*. London: Grubb Institute.

Reynolds, D. (1976) 'The delinquent school', in P. Woods (ed.), *The Process of Schooling*. London: Routledge & Kegan Paul.

Reynolds, D. and Creemers, B. P. M (1990) 'School effectiveness and school improvement', *School Effectiveness and School Improvement*, 1 (1): 1–3.

Reynolds, D. and Cuttance, P. (eds) (1992) *School Effectiveness Research Policy and Practice*. London: Cassell.

Reynolds, D. and Murgatroyd, S. (1977) 'The sociology of schooling and the absent pupil. The school as a factor in the generation of truancy', in H. C. Carrol (ed.), *Absenteeism in South Wales: Studies of Pupils, Their Homes and Their Secondary Schools*. Swansea: Faculty of Education, University of Swansea.

Reynolds, D. and Sullivan, M. (1979) 'Bringing schools back in', in L. Barton (ed.), *Schools, Pupils and Deviance*. Driffield: Nafferton.

Rice, A. K. (1963) *The Enterprise and Its Environment*. London: Tavistock.

Riley, P. (1983) 'A structurationist account of political culture', *Administrative Science Quarterly*, 28: 414–37.

Roberts, S. and Pruitt, E. (2003) *Schools as Professional Learning Communities*. London: Sage.

Roberts, V. Z. (1994) 'The organisation of work: contributions from open systems theory', in A. Obholzer and V. Z. Roberts (eds), *The Unconscious at Work*. London: Routledge.

Roethlisberger, F. J. and Dickson, W. J. (1939), cited in Mullins, L. J. (1993) *Management and Organisational Behaviour*, 3rd edn. London: Pitman.

Rutter, M., Maughan, B., Mortimore, P. and Ouston, J. with Smith, A. (1979) *Fifteen Thousand Hours: Secondary Schools and Their Effects on Children*. London: Open Books.

Sammons, P. (1994) 'Findings from school effectiveness research: some implications for improving the quality of schools', in P. M. Ribbins and E. Burridge (eds), *Improving Education: The Issue of Quality*. London: Cassell.

Sammons, P. (1999) *School Effectiveness Coming of Age in the 21st Century*. London: Swets & Zeitlinger.

Sammons, P. Cuttance, P., Nuttall, D. and Thomas, S. (1994) 'Continuity of school effects: a longitudinal analysis of primary and secondary school effects on GCSE performance', *School Effectiveness and School Improvement*, 6 (4): 285–307.

Sammons, P., Hillman, J. and Mortimore, P. (1995) *Key Characteristics of Effective Schools: A Review of School Effectiveness and Research*. London: Office for Standards in Education.

Scheerens, J. (1992) *Effective Schooling: Research Theory and Practice*. London: Cassell.

Schneider, S. C. (1991) 'Managing boundaries in organizations', in M. F. R. Kets de Vries (ed.), *Organizations on the Couch*. San Francisco: Jossey-Bass.

Schön, D. A. (1983) *The Reflective Practitioner: How Professionals Think in Action*. New York: Basic Books.

Scott, W. R. (1998) *Organizations – Rational, Natural and Open Systems*. Englewood Cliffs, NJ: Prentice Hall.

Segal, H. (1979) *Klein*. London: Fontana.

Senge, P. (1990) *The Fifth Discipline: The Art and Practice of the Learning Organisation*. London: Random House.

Sergiovanni, T. J. (1987) *The Principalship: A Reflective Practice Perspective*. Newton, MA: Allyn & Bacon.

Smircich, L. (1983) 'Concepts of culture and organisational analysis', *Administrative Science Quarterly*, 28: 339–58.

Smyth, J. (1991) *Teachers as Collaborative Learners*. Milton Keynes: Open University Press.

Stapley, L. (1996) *The Personality of Organisation*. London: Free Association Books.

Stoll, L. and Fink, D. (1996) *Changing Our Schools: Linking School Effectiveness and School Improvement*. Milton Keynes: Open University Press.

Teddlie, C. and Reynolds, D. (2000) *The International Handbook of School Effectiveness Research*. London: Falmer.

Teddlie, C. and Stringfield, S. (1985) 'A differential analysis of effectiveness in middle and lower socio-economic schools', *Journal of Classroom Interaction*, 9 (2): 12–14.

Teddlie, C., Stringfield, S. and Reynolds, D. (2000) 'Context issues within school effectiveness research', in C. Teddlie and D. Reynolds (eds), *The International Handbook of School Effectiveness Research*. London: Falmer.

Teddlie, C., Reynolds, D., Creemers, B. and Stringfield, S. (2002) 'Comparisons across country case studies', in D. Reynolds, B. Creemers, S. Stringfield, C. Teddlie and G. Schaffer (eds), *World Class Schools: International Perspectives on School Effectiveness*. London: RoutledgeFalmer.

Thomas, S. and Mortimore, P. (1996) 'Comparison of value-added models for secondary school effectiveness', *Research Papers in Education*, 11: 15–33.

Thomas, S., Sammons, P. and Mortimore, P. (1995) *Stability and Consistency in Secondary School Effects on Students' Outcomes over Three Years*. Paper presented at the Annual Conference of the International Congress for School Effectiveness and Improvement, 3–6 January, Leeuwarden, The Netherlands, cited in

Sammons, P. (1999) *School Effectiveness Coming of Age in the 21st Century*. London: Swets & Zeitlinger.

Thomas, S., Sammons, P., Mortimore, P., Thomas, S. and Smees, R. (1995) *Differential Secondary School Effectiveness: Examining the Size, Extent and Consistency of School and Department Effects on GCSE Outcomes for Different Groups of Students over Three Years*. Paper presented at the ECER/BERA Annual Conference, Bath, September, cited in Sammons, P. (1999) *School Effectiveness Coming of Age in the 21ˢᵗ Century*. London: Swets & Zeitlinger.

Thrupp, M. (1999) *Schools Making a Difference: Let's Be Realistic!* Buckingham: Open University Press.

Turquet, P. ([1974] 1985) 'Leadership: the individual and the group', in A. D. Coleman and M. H. Geller (eds), *Group Relations Reader 2*. Washington, DC: A. K. Rice Institute.

Van Maanen, J. and Schein, E. H. (1979) 'Towards a theory of organisational socialisation', in B. Staw (ed.), *Research in Organisational Behaviour*, Vol. 1. Greenwich, CA: JAI Press.

Van Manen, M. (1977) 'Linking ways of knowing with ways of being practical', *Curriculum Enquiry*, 6: 205–88.

Vann, B. J. (1999) 'Micropolitics in the United Kingdom: can a principal ever be expected to be "one of us"?', *School Leadership and Management*, 19: 201–4.

Von Bertalanffy, I. (1968) *General Systems Theory*. New York: George Brazillier.

Walberg, H. J. (1984) 'Improving the productivity of American schools', *Educational Leadership*, 41 (1): 19–27.

Wallace, M. and Hall, V. (1994) 'Promoting collaboration among schools and colleges', in I. Lawrence (ed.), *Education Tomorrow*. London: Cassell.

Weeks, J. (2004) *Unpopular Culture: The Ritual of Complaint in a British Bank*. Chicago: University of Chicago Press.

Weick, K. E. (1979) *The Social Psychology of Organizing*, 2nd edn. New York: Random House.

Weick, K. E. (1995) *Sensemaking in Organizations*. Thousand Oaks, CA: Sage.

Welsh Assembly Government (2002) *Narrowing the Gap in the Performance of Schools*. Cardiff: Welsh Assembly Government.

Wenger, E. (1998) *Communities of Practice: Learning, Meaning and Identity*. Cambridge: Cambridge University Press.

Williams, A., Dobson, P. and Walters, M. (1989) *Changing Culture*. London: Institute of Personnel Management.

Willms, J. D. (1986) 'Social class segregation and its relation to pupils' examination results in Scotland', *American Sociological Review*, 51: 224–41.

Willms, J. D. (1992) *Monitoring School Performance: A Guide for Educators*. London: Falmer.

Wilmott, H. (1993) 'Strength is ignorance; slavery is freedom: managing culture in modern organizations', *Journal of Management Studies*, 30 (4): 515–52.

Zeichner, K. and Liston, D. (1987) 'Teaching students to reflect', *Harvard Educational Review*, 57: 23–48.

Zeichner, K. M. and Gore, J. M. (1995) 'Using action research as a vehicle for student reflection', in S. Noffke and R. B. Stevenson (eds), *Educational Action Research*. New York: Teachers College Record.

Index